THE LABOUR PARTY
SINCE 1979

When Neil Kinnock took over the leadership of the Labour
Party in 1983, he inherited a divided organisation, saddled with
an array of unpopular left-wing policies. When he resigned in
1992, Labour was a radically different party, tightly organised
and committed to working within the framework of a privately-
owned market economy. *The Labour Party since 1979* tells the
story of Labour's struggle to survive during the turbulent years
in opposition. The book charts the internal strife of the early
1980s, the transformation of Labour's structure, strategy and
policies under Kinnock's leadership, and the Party's rise to a
position at the brink of power in the run-up to the 1992 election,
at which its hopes were dashed again.

Eric Shaw has provided the first systematic analysis of the
evolution of Labour's policies, power structure and strategies
during the 1980s and up until the present day. Using new
sources and documents, he looks at how and why the transformation occurred, examining the pressures and constraints imped-
ing the modernisation process of the Party, its shift to the
political middle ground and the new professionalism of
Labour's campaigning and communications strategies.

The book analyses major events in the Party's evolution such
as the miners' strike, the fragmentation of the left and the 1987
Policy Review. Shaw argues that the shedding of key social
democratic policies has left Labour bereft of any clear purpose
or direction, and that the strategy of seeking to project a
'moderate' and 'responsible' image of the Labour Party today is
seriously flawed.

Eric Shaw is the author of *Discipline and Discord in the Labour
Party*. He lectures in the Politics Department of the University of
Stirling.

THE
LABOUR PARTY
SINCE 1979

Crisis and transformation

Eric Shaw

London and New York

First published 1994
by Routledge
11 New Fetter Lane, London EC4P 4EE

Simultaneously published in the USA and Canada
by Routledge
29 West 35th Street, New York, NY 10001

Typeset in Baskerville by Florencetype Ltd, Kewstoke, Avon

Printed and bound in Great Britain by
T. J. Press (Padstow) Ltd, Padstow, Cornwall

British Library Cataloguing in Publication Data
A catalogue record for this book is available from the
British Library

Library of Congress Cataloging in Publication Data
Shaw, Eric, 1949–
The Labour Party since 1979 : crisis and transformation /
Eric Shaw.
p.   cm.
Includes bibliographical references and index.
ISBN 0–415–05614–4. – ISBN 0–415–05615–2 (pbk.)
1. Labour Party (Great Britain) – History. 2. Great
Britain – Politics and government – 1979– I. Title.
JN1129.L32S457 1994
324.24107′09′048 – dc20   94–8635
CIP

ISBN 0–415–05614–4 (hbk)
ISBN 0–415–05615–2 (pbk)

To Susan

CONTENTS

PREFACE

When Neil Kinnock was elected leader in 1983, he inherited a party which was hopelessly divided, appeared to be totally unmanageable, and was saddled with an array of unpopular left-wing policies. By the time of his resignation in 1992 Labour was a radically different party, tightly disciplined, firmly in the hands of the Parliamentary leadership and wholly committed to working within the framework of a privately owned market economy. Most commentators concur that Labour has undergone a transformation, removing 'from a party which would often call itself socialist . . . any basis for being so' (Lloyd, 1990). However, although there have been many publications on aspects of Labour politics there is as yet no book-length study of the Party as a whole since 1979, nor one that seeks to trace, in an integrated and systematic manner, the way in which this transformation occurred. One intention of this book is to try and fill this vacuum.

The choice of the title, *Crisis and Transformation*, has been deliberate, since rather than offering a general survey of the Labour Party the book is organised around the exploration of these themes. What was the nature of the crisis that overwhelmed Labour from 1979 to 1983? How did its leaders seek to surmount it? And, most important of all, in what sense has the Party been transformed? What has it ceased to be and what has it now become? For most commentators, the party that it has left behind is one that favoured 'detailed planning. . . . the goal of common ownership of the means of production' and the destruction of capitalism (Smith, 1992: 27–8). Similarly, there is broad agreement that Labour had now 'sided firmly with the social democratic tradition' (Smith: 223, 224). We suggest that these answers are, at most, partially correct. They exhibit a curiously ahistorical approach in that they take as their point of departure the period immediately preceding the Kinnock leadership (from 1979 to 1983) when the left was temporarily in the ascendant. Yet this period was thoroughly atypical. The degree of control the left exerted over decision-making was unprecedented and the 1983 Manifesto, as a document produced in the teeth of the opposition of the majority of the PLP, and with only a slim input from the Shadow Cabinet and the leader, Michael Foot, was in many ways unique. We argue that a much more appropriate yardstick for evaluating the scale and nature of change since 1983 is the body of beliefs which actually influenced the behaviour of Labour governments and represented the ideological viewpoint of those who ran the Party for the generation before 1979, which we call revisionist or Croslandite social democracy. We also contest the view that Labour has now definitively become a revisionist party.[1] We propose to show that the new ruling doctrine is in fact 'post-revisionist' and that, far from embracing Croslandite goals and values, it has departed from this tradition in a number of crucial respects. We present two further arguments: firstly, that the Policy Review was not the clean rupture it has often been portrayed as, but the acceleration of processes of change that were already underway after 1983. Secondly, whereas most commentators on the Policy Review have concentrated on the clash between the leadership and the custodians of the traditional socialist faith, we point out that the real debate that took place, and one of very considerable moment for Labour's ideological odyssey, was between Kinnock and the right-wing advocates of post-revisionism on the one hand and the so-called 'soft-left' advocates of Keynesianism and state intervention on the other.

Programmatic change was only one aspect of Kinnock's modernising project[2] since he also sought radical changes in Labour's constitution, organisation and power structure (for short, we refer to this as organisational change). As in the policy sphere, so here too, Labour was transformed. In 1981 Drucker wrote that 'Labour has become yet more closely tied to the unions, more the plaything of its decreasingly numerous but increasingly leftist local activists, more disputatious. . . . All of these trends have tended to undermine the position of the leader.' He concluded by pronouncing the end of 'elite domination' by the Parliamentary leadership (Drucker, 1981: 375–6). Less than a decade later the *Guardian* reported that 'Mr Kinnock appears in Blackpool, too, more perhaps than any of his predecessors, as the undisputed voice of the Labour Party. By cunning and patient strategies he has achieved a control of the Party which even Harold Wilson never matched. What he says usually goes. In the Party's National Executive he wins vote after vote by truly crushing majorities' (*Guardian* leader, 1 October 1990). In seeking to explain this transformation, we draw attention to the landmark year of 1985 which witnessed the defeat of the miners' strike and the collapse of resistance to rate-capping, events which demoralised and fragmented the left, speeding up the so-called realignment of the left and thus contributing significantly to the consolidation of leadership power. Organisational transformation was no less significant than programmatic, not least because sweeping changes in ideology and policy could not have been accomplished in its absence. We examine the complex of factors, such as Labour's power structure, party culture, the pattern of internal alignments and environmental forces which shaped the pace and direction of change.

The crucial catalyst was undoubtedly successive electoral defeats, reflecting the impact of social, economic, cultural and political developments whose impact on Labour's vote has been extensively analysed (see, for example, Heath, Jowell and Curtice, 1985; Heath *et al.*, 1991; Johnston, Pattie and Allsopp, 1988; Franklin, 1985; Dunleavy and Husbands, 1985; Crewe, 1984). Some commentators have claimed that social trends, especially the shrinkage and fragmentation of the working class, have doomed Labour to ineluctable decline (Rose, 1992) but this assumes causal relationships between societal factors and electoral performance which evidence outside Britain indicates do not hold.[3] Rather, these trends coupled with class and partisan dealignment had released millions of voters from their social and political anchorage and created a massive reservoir of floating voters affording the parties opportunities to expand their constituencies through political mobilisation. As Miller *et al.* explain: 'The British political system is now one where the alignment between social classes and partisan support is sufficiently weak to give major play to highly mutable short-term forces. As such, it places a premium on waging successful campaigns – both long and short campaigns' (Miller *et al.*, 1990: 267).

Hence, much of this study is devoted to a third dimension of change, whose importance has not been fully grasped and which has not as yet been systematically explored: the transformation of Labour's approach to campaigning strategy. It is often assumed that the most rational (or vote-maximising) electoral strategy can easily be identified and that the main problem is securing party approval (Strom, 1990). We contend, in contrast, that neither the meaning of external settings nor therefore the nature of the most appropriate strategic response is self evident. In contrast, we hold – and this is a major thesis of this volume – that the crucial intervening factor, mediating the impact of environmental pressures on Labour and influencing the selection of electoral strategy, was the frame of reference employed by its strategists. We label this 'the new strategic thinking' (or paradigm) and enumerate five main components: a model of electoral behaviour; a conception of policy development that viewed it largely in terms of 'positioning'; an approach to electioneering that identified control of the political agenda as the prime campaigning object; an emphasis on the indispensability of securing maximum media exposure; and, finally, the methodical application of modern, commercially-inspired, communication techniques.

We shall argue that the emergence of a new strategic decision-making community was primarily responsible for formulating and implementing the new strategic thinking. Not only was this revolution in the Party's campaigning and communications profoundly important in its own right but it also supplied the driving force behind the modernisation of Party organisation, programme as well as strategy. It encouraged a steady drift to the right entailing not only the shredding of the radical commitments inherited from the left but also the discarding of central elements of revisionist social democracy. The organisational changes it promoted culminated in a tighter disciplinary regime, a more centralised decision-making structure and the restoration and, indeed, the intensification of control by the Parliamentary elite.

Crewe has written that: 'by 1992 the Labour Party was united, disciplined, moderate and modern. The Trotskyist Militant faction had been purged; the socialist left was marginalised; and a wide-ranging policy review had jettisoned its former policy liabilities, including unilateralism, nationalisation and central economic planning.' Further, the Conservatives had suffered dissension, the economy was in deep recession and the Liberal Democrats had lost credibility as an alternative government. Labour – which most commentators agreed had out-campaigned the Tories – in short, 'fought the election in as ideal conditions as an opposition could hope to find' (Crewe, 1992b: 3). Despite this, in terms of votes, the Party lost conclusively. For some this attests the inevitability of Labour's decay, whilst to others – for example Labour's modernisers – it was because the Kinnock modernisation project had not proceeded far enough. In the course of an assessment of Labour's campaigning and communications strategy, we shall contend that, insofar as the outcome of the election was affected by Labour's own actions, weaknesses in its overall strategic design played a significant part.

Chapter 1 examines the onset and characteristics of Labour's crisis. We begin by outlining revisionist social democracy and note how it decomposed during the years of the 1974 to 1979 Labour Government. After the fall of the Government, control of Labour's policy-making fell to a large extent into the hands of the left. We discuss the main components of the left alternative programme and indicate why it failed to provide a feasible and credible alternative to revisionism. We then turn to Labour's crisis of governance, and its two main constituent elements, a paralysis of leadership and extreme polarisation. Finally, we trace the ascendant left's strategic response to Labour's electoral decline and briefly consider the mismanaged campaign of 1983.

Chapter 2 examines the process of organisational and pro-grammatic change between 1983 and 1987. It draws attention to the hitherto largely unnoticed significance of the shift in gear from late 1985, when the defeat of the miners' strike and of the campaign against rate-capping combined with the accommo-dation of a section of the left with the leadership eased internal pressures and restraints thereby considerably augmenting the leadership's innovating capability. Not only was much of the 1983 programme cast aside, but several of the themes of the Policy Review, such as the move to a more market-oriented economic approach, were clearly prefigured. The contrast

between the proficiency and professionalism of the Conservatives' campaign and Labour's lacklustre and disorganised efforts
struck the new leadership very powerfully, and the main theme
of Chapter 3 is the transformation in its own approach to
electoral mobilisation and communications. It discusses the
emergence of a new strategic community, whose key members
included Party officials, leadership aides and members of
the newly formed Shadow Communications Agency. It then
analyses the emergence of the new strategic thinking and the
revolution in the Party's approach to campaigning and
communications.

In Chapter 4 we examine the Policy Review of 1987 to 1990
which represented Labour's most systematic effort to address
the crisis of social democracy and adapt to the new world of the
1990s. To most commentators its outcome marked Labour's
belated embrace of continental social democracy. We shall
suggest that the Review led not to Labour's social democratisation but to the adoption of a 'post-revisionist social democracy' in
which several of the key tenets of Croslandite revisionism were
discarded. The leadership sought to achieve organisational as
well as policy modernisation, that is the creation of a more
disciplined and cohesive party, and the extinction of the political
influence of the left by means of more stringent central control
and the extension of direct membership enfranchisement.
Kinnock, we shall suggest, enjoyed a substantial measure of
success and, in doing so, strengthened the oligarchical tendencies endemic in parties. These form the main themes of Chapter
5. In Chapter 6 we examine Labour's campaigning and communications strategy between 1987 and 1992 and the messages,
techniques and objectives selected. We then turn to the planning
for the 1992 election and conclude with a discussion of the
campaign. Chapter 7 explores the main factors shaping the
course, pace and direction of party modernisation or transformation. The eighth chapter analyses those features of the communications environment which impair Labour's capacity to
convey its messages and then proceeds to scrutinise in some
detail the elements of the new strategic thinking and the premises underpinning the Party's campaigning and communications
strategy. The conclusion summarises the main themes and considers briefly the problems raised by modernisation and the
switch to post-revisionist social democracy.

ACKNOWLEDGEMENTS

I would like to express my great appreciation to the people who allowed me to interview them (most on two and several on more than two occasions). Their names are listed below. I am particularly grateful to the following who made helpful comments on sections of earlier drafts of the work: Elizabeth Bomberg, Bryan Gould, Peter Mandelson, Chris Pierson, Chris Powell, Tom Sawyer, Len Scott, Adam Sharples and Nigel Stanley. My thanks are also due to Tony Benn and Ruth Winstone for access to and assistance in using the fascinating Benn Archives, and to Charlotte Atkins, Liz Atkins, Geoff Bish and Nick Sigler who helped in a variety of ways. I would like to acknowledge financial assistance from the Carnegie Foundation and the University of Stirling. I owe an especially heavy debt of gratitude to Lewis Minkin (whose two magisterial works, *The Labour Party Conference* and *The Contentious Alliance* are indispensable sources for all students of Labour politics) both for reading and making very valuable comments on the whole of an earlier draft of the book and for the advice given and thoughts shared in conversations over the years. I am most indebted of all to Susan who coped so well with the stresses and strains of – it often seemed – the interminable number of years I spent on writing this book.

SOURCES

I have sought to ensure that every point made, interpretation advanced or conclusion reached is supported by evidence. I have utilised four major types of source. Firstly, secondary material, which has been referenced in the text. Chapter 8 relies to a much greater degree than the rest of the book on the findings of (mainly American) secondary literature though these were, in large part, supported by a large body of (largely quantitative) research. Secondly, published Labour Party documents such as Annual Conference Reports and policy statements. Thirdly, the files of the *Guardian*, the *Observer*, the *New Statesman* (later the *New Statesman and Society*) and *Tribune* and, more selectively *The Times*, the *Independent*, the *Sunday Times* and *Independent on Sunday*. Fourthly, and most importantly, primary sources. I was able to consult a substantial body of internal Labour Party documentation, including NEC minutes and papers and a variety of memoranda and reports. In addition the work draws extensively upon a series of interviews. Since all interviews were held on an off-the-record-basis, I have used an appropriate label to designate the interviewee.

PEOPLE INTERVIEWED

Andy Batkin, Geof Bish, Ewan Cameron, Charles Clarke, Mike Craven, John Cruddas, Murray Elder, Mike Gapes MP, Roger Glendenning, Bryan Gould MP, Philip Gould, Anna Healey, Partricia Hewitt, David Hill, Keith Hill MP, Roger Jowell, Michael Meacher MP, Peter Mandelson MP, Henry Neuberger, Rex Osborne, Jim Parish, Chris Powell, George Robertson MP, Tom Sawyer, Len Scott, Adam Sharples, Nick Sigler, Nigel Stanley, John Underwood, Mary Walker, Larry Whitty, Bob Worcester.

ABBREVIATIONS

AUEW	Amalgamated Union of Engineering Workers
CLPD	Campaign for Labour Party Democracy
CMT	Campaign Management Team
CSC	Campaign Strategy Committee
GMB	General and Municipal Workers
IPPR	Institute of Public Policy Research
LCC	Labour Co-ordinating Committee
LPCR	Labour Party Conference Report
MSF	Manufacturing, Science, Finance
NEC	National Executive Committee
NEDC	National Economic Development Council
NUM	National Union of Miners
NUPE	National Union of Public Employees
Org. Sub.	Organisation Sub-Committee (of NEC)
PD	Policy Directorate
PLP	Parliamentary Labour Party
PPB/PEB	Party Political/Election Broadcast
PRG	Policy Review Group
RD	Research Department
SCA	Shadow Communications Agency
TGWU	Transport and General Workers' Union
TUC	Trades Union Congress
UCW	Union of Communication Workers

1

LABOUR'S MULTIPLE CRISES 1979–83

The period 1979 to 1983 was one of the most stormy and eventful in the Labour Party's history. With the left in control of the policy-making machine, it engaged in an extensive process of policy innovation which culminated in the supplanting of many of the governing ideas and policies of the past generation by a considerably more radical programme. In order to establish a benchmark against which to measure the scale of programmatic change both under the left and subsequently when the right regained control, this chapter opens with an outline of revisionist social democracy, Labour's ruling body of ideas until decomposition set in from the mid-1970s. It then assesses the left's alternative programme which took definitive form in the 1983 manifesto. After Labour's defeat in 1979 the smouldering tensions between left and right ignited into a veritable civil war encompassing organisational as well as ideological and policy matters. Further, the success of the left precipitated a major schism as senior right-wingers quit to form the Social Democratic Party (SDP). An analysis of these issues forms the second part of this chapter. The ferocity of the internal struggle coupled with the advent of the SDP shattered Labour's standing in the polls, reversing any hope of recovery after its ousting from government in 1979. This intensified the process of electoral decline, from which Labour was already suffering and, in conjunction with one of the most ramshackle campaigns it has ever mounted, led to the electoral disaster of 1983: this constitutes the subject matter of the third part of the chapter.

REVISIONIST SOCIAL DEMOCRACY AND ITS DECOMPOSITION

For a generation, from the late 1940s to the end of the 1970s, the political thinking and practice of the Labour Party were governed by the precepts of revisionist social democracy. It constituted what Kitschelt has called a social democratic 'discourse', that is, 'the set of key organising principles and axiomatic propositions that drive the programmatic vision of socialist parties and is invoked by socialist politicians to propose solutions for concrete policy problems in the economic, social or cultural realm' (Kitschelt, 1992: 194). Labour's 'discourse' whilst in part the sedimentation of its history and experiences also incorporated the thinking of revisionist intellectuals, most notably that of Tony Crosland, who was a prominent theoretician, a confidante of one leader (Hugh Gaitskell) and a senior minister in administrations formed by his two successors, Harold Wilson and James Callaghan.

Keynesianism and public ownership

Prior to the War, socialists had contended that capitalism was incapable of providing either full employment or decent living conditions for the mass of the population because it suffered from an endemic propensity to swing between boom and slump and because it distributed income and wealth in a highly inegalitarian manner. These ills were innate in a private enterprise system and thereby could only be overcome by a major extension of public ownership. It followed, as the post-war leader of the Labour left, Aneurin Bevan, put it, 'that one of the central principles of socialism is the substitution of public for private ownership' (*Tribune* 13 June 1952, quoted in Greenleaf, 1983: 471). This belief was challenged by revisionist social democracy which contended that the defects to which capitalism was prone (inequality, unemployment and economic instability) could be surmounted by the application of Keynesian economics, rendering alterations in the ownership structure superfluous. By manipulating the level of aggregate demand a social democratic government could smooth out the oscillations of the business cycle and, by preventing the recurrence of inadequate demand and excess savings, maintain higher levels of consumption,

2

investment and employment. Further, Keynesian macro-economics provided the state with the means to establish social control of the economy – that is to say, impress upon the prevailing economic pattern priorities other than short-term profit maximisation – through the use of fiscal, monetary and regulatory instruments. As Crosland argued, 'political authority has emerged as the final arbiter of economic life' (Crosland, 1964: 29). Hence social democracy could combine private ownership and the market, on the one hand, with the pursuit of full employment, economic growth and equality on the other. Whilst nationalisation – of natural monopolies and of vital but economically insecure industries – might be advisable to protect the interests of the economy as a whole or to avert major job losses, it was not a necessary means to achieve socialist ends.

Keynesianism, in short, supplied the basis for a rapprochement between private corporate interests and the common good. In Przeworski's words, it 'held out the prospect that the state could reconcile the private ownership of the means of production with democratic management of the economy' (Przeworski, 1985: 207). It performed a triple function: firstly, it showed that the basic goals of the labour movement – full employment, decent wages and the public provision of social goods – need not be placed at the mercy of market forces but could be achieved by the purposive use of state power. Secondly, it provided a sound basis in economic theory for the sustained pursuit of social democratic goals: as Padgett and Paterson commented, it 'legitimised the doctrine of equality, since it demonstrated that economic expansion depended on broadening the basis of consumption through a diffuse distribution of income and wealth' (Padgett and Paterson, 1991: 23). Thirdly, it greatly enhanced the economic credibility of social democratic politicians by inviting the voters to decide not who was most qualified to manage a market economy but who was best equipped to use the power of the state to advance economic performance.

Capital, labour and the state

The Labour Party had never subscribed to the theory of class struggle: rather it saw its role as to secure for the working class the full right to participate in the established social order. With

3

the emergence of the Keynesian state able to countermand the power of capital, and with the arrival of full employment which had transformed the balance of industrial power between management and the unions, revisionism held that this had largely been achieved. Because of the organic link between the Party and the unions, and because the bulk of its electorate was composed of working class voters, revisionism accepted (though with a degree of unease) that Labour had to some degree to operate as a vehicle for working class interests, as defined by the unions. But it believed that the Party's ultimate responsibility was to foster social cohesion and industrial harmony, a balancing of roles which could never be wholly free of friction.

The inflationary upsurge of the 1970s following the huge increases in the price of oil exacerbated the friction and greatly complicated Labour's task. Following the pattern of more successful social democratic parties in Northern Europe, the revisionist response was 'the social contract', a corporatist experiment in policy-making. At its core was a bargain between the government and the unions in which wage restraint was exchanged for legislative concessions and the grant to the TUC of guaranteed rights of access to key policy-making centres. In part, corporatism was a device to master inflationary pressures, but, in a broader sense, it was a new means to achieve industrial order through an institutionalisation of co-operation between the unions, business and government.

State and market

The central economic proposition of revisionist social democracy thinking was that an appropriately regulated, predominantly privately-owned market system could attain most of the objectives that socialists regarded as desirable. In the late 1980s it became fashionable both for Labour's leaders and for many commentators to interpret the new economic stance outlined in the Policy Review as a rupture with the Party's traditional preference for planning and state intervention and thus a belated recognition of the superiority of the market economy. This is an inaccurate judgment: Labour's 'discourse' had long presupposed, as Hirst has pointed out, that, within the appropriate demand regime, 'private management in industry could be left to make the right decisions about levels of investment and

4

manufacturing methods' (Hirst, 1991: 250, 251). Thus Labour never sought to challenge the market as the organising principle of economic life. Whilst it advocated state intervention to remedy market defects, or (to use Marquand's phrase) 'hands-on Keynesianism' (Marquand, 1988: 45–7) it rejected what Crosland called 'the traditional socialist case for planning' – that is, an assumed conflict between production for use and production for profit – accepting that 'the price mechanism is now a reasonably satisfactory method of distributing the great bulk of consumer-goods and industrial capital-goods' (Crosland, 1964: 346). Beer summed up the process of programmatic change accomplished by the revisionists when he commented: 'In revisionist thinking and in the Party documents that reflected it there was during the 1950s a growing emphasis not only upon the private sector of the economy and the mechanisms of the market but also upon the incentives of gain and competition' (Beer, 1969: 237). Revisionist social democracy, in short, sought not to displace the market but to use state power to render it more responsive to social ends.

Social democratic values and the welfare state

Although revisionism abandoned the traditional view that socialism entailed the transformation of the economic system, it retained a distinctive and radical ideological edge. Crosland identified two key aspirations which demarcated a socialist party from its rivals. The first was social welfare: the relief of distress and squalor was, he argued the main object of social policy and 'a socialist is identified as one who wishes to give this an exceptional priority over other claims on resources' (Crosland, 1964: 76–77). The second was equality. This involved challenging the class system which he defined in terms of pronounced inequalities in access to social resources arising from deep, cumulative and reinforcing social disparities. The belief in social equality, Crosland declared, was 'the most characteristic feature of socialist thought', its promotion Labour's prime task (Crosland, 1964: 77).

The major instrument to accomplish these objectives was the welfare state. Whilst production was to be left mainly in private hands, revisionism advocated the socialisation of consumption in which the economic surplus of the private sector could be re-

5

cycled to meet social needs. This strategy was based on the notion that in a capitalist democracy resources are allocated by two mechanisms: the market and a democratically controlled state. The inequality and hardship generated by the former could be effectively balanced by the latter's endeavour (under Labour control) to advance equality and social justice. The welfare state constituted the goal, Keynesianism the vital means which provided the funds to finance it, whilst at the same time positively aiding, rather than impairing, the accumulation function which drove the market economy.

However, precisely since revisionism wished to avoid damaging capital accumulation or heightening social tensions, redistribution was seen as politically and economically feasible only when the economy was growing. The increments of growth would furnish the resources to finance an expanding social services, tackle social deprivation and spur the moves towards greater equality without imposing any additional burdens on higher income groups, who could then be expected to acquiesce in the process. It followed that it was upon the ability of Keynesianism to foster economic growth and maintain full employment, that the viability of revisionist social democracy ultimately rested. This programme was never formally adopted – unlike the SPD's Bad Godesberg programme – and therefore lacked an official status. But it provided the motive force behind successive Labour election manifestos and – more haltingly – its conduct in government.

Revisionism in disarray

However, the emergence of stagflation – a combination of high inflation and unemployment – shook confidence in the verities of Keynesian demand management. By the mid-1970s, a mix of monetarism and economic liberalism had become the ruling economic wisdom throughout the West. It was in this unpropitious environment that the Labour Government in 1976 blundered into a speculative crisis culminating in a request for an IMF loan. The IMF insisted upon drastic cuts in public spending and tighter control of the money supply, conditions which were only accepted after a long struggle in Cabinet and on the insistence of the Prime Minister, Jim Callaghan and his Chancellor, Denis Healey. Along with Tony Benn, Michael Foot and Peter Shore, Crosland was a staunch opponent of the loan but eventually capitulated on the grounds that rejecting the Prime Minister's advice on such a crucial matter would precipitate a sterling crisis and shatter Party unity. But as for the loan and its attached conditions he remained convinced that it was 'wrong economically and socially, destructive of what he had believed in all his life' (Benn, 1989: 674).[1] He understood that the loan signalled the abandonment of revisionism. In a few jotted notes he summed up the consequences: 'unemployment, even if politically more wearable = grave loss of welfare, security, choice' (quoted in Marquand, 1991: 176). Six weeks later, Crosland died suddenly of a stroke.

Unlike the Conservatives, the Labour Government's switch to monetarism was pragmatic, and hope lingered that, once the economy was set on the road to recovery, more resources could be committed to welfare programmes and cutting unemployment. Although steady progress was in fact made towards lower inflation, a stronger balance of payments and a lower budget deficit, the misjudged 5 per cent pay policy insisted upon by Healey in the autumn of 1978, and the decision to delay the election until 1979, contributed to the explosion of pay claims and the industrial strife of the winter of 1978–9: the Winter of Discontent. The Winter of Discontent eliminated any prospect of Labour holding on to power, and, indeed, has dogged it ever since. Just as the IMF loan marked the disintegration of Keynesianism as the governing economic doctrine so too the Winter of Discontent signified the collapse of corporatism. Without these two pillars, revisionist social democracy fell to pieces. The election was held shortly after and Labour tumbled to an inevitable and major defeat.

THE SOCIALIST ALTERNATIVE

The left had always been critics of revisionism. They claimed that it exaggerated the capacity of the Keynesian state to control corporate behaviour and was far too sanguine in its belief that the market and the private sector could achieve sustained growth or that social policy of itself could bring about effective progress towards equality without challenging the ownership of property (Holland, 1975). *Labour's Programme 1973* (drawn up by the left-leaning National Executive Committee (NEC))

7

reasoned that since the interests of large corporations 'cannot be expected to coincide with the interests of the national economy' and since fiscal and monetary policy or tax incentives alone were incapable of modifying their behaviour, a future Labour government would have to 'act *directly* at the level of the giant firm itself.' Objectives such as higher investment, increased exports, full employment and regional balance could only be achieved by a substantial expansion of public ownership in profitable industries.[2] The 1974–9 Labour Government took little notice of this argument but defeat at the polls in 1979 transferred the initiative to the left-controlled NEC, constitutionally responsible for policy formulation. It moved with alacrity and embarked on an ambitious programme of policy renewal culminating in the compendious *Labour's Programme 1982*.

The greatest source of the left's influence in this period lay in the fact that it was their experiences as largely impotent critics of the 1974–9 Government, their belief that it demonstrated the bankruptcy of revisionist social democracy and their frame of reference that governed the way in which most policy matters were considered. In contrast, predominantly right-wing former ministers had a limited input: many were demoralised, intellectually fatigued and could only rely on the exiguous organisational and constitutional resources of the Parliamentary Labour Party (PLP). Hence the conclusions they drew from their time in government and their definition of the problems Britain faced were of little relevance. The leading critics of the key IMF loan decision within the cabinet were, as we have noted, Crosland, Benn, Shore and Foot. By November 1980, Foot was leader of the Party, Shore the shadow chancellor and Benn the chairman of the Home Policy committee and effectively the senior policy-maker on the NEC.

However, the NEC was not the only policy conduit. A second channel of policy formation was the TUC–Labour Party Liaison Committee, which comprised representatives of the unions, the NEC and the Parliamentary leadership. It had been established in 1972 in order to repair the breach between the Labour Government and the unions which had occurred in the 1960s, although it served an additional purpose of reducing the left NEC's hold over policy. It had a particular responsibility for matters of especial interest to the unions, like pay and labour law, and in this period its influence reached a peak as it shaped policy on industrial matters as well as participating in the devising of Labour's overall economic strategy. This, as we shall see, ensured that Party policy did not solely reflect the thinking and preferences of the left.

Keynesianism

The left's macro-economic policy was unashamedly Keynesian. It promised 'a major increase' in public investment, 'a huge programme' of construction and 'substantial' increases in social expenditure. By boosting demand, public spending-driven reflation would, it was anticipated, generate more investment growth and job opportunities, and (via higher tax yields) the greater revenue needed to refurbish the public services.[3] The crucial objective was to reduce unemployment to below one million within five years of taking office. Policy-makers recognised that a substantial injection of demand was bound to suck in more imports, whilst the programme as a whole would shake the confidence of the money markets, but the left's response was not to bend before such pressures but to seek to restrict the economy's exposure to international pressures by introducing import and exchange controls. However, on this point, the left's preference for protection was checked by the free trader Shore, who, as shadow chancellor, favoured the standard Keynesian response of devaluation. Labour's final policy, as agreed in the 1983 Manifesto, was a compromise between the two stances, calling for 'a realistic and competitive' exchange rate, import controls if necessary and exchange controls to counter currency speculation and redirect capital from overseas to domestic investment.[4] Whether this would have enabled a Labour Government to resist international pressures is a question to which we shall return.

Pay, inflation and the unions

Pay policy had been the issue which had brought the last Labour Government crashing to the ground and it continued to be a cause of difficulties after 1979. But the twin questions of pay and inflation were, in this period, viewed very much from the perspective of that Government's left-wing critics who viewed incomes policy as simply a form of wage restraint designed to ensure that workers bore the main brunt of the economic crisis. Both Shore and Party officials, in contrast, were well aware of the inflationary pressures that would confront an incoming Labour Government: the Party's public spending programme and devaluation would fuel inflationary pressures and if workers sought to recoup lost earning power caused by higher prices of imported goods then devaluation would be self-defeating since Labour's priorities of improved welfare services, full employment and more investment left little room for wages growth. The NEC paid scant regard since it did not accept that excessive wage demands were a major cause of inflation, and at a special Home Policy Committee meeting to discuss inflation Benn dismissed wages policy as 'rigid, unfair and unacceptable for a Labour electorate'.[5]

The solution which eventually emerged was the National Economic Assessment, an idea which originated with TUC and Party staff (Minkin, 1991: 426). It was an experiment in what we can call 'social corporatism', a form of tripartite government–unions–employers bargaining system in which the central axis would be a partnership between the unions and the Labour Government. Whilst the revisionist brand of corporatism offered unions an institutionalised right to participate in policy formation in return for wage restraint within the contours of the existing economic order, social corporatism envisaged a substantial alteration in the nature of that order by extending tripartite bargaining over key economic decisions. Thus the NEA would form the basis of a five-year planning strategy and would cover 'the allocation of resources, and the distribution of income between profits, earnings from employment, rents, social benefits and other incomes.'[6]

But would social corporatism provide a barrier to inflationary pressures? Considerable faith was reposed in the willingness of the unions to refrain from utilising to the full their industrial leverage and 'where necessary, to make sacrifices' to achieve wider social goals.[7] But did unions have the power to trade wage restraint against broader social advances? Labour's answer was to advocate the devolving of responsibility for wage moderation to those most closely involved, the pay bargainers themselves. Wage determination at plant and company level would become part of a much broader process as collective bargaining would be extended – under Labour's ambitious programme for economic planning and industrial democracy – to encompass a much wider range of matters. The problem here was that local union negotiators were more likely than national union organisations to define their role primarily in terms of representing the interests of their members. As a result, the National Economic Assessment rested on brittle foundations since the unions lacked the organisational capacity or, indeed, the ideological traditions to justify and enforce the subordination of sectional concerns to wider societal ones. The lack of a credible anti-inflation strategy was a problem which was never resolved.

The market, planning and the state

Revisionist social democracy, as we have seen, believed that Keynesian demand-management afforded sufficient means to secure collective control over the economy. The left, in contrast, favoured a considerably more active supply-side role for the state and this was the stance taken by Labour after 1979.[8] Labour's major policy statement spelling out its industrial strategy was entitled *Economic Planning and Industrial Democracy* and these two policies were deemed to constitute 'an essential framework for full employment, industrial revival and greater social justice.'[9] The strategy involved a *dirigiste* approach to state intervention and held that while the market might be a useful means of enhancing corporate efficiency, it was incapable of resolving major economic and social problems. Planning was designed, firstly, to provide a framework in which corporate plans in the private sector could be aligned with the Government's expansionary macro-economic policy; secondly, to steer investment into new growth sectors and encourage the exploitation of new technologies; and thirdly to ease the process of adjustment in failing industries and rectify regional imbalances.[10] The government would seek agreement with business and the unions via a revamped National Economic Development Council to be renamed the National Planning Council whilst a new Planning Department would be charged with drawing up a rolling five-year macro-economic and sectoral plan. The Planning Department would negotiate Agreed Development Plans (ADPs) with major companies (and with the unions) on matters such as pricing, training, investment and imports with the object of boosting competitiveness. Planning was not, however, intended to replace the market, for, as the then Party Research Secretary, Geoff Bish later recalled, it was 'always meant to be market-driven – to take place within a market framework.'[11] The aim was to modify the way in which the market system operated in order to compel it to take account of motive-forces other than immediate commercial gain but this, nevertheless, represented a major break with revisionism's scepticism about economic planning.

Radicalising the pursuit of equality: industrial democracy and public ownership

Revisionism confined its egalitarian efforts largely to matters of social policy. The left sought to transcend the traditional social democratic objectives of full employment, greater equality and social justice by a more wide-ranging attack on inequality, aiming at 'a fundamental and irreversible shift in the balance of power and wealth in favour of working people and their families.'[12] Thus the democratisation of industry – a matter that hardly figured on the revisionist agenda – was designed to enfranchise the workforce and challenge the great constellations of corporate economic power. Nevertheless, it did not entail the substitution of public for private ownership – here it marked a retreat from schemes for workers' control advocated by the left in the 1970s – but the sharing of power between employees and management. The ideological premise was a distinctly non-Marxist one – that capital and labour could co-operate for the greater good of the country. However this co-operation could only take place in the context of a more equal balance of power between capital and labour. Thus rights to information would be greatly widened, management would be obliged to consult with the workforce on any matters which might affect the operations of the enterprise and, more boldly, workers would be given representation rights to be exercised through a Joint Union Committee 'at all levels of decision-making up to and including board level.' Workers would be able to build up to 50/50 representation on the board of directors or with a third element where this was mutually agreed.[13]

A view widely propagated by commentators later in the decade was that, in this period, public ownership lay at the heart of the 1983 Manifesto. *Labour's Programme 1982* did indeed argue that 'our social and economic objectives can be achieved only through an expansion of common ownership substantial enough to give the community decisive power over the commanding heights of the economy.'[14] However, although Labour was pledged to restore to the public sector all privatised industries, in Labour's 1983 Manifesto precisely one sentence (in the Party's longest Manifesto on record) was devoted to fresh public ownership calling for 'a significant public stake in electronics, pharmaceuticals, health equipment and building materials and in other important sectors, as required in the national interest.'[15] No reason was given for the choice of these industries, the purpose of nationalising them was not spelt out and there was no obvious relation to Labour's planning objectives. This represents a contrast with the industrial policy of the early 1970s, which viewed an extension of public ownership into the most profitable manufacturing sectors as an essential component of its strategy. Hence, in this respect – a point invariably overlooked – Labour's programme in 1983 amounted to a move towards accepting a predominantly privately owned economy, albeit one which subjected market forces to a complex system of state regulation.

A viable programme?

This programme, as summed up in the 1983 Manifesto, was certainly the most left-wing for many years, yet not wholly the left's programme but rather a compromise between two positions. Shore and Foot basically wanted a Keynesian programme – with some supply-side additions – to create jobs and boost growth but the Bennite left, in contrast, wished to go considerably further in encroaching upon the prerogatives of capital. The outcome was, in key areas of policy, a hybrid. Thus on macro-economic policy, the left's preferences for tough controls on exchange and capital movements were watered down to a pledge to revive the more limited exchange control regime scrapped in 1979; similarly, the commitment to comprehensive import controls tied into Labour's planning strategy was replaced by devaluation backed up by partial restrictions on imports. Labour's proposals on industrial democracy fell considerably short of the notions of workers' control pressed by the Institute for Workers' Control and others on the left whilst its complex planning policy owed as much to continental and Japanese experience as to any specifically socialist blueprint. Most notably of all, in contrast to Labour's industrial programme of the early 1970s, public ownership was relegated to a single sentence in *New Hope for Britain*. Nevertheless one can conclude that the general thrust of Labour's economic strategy was towards a far greater degree of collective control of the economy than the Party at the end of the decade would entertain.

Revisionist social democracy had been overturned in part by domestic and international pressures: the left's response was that, if greater determination were displayed, a more audacious programme could overcome them. They were slow to grasp the fundamental challenge posed by Thatcherism and their belief that the election defeat of 1979 was primarily due to the discarding by a supine Labour Government of the radical platform upon which it was elected deflected them from engaging in a more complete analysis. They deduced from Mrs Thatcher's successes in driving through her own brand of radicalism the simple lesson that, given decisive leadership, sweeping innovations could be achieved by the left as well. This promoted a voluntarist faith in forceful leadership which disregarded objective constraints. There is little doubt that a Labour Government seeking to implement the 1983 manifesto would have encountered very stiff resistance from extremely powerful forces, both at home and abroad. Yet insufficient thought was given, for instance, to the predictable storm of resistance that the Party's planning proposals would provoke from a private sector which, unlike in France and Japan, was traditionally very hostile to an interventionist state. Domestically, the problem was not only business distaste for such policies as planning and industrial democracy which infringed its prerogatives but also the sheer range of Labour polices – including reflation, labour law, import and exchange controls, withdrawal from the EC – which it found objectionable. Equally, the Party took little account of developments in the international environment which were progressively undermining the control of nation-states over their own economic destinies, such as liberalisation, deregulation and the massive expansion of global money markets though many of its policies flew in the face of received wisdom in both the world financial community and foreign governments. Could a Labour government survive a massive flight of capital, intense speculative pressure against sterling, turbulence on the money markets and a collapse of business confidence? Was not Britain now so entangled in the web of an open, highly interdependent world economy where vast power was wielded by the financial markets that a socialist or social democratic national economic strategy had ceased to be a viable option? The matter was hardly an academic one since precisely at the moment that the Party was putting the finishing touches to its economic programme (1982/3) the French Socialist government was being forced by external pressures to abandon an economic strategy similar in many ways to Labour's own. In addition, there was little evidence of any mass support for radical polices within the electorate even if it had been persuaded to reject the Conservatives.

The left – oddly in a way – failed to grasp that Labour and the Conservatives were not on a level playing field, that drastic reforms could be accomplished by Mrs Thatcher because they had the sympathy of the holders of economic and financial power at home and abroad. The left, in contrast, suffered from a double handicap: *any* left of centre government was regarded by industry and the financial markets as suspect and one equipped with a radical programme as beyond the bounds of the reasonable. The left, in fact, had an exaggerated view of the amount of power that victory in the electoral process, and the possession of a democratic mandate actually conferred upon a government in an internationally integrated market system. In the event, Labour was totally repudiated by the voters, the scale of the defeat demonstrating that the radical manifesto of 1983 far from resolving its ideological crisis had immeasurably deepened it.

LABOUR'S CRISIS OF GOVERNANCE

The constitutional crisis

The indifference displayed by successive Labour governments to Party manifestos and Conference declarations had by 1979 convinced many, amongst unions as well as activists, that formal control over the programme was pointless unless the wider Party had the power to compel a Labour cabinet to put it into effect.The left in particular concluded that if the rules had failed to protect democracy, then the rules had to be changed. The campaign for constitutional reform, already being pursued before Labour's loss of office (and quite inaccurately attributed to Tony Benn) was masterminded by the Campaign for Labour Party Democracy (CLPD) an organisation of grass-roots activists set up in 1973. It sought three main reforms: mandatory re-selection of Labour MPs so that they would have no automatic right to remain as Labour representatives beyond the life of one parliament; the placing of the right to frame the manifesto – theoretically shared between the parliamentary leadership and the NEC, but with the former's influence usually paramount – solely in the hands of the latter; and extending the franchise for selecting the leader beyond the PLP to the Party at large. The constitutional reformers had three interlinked aims: to weaken the right's hold on the Party, to redistribute power from the parliamentary establishment to the rank and file and to end the effective independence of the PLP upon which right-wing control of the Party was seen ultimately to rest. The central reform, mandatory reselection, was designed to enforce MPs' accountability to their individual parties – in the knowledge that constituency General Committees were predominantly left-wing; the electoral college aimed to render the leader more sensitive to Party and union opinion and NEC control of the manifesto to remove the leader's power of veto. The Parliamentary leadership and the right stridently opposed the constitutional reforms. Far from extending democracy, they would undermine it by swelling the power of a small number of activists and of the 'barons' of the trade unions. They argued that MPs were properly accountable to the voters, not to a narrow party caucus; and that MPs were elected to exercise their judgment and discretion and should not be trammelled by Party mandates. Further, they claimed that the shrunken number of Party activists was unrepresentative of Labour voters and that MPs were far more sensitive to the currents of public opinion.

The policies that a triumphant left-led NEC swept through Conference from 1979 to 1981 – unilateralism, withdrawal from the EC, extending public ownership – convinced the right that Labour under the command of the left was heading for electoral disaster, and influential figures, notably former cabinet members David Owen, Shirley Williams and Bill Rodgers, dismayed by the left's success, began to consider quitting the Party. At the

1980 Annual Conference and the special conference of January 1981, mandatory reselection, and a new method of electing the leader (the electoral college which gave 40 per cent of the votes to the unions, 30 per cent to the constituencies, hence reducing the PLP's share to 30 per cent) were adopted. (NEC control over the manifesto was narrowly rejected). Their lingering doubts resolved by the left's triumph, the three former ministers, together with another former senior Labour politician, Roy Jenkins, decided to establish a new party, the SDP, and were joined by almost two dozen Labour MPs. This was the worst split in the Party for half a century with devastating electoral consequences as former Labour voters flocked to the new party.

The paralysis of leadership

Constitutionally, Labour was a highly pluralist organisation with decision-making powers apportioned amongst a variety of institutions: the leader, the shadow cabinet or front bench, the NEC, and, as possessors of large blocks of votes at Conference and the right to elect the majority of NEC members, the larger unions. In fact, for most of Labour's history, the Party was dominated by its Parliamentary leadership whose rule rested upon right-wing majorities in all key institutions which gave rise to a system of integrated organisational control. After 1979 this disintegrated and bereft of the powers which it had only enjoyed by virtue of its grip over the NEC, the leadership lacked the constitutional authority to block the adoption of policies to which it was fundamentally opposed. It was by exercising its right to formulate policy statements and present them to Conference that the left NEC helped steer such controversial policies as unilateralism, withdrawal from the EC and the interventionist economic strategy through Conference. Equally, it was the NEC, as custodian of the Constitution, which used its constitutional prerogatives to ensure that the momentum of constitutional reform was not stalled. Callaghan's inability to dissuade Conference from approving these constitutional reforms and adopting left-wing positions on major policy matters demonstrated the extent to which the authority of both the Leader and the front bench as a whole had dwindled. 'I have as little authority in the PLP as I have in the NEC', Callaghan lamented to an aide who replied: 'The left are the masters now' (Jenkins, 1987: 113).

17

Callaghan was discredited by what was perceived as his meagre record of achievement as premier and was obviously a lame duck. He resigned the leadership before a new leadership election procedure was installed in the hope that, with the franchise still precariously in the PLP's hands, Healey would enter into the inheritance for which, by experience and talent, he seemed eminently well-qualified. But he was defeated by Michael Foot, largely because sufficient numbers of right and centre MPs feared that the ebulliently abrasive Healey would so infuriate the left as to finally rupture the Party. (Also, some MPs intending to defect to the SDP backed Foot on the grounds that Healey would be a more formidable opponent.) Despite the enthusiasm with which many greeted his election, Foot proved to be an ineffectual leader who lacked either the power base or the political gifts to stamp his authority on the Party; furthermore, his position was constantly undermined by his derisory showing in the opinion polls. Once an unrepentant rebel, Foot had for a decade performed the role of conciliator: he saw his mission above all to maintain Party unity. However, even his emollient gifts proved inadequate to the task as he could neither prevent a large segment of the right seceding to form the Social Democratic Party nor end the civil strife that raged within the Party and far from restoring the authority of the leadership, under his aegis it fell to its nadir. He was regarded as an apostate left-winger by most of the Bennites because of his defence of the last Labour Government, and he further alienated them by his attempts to protect the prerogatives of the PLP and staunch the tide of constitutional change. But his sympathy for left-wing polices on a number of vital issues put him at odds with the right-wing majority of Labour MPs and his own shadow cabinet whose support for him him was at most tepid.

The paralysis of leadership power under Foot was illustrated by a series of episodes. In 1981, Benn decided to invoke the electoral college and challenge the incumbent Denis Healey for the deputy leadership. Foot bitterly opposed the move, rightly anticipating that a further bout of internal strife between embattled left and right would inflict immense electoral harm on the Party. But Benn was unmoved by the pleas of the leader whose repeated and insistent condemnation of the contest failed to dissuade the mass of constituency activists nor considerable numbers of trade unionists from voting for Benn who was only very narrowly held at bay by Healey. A second instance was the Peter Tatchell affair. Foot in December 1981 rather impetuously announced in the House of Commons that the strongly left-wing young Australian, selected as Labour candidate for the safe seat of Bermondsey, was wholly unsuitable and would never be endorsed. Constitutionally, the power of endorsing parliamentary candidates lay with the NEC and it refused to accept Foot's judgment. Tatchell was approved, and Foot had no option but to back his candidature at a bye-election called shortly after – at which Labour suffered a devastating defeat. A third rebuff was from the right. A longstanding power of the Party leader derived from his control over appointments, but when Foot tried to replace Eric Varley as Employment spokesman with his protégé, and the organiser of his leadership campaign, Neil Kinnock, he was thwarted by right-wing members of the shadow cabinet who threatened to resign. As a result, he was forced to back down, and his prestige dwindled even more. A final example was afforded by the impasse into which the first disciplinary drive against the Trotskyist Militant Tendency fell. The influence of this organisation was often wildly exaggerated but there was no doubt that it was growing and many centre and right-wing MPs were deeply alarmed. Whilst under left control, the NEC was unwilling to act but as the right recouped its forces, an alliance between them and the centre–left on the Executive won enough votes to tow an initially reluctant Foot behind it, and instigate measures against Militant. An enquiry was held and, after some delay, the NEC proscribed the Trotskyist body and expelled some of its leaders but in the teeth of fierce criticism from most of the left. Further disciplinary action was bogged down in procedural wrangles and although by the following year the NEC was able to claim a few scalps, the sheer problems it encountered and pain it had suffered in achieving this very modest outcome (which enhanced rather than diminished the influence of Militant) merely underlined the limits of leadership power. (For a full account, see Shaw, 1988: 218–53.)

The crisis of legitimacy

Power in the Labour Party, as in any voluntary organisation in the last resort rests on the consent of the rank and file. By 1979 this was crumbling as the failure of successive Labour

Governments to fulfil their aspirations had bred a deep disenchantment with the Party's leaders. Not only could they boast few substantial strides towards the socialist commonwealth, even the core goals of full employment and expanding social services seemed by the close of the 1970s to have been abandoned. The fact, too, that the leadership had ignored Conference decisions and (it was felt) shed key manifesto pledges convinced many that they were exercising their power in a way that contradicted the canons of Party democracy. This, in turn, led many to deny the right of the Parliamentary leadership to operate as the main repository of power within the Party and Labour succumbed to a crisis of legitimacy. This crisis of legitimacy was exacerbated by other changes in the cultural landscape of the Party. For much of its history Labour adhered to a common culture or (in Drucker's terminology) 'ethos' (Drucker, 1979: 9). From this emanated a distinct pattern of norms, or expected standards of conduct on the part of members which included loyalty to the leader (Drucker, 1979: 12). By the end of the 1970s, however, Labour had undergone a cultural transformation as a new cohort of activists entered the Party, predominantly young, educated and employed in public sector white collar occupations. They had not been exposed to the types of socialising experiences that had inculcated traditional labourist norms and were far more assertive and more rebellious than earlier cohorts, much more impatient of the rules and those who sought to enforce them. Whereas Drucker had discerned as part of Labour's culture a sense of 'a shared past, [of] a series of folk-memories or shared expression of exploitation, common struggle and gradually increasing power' (Drucker, 1979: 31), these new activists tended to regard Labour's history in terms of the unfolding of a series of betrayals by an opportunistic leadership. Imbued with a participatory ethos they were singularly free of any trace of deference to the Party establishment and espoused demands not only for greater involvement in the policy process but for radical changes in the whole structure of authority within the Party. The right-wing Labour MP, Austin Mitchell, was not far off the mark in his portrayal of left-wing attitudes: 'To lead was to betray. Leadership itself was an anti-social act, an indictable offence. Leaders would sell out – unless they were stopped' (Mitchell, 1983: 35).

Polarisation

This animosity to the leadership both reflected and was compounded by the sheer range and depth of the conflicts rending the Party. Labour turned inwards as it was embroiled in an unrestrained struggle for power between left and right with the mass of the Party split into two hostile camps locked in combat over an extensive range of issues producing fault lines that were deep and mutually reinforcing. Thus the crisis was ideological, institutional and normative: a clash between right and left, a jurisdictional struggle as the institutions of the parliamentary and extra-parliamentary parties contended for supremacy and a contest between opposing notions of party democracy. Left and right viewed each other through a polarised prism, perceiving each other as antagonists adhering to radically different conceptions of the Party's role and purposes. As a result attachment to the rival camps often overshadowed that to the Party and leaders were seen as purely 'partisan' figures pursuing their own factional ends rather than as representatives of the Party as a whole. The result was that the capacity of the leadership to secure compliance by appeals to loyalty and solidarity disintegrated.

To much of the right, the triumph of the campaign for constitutional change was (in Healey's words) primarily the work of a 'handful of conspirators' (Healey, 1989: 469). This overlooks the appeal of the left in this period: packed left-wing fringe meetings at Conference, the large audiences that Tony Benn was able to command, his success in sweeping up the constituency vote for the deputy leader contest all testify to the popularity of the 'Bennite' left's cause amongst the Party activists. Yet the rank and file challenge to the traditional pattern of leadership may yet not have prevailed without the addition of a further factor: the effective mobilisation of discontent. A range of ginger groups, notably CLPD and the Labour Co-ordinating Committee (LCC) acted as arenas in which new ideas were generated and debated, as communications networks disseminating information and tactical advice and, above all, as organisational bases for the sustained articulation and mobilisation of opposition to the leadership. In addition, the left displayed in this period a rare ability to co-operate: thus a whole host of left-wing groups ranging from CLPD and the LCC to a medley of

21

Trotskyist sects worked together in the umbrella Rank and File Mobilising Committee which later became the organising centre of the Benn deputy leadership campaign. This broad coalition was held together not by any common ideology (which did not exist) but by agreement over the pursuit of a limited number of clearly-specified goals. Conversely, the standing of the right was damaged by the defection of some of its ablest and most energetic leaders to form the SDP and by the questioning of the loyalty of those who had remained due to their close association with these defectors. Hence there was a widespread sense of demoralisation aggravated by the disorganisation and poor leadership of the right-wing trade union allies.

By 1983, the power of both the leader and the Parliamentary elite had been drained to an unprecedented degree. The constitutional reforms, it seemed likely, would (as intended) institutionalise the transfer of power from the centre to the rank and file. The left's triumph over reselection and the election of the leader, Benn recorded in his diary in January 1981, had wrought 'an enormous change, because the PLP, which has been the great centre of power in British politics, has had to yield to the movement that put members there' (Benn, 1992: 69). Of the two changes, mandatory reselection was of greater significance since parliamentary selection is one of the key functions performed by political parties. As a result of the 1980 rule-change, the constitutional rights of constituency parties were considerably enlarged and sitting MPs rendered far more dependent on the goodwill of their local activists than had hitherto been the case. Not only did mandatory reselection erode the security of the MP, it also constituted a formidable countervailing power to the sanctions and incentives available to the leader. Most commentators concluded that Labour's power structure had been permanently altered: in Denver's words, the constitutional reforms of the early 1980s had 'decisively shifted power in the Party away from the PLP to the constituency activists and the trade unions' (Denver, 1987: 88).

The effect however was not a transfer of power to the extra-parliamentary party but the paralysis of power. To be able to pursue its goals, a party must be able to co-ordinate the efforts of its members as effectively as possible, which requires a degree of internal order and centralised direction. Further, to be able to cope with the pressures and exploit the opportunities emanating from its environment, a party leadership needs flexibility and discretion to formulate the party's response to external challenges. Labour in this period lacked both, a rudderless ship that drifted aimlessly in dangerous seas buffeted by storms which it was helpless to resist. This was the internal crisis of Labour – its crisis of governance.

THE LEFT'S ELECTORAL STRATEGY AND THE ELECTORAL CRISIS

The 1979 election, according to Crewe, 'marked the most emphatic rejection of the Labour Party for almost half a century' with particularly heavy losses sustained amongst the working class (Crewe, 1982: 11). A process of class dealignment was underway, diminishing the numbers of habitual Labour voters amongst the working class (Crewe, 1982: 20, 23; Crewe, 1983a). Most worrying of all, on most key issues the views of working class voters coincided more closely with Conservative policy-stances: Crewe noted that 'among Labour's voters there had been a spectacular decline in support for the collectivist trinity of public ownership, trade union power and social welfare' (Crewe, 1982: 37). This analysis – accepted by Labour's right (e.g. Mitchell, 1979) – implied that to recover lost ground, the Party ought to shift to the right. The left, however, offered a quite different interpretation. As Tom Litterick (a former Tribunite MP and one of the casualties of the 1979 election) put it during the 1979 Conference debate on the election: 'Governments and only Governments, win or lose elections. Oppositions do not.'[16] The left believed that weakly-aligned voters cast their ballots on the basis of retrospective judgments as to how well their interests (collectively defined) had been served by the government. The blame for the triumph of the Conservatives, it followed, lay unambiguously with the outgoing government: its record had disillusioned millions of normally Labour voters since it had allowed the unemployment toll to rise, presided over the deterioration of the public services as expenditure was repeatedly cut, reduced working class living standards by the imposition of incomes restraint and, by abandoning the policies on which it fought the 1974 elections, had proved unable to achieve sustained economic recovery. Responsibility for the disastrous Winter of Discontent was attributed neither to the strikers nor to

23

the unions but to Labour ministers. In the words of the Party's left-of-centre General Secretary Ron Hayward: 'the reason was that, for good or ill, the Cabinet, supported by MPs, ignored Congress and Conference decisions.'[17] By persisting in deflationary economic policies and by demanding a wholly unrealistic 5 per cent pay limit, the Government had driven the low paid to a spontaneous outburst of protest. The strategic conclusions the left drew flowed from this analysis. Voters often sympathised with the Party's policies and values but lacked confidence in its willingness to realise them. The reversal of Party policy by the outgoing government had created a problem of trust and credibility: of trust, because voters did not now believe that Labour meant what it said; and credibility, since the Tories could argue that the former cabinet's espousal of monetarist polices proved that there was no real alternative. 'If we keep faith with those we represent,' Benn contended, 'and if we keep our nerve, there is nothing that can stop us from restoring our society to a new and fairer basis . . . The greatest problem we face is not that our polices are unpopular. The problem is that many people don't believe what we say and don't know whether we would do it if we were elected' (*Guardian*, 5 September 1981).

The key to overcoming the problems of trust and credibility was the creation of a leadership which could be relied upon to promote and implement a radical programme – and the ousting from power of those who had failed to do so. Constitutional reform, Benn concluded, was 'indissolubly linked with Labour's integrity and credibility as a Party trying to win popular support. We cannot convince others that we will establish social justice if we doubt our own capacity, as a Party, to adopt an effective policy or to carry it out once we have adopted it' (Benn, 1980: 15). Since the roots of right-wing domination lay in the autonomy of the PLP from the extra-Parliamentary party, it followed that this autonomy must be curtailed. Austin Mitchell accurately summarised the left's project: 'Policy would be formulated through the wishes of the activists coming up in resolutions passed by Conference, then welded into a Manifesto, not by the parliamentary party which had abused its independence, but by a National Executive dependent on the Party activists. That Manifesto would then become a binding mandate' (Mitchell, 1983: 37).

The left's political strategy drew additional sustenance (though rather loosely and haphazardly) from a class politics perspective which held that not only was class an objective factor of great prominence but that sentiments of class solidarity and shared interests had survived and could be readily translated into enthusiastic support for a socialist programme based on pledges to redistribute wealth and power, extend the welfare state and revive the economy through interventionist means. If class had appeared to fade as a spur to voting this was because Labour cabinets had often been hostile to working-class interests, denounced strikers and perpetuated the myth of a national interest that transcended class. The salience of class and class solidarity was not socially determined but was contingent upon the efforts of the Party to define political issues in class terms, and to propagate socialist ideas. Since the triumph of revisionism, if not earlier, both the discourse and the governmental conduct of Labour has actually discouraged class solidarity and disconnected industrial disputes from their wider class dimension – hence the importance of the Party's willingness now to support workers in dispute and explain the broader social and political context in which struggles against employers occurred.

Such was the left's case. But to leave the impression that their political strategy was rooted in a systematic class analysis would be misleading. The complex issue of the relationship between social location, class solidarity and political commitment was hardly ever explored and little attempt was made to analyse the impact of factors such as the break-up of occupational communities, changes in workforce composition and in patterns of wage bargaining, the erosion of working class sub-cultures and the enhanced penetrative power of the mass media. The left's diagnosis of the 1979 defeat congealed into a fixed set of beliefs which seemed to have rendered them incapable of responding to the formidable challenge to the Party's very survival as an alternative government posed by the formation of the SDP and the Alliance. Even when the Falklands campaign led to a dramatic turnaround in the Government's fortune and more or less eliminated any remaining hope of a Labour revival, the left were slow to draw any strategic lessons; and their faith in the capacity of the Party to mobilise opinion appeared not to have been dented by the mounting evidence that many of its central policy planks were wholly out of line with public sentiment.

Almost universally the left – and Benn in particular – were caricatured and vilified by the press and treated coldly by television (Hollingworth, 1986; Glasgow University Media Research Group, 1982) but whilst bitterly resenting this, they failed to comprehend the extent to which they became tarnished in the public mind. Instead they concentrated on pushing through a radical manifesto which the right for the most part (despite having greatly increased their representation on the Executive) hardly bothered to resist. The right-wing trade unionist John Golding (who had replaced Benn as the chairman of the key Home Policy sub-committee of the NEC) insisted that the will of Conference must be obeyed – but as a tough and wily operator, doubtless grasped that if Labour was heading for a major defeat it might be a sizable political bonus for the right if it did so with a left-wing manifesto unambiguously pinned to it.

The 1983 election

The constitutional disputes, the deputy-leadership contest and the disciplinary steps against Militant had so distracted Labour that only sporadic attention was given to organising for the election. The left had traditionally been highly sceptical of opinion research and the use of advertising techniques and MORI, which had acted as the Party's pollster since 1970, was only awarded a contract in February 1983 together with the Johnny Wright advertising agency (Butler and Kavanagh, 1984: 57). Nothing was done to establish an effective campaign machinery at Head Office and the campaign itself was ill-prepared, disorganised, uncoordinated and incoherent, destitute of any central themes or thought-out communications strategy (M. Linton "Disaster Snatched from the Jaws of Defeat", *Guardian*, 30 June 1983). Foot was obviously ill-at-ease with television, unwilling to adapt his behaviour and ridiculed in a virulent media assault which totally destroyed his poll ratings. No real effort had been made to expound the case for the highly controversial non-nuclear defence policy adopted in 1981 which was further discredited by public disagreement between Foot and his Shadow Foreign Secretary, Denis Healey, over its precise meaning and by a withering attack from Callaghan, exploiting all his prestige as a former Labour Prime Minister.

It was in a mood of pessimism that Labour entered the election fray of 1983, but few anticipated the cataclysm that occurred. Only 209 chastened MPs survived, and the Party's vote slumped to a dismal 28 per cent, a mere 2 per cent more than the Liberal–SDP Alliance and its worst performance (in terms of votes per candidates) since 1900 (Butler and Kavanagh, 1988: 47). A whole range of factors contributed to this outcome: these included social structural changes, like the contraction of the working class, the decay of Labour's urban heartlands and changing patterns of housing tenure; a battery of unpopular policies; the violent turbulence within the Party, coupled with a leader, Michael Foot, regarded with incredulity by most of the electorate; a totally ramshackle election campaign; and the emergence of a third force, the Liberal–SDP Alliance, rendered, by the accession of former Labour cabinet ministers, a far more credible alternative governing formation. (See e.g. Crewe, 1983a; Crewe, 1983b; Crewe, 1984; Heath, Jowell and Curtice, 1985.)

Using Heath, Jowell and Curtice's categories, Labour's share of the working-class vote fell from 55 per cent in 1979 (itself a decline in 9 per cent since 1974) to 49 per cent; of the routine non-manuals from 32 per cent to 29 per cent, and of the salariat from 22 per cent to 13 per cent (Heath, Jowell and Curtice, 1985: 68–9). Using the A to E market research classification scheme, Crewe found that the Conservatives drew more support than Labour from workers in the South (42 per cent to 26 per cent with the Alliance at 32 per cent) and owning their own homes (47 per cent to 25 per cent with the Alliance at 28 per cent) whilst almost drawing level amongst those employed in the private sector (36 per cent to 37 per cent with the Alliance at 27 per cent). He concluded that while 'the Labour vote remains largely working class . . . the working class has ceased to be largely Labour' (Crewe, 1983a). As a result of the dramatic fall in the working-class vote (if the results for 1979 and 1983 are combined) Labour had been driven back to its heartlands. 'By 1983 it would be more accurate to describe Labour as the party of a segment of the working class – the "traditional working class" of Scotland and the North, the public sector and the council estate' (Crewe, 1984: 195). What was especially disturbing was that the party tended to perform least well in the social groups, employment sectors and geographical areas where numbers were growing – demographically, it seemed to be the party of the past, and politically, with a dynamic new political formation snapping at its heels, it appeared to have little future. This was Labour's electoral crisis.

2

TRANSITION: ORGANISATIONAL AND POLICY CHANGE 1983–7

KINNOCK'S INHERITANCE

Shortly after the election Foot announced his resignation as leader. Four contestants entered the race for the succession, Neil Kinnock (from the centre-left), Roy Hattersley, Peter Shore (both from the right) and Eric Heffer (from the left). Tony Benn's loss of his seat had removed the only serious threat to Kinnock from the left and the Welshman's personal popularity, the weakness of the right and the widespread desire for an end to in-fighting all combined to accord him an easy victory over his main opponent, Hattersley: he beat him in all three sections of the electoral college, with no less than 71 per cent of the total vote. Hattersley, anticipating this, had concentrated his efforts on the deputy leadership with – in what was dubbed the 'dream ticket' – the active support of Kinnock. Hattersley crushed his main opponent and standard-bearer of the left, Michael Meacher, with surprising ease, by 67 per cent to 28 per cent.[1] It was the first unequivocal evidence, in the wake of the electoral cataclysm, of a new yearning for peace and unity within the Party.

But Kinnock's inheritance in 1983 was, as he was acutely aware, in many ways an impoverished one – a badly-divided and demoralised Party permeated with intense suspicion of the leadership, and a programme that had been decisively repudiated by the electorate. He was convinced that dissension, lack of self-discipline and the lurch to the left had offended millions of potential Labour voters and that these weaknesses had to be remedied by changing policy and strategy and, above all, internal organisation. He sought to revive effective governance by re-establishing the authority of the leadership, restoring the supremacy of the Parliamentary Party over policy-making, bringing the NEC to heel, marginalising the left and ridding the Party of the Militant Tendency. Attaining these objectives was to be no easy task. The new leader faced a range of pressures with limited resources: his base within the Party was broad but shallow and, although the pendulum had moved to the right, the political equilibrium remained such as to continue to impose significant limits on his room for manoeuvre. As a result – until the end of 1985 – he could not rely on a majority in the NEC or in Conference.

The first period of Kinnock's leadership can be divided into two parts: from 1983 to 1985 and from 1985 to 1987. In the first part, his capacity to realise his programme of change was heavily constrained both by externally generated problems and by the strength of internal resistance. From the second half of 1985, the constraints eased and he was able to obtain significant movement in both organisation and policy.

THE LIMITS OF LEADERSHIP 1983–5

Kinnock was determined to fasten the leadership's grip on the Party by overhauling organisation and wresting power from left-wing constituency activists. A central priority was altering the system of selecting MPs, a key function performed within political parties and a significant source of power. As a result of the 1980 rule-change, the constitutional rights of constituency parties were considerably enlarged and sitting MPs rendered far more dependent on the goodwill of their local activists than had hitherto been the case, hence both eroding the security of the MP and weakening the pull of parliamentary discipline. Many within the PLP had never been reconciled to mandatory reselection and early in 1984 Kinnock came under pressure to alter the selection rules from senior members of the shadow cabinet, backed by many right-wing back-benchers who feared that a goodly proportion of the PLP, including front-benchers Peter Shore, Gerald Kaufman and John Silkin, were in serious danger of losing their seats (*The Times*, 1 March 1984).

Kinnock personally wished to institute what came to be called 'OMOV' (One Member, One Vote). This involved transferring the right to select Parliamentary candidates and deselect MPs from Constituency General Committees (GCs) (composed of delegates from branches, affiliated trade unions and other organisations) to ordinary fee-paying members. He believed that this would both succour imperilled MPs and undermine the left's main power base since it was assumed that passive members were more 'moderate' than activists. Precisely for this reason Kinnock knew that 'OMOV' would provoke the wrath of the activists and their supporters in the left-wing unions who considered mandatory reselection as their foremost achievement. But since delay would mean that the next round of selections would be well under way before the rules could be altered Kinnock opted for a compromise system of 'voluntary OMOV' in which General Committees could, if they so chose, delegate the right to determine the fate of a sitting MP to Party members as a whole. The scheme, however, provoked almost universal hostility from the left. They claimed that the GC was the only body able to ensure the accountability of an MP, that raising the issue was divisive, that the formula chosen was half-baked (thus it would apply only to MPs and not to parliamentary selections in general) and administratively burdensome and had been rushed through without adequate consultation (see, for example, Audrey Wise, a left-wing NEC member in *Tribune*, 13 July 1984). Only with difficulty did Kinnock secure a majority on the NEC, but it soon became evident that the success of the project hinged on the support of the TGWU. Despite backing from its two senior leaders, Moss Evans and Alex Kitson, the union's conference delegation voted against the proposal and as a result, it was rejected at the 1984 Conference by 3,992,000 votes to 3,041,000.[2] Kinnock had failed to prepare the ground, but notwithstanding the episode indicated the magnitude of the task he faced in seeking to impress his authority on the Party.

Events too were to conspire against him. For a number of years the Tory Government had been imposing tighter controls on local authority spending, culminating in its decision to 'rate-cap', or set legally-binding limits to the amount that rates could be raised, as a result of which 'overspending' councils would have to cut services or manpower. How was Labour to respond? The initiative – significantly – was taken not by the national Party leadership but by 16 rate-capped and mostly left-led Labour local authorities who jointly agreed to defy the Government by refusing to set a rate (known as 'non-compliance'): a course which entailed defying the law and risked fines and disqualification from office. The strategy, set by prominent left-wing local government leaders such as Ken Livingstone of the GLC (Greater London Council), Ted Knight of Lambeth and David Blunkett of Sheffield, was designed to force the Government (already engrossed in the miners' strike) to back-track by mobilising concerted mass opposition to rate-capping.

Kinnock and the bulk of his front-bench colleagues rejected the strategy both on practical grounds and because they were opposed in principle to illegality. But they were helpless to block a range of motions at the 1984 Conference giving it official approval. One urged support for any Labour council budgets which defended jobs and services even if they involved policies 'which can be defined as technically illegal' whilst another, moved by the deputy leader of Liverpool council, and a leading member of the Militant Tendency, Derek Hatton, even more unequivocally pledged Conference's support for any council 'forced to break the law as a result of the Tory government's policies'.[3] A third – also spurning the NEC's advice – applauded the Militant controlled Liverpool council for its defiance of the Government. Already locked in combat with many in the Party over reselection procedures and the miners' strike (as we chron-icle below) Kinnock did not feel strong enough to resist. He immediately came under intense pressure from left-wing Labour local authorities, now able to claim an official Party mandate, to support their challenge to government authority. He refused to do so yet nevertheless felt compelled to proceed gingerly and in a speech to Labour's Local Government con-ference in February 1985 he took an equivocal line on non-compliance, commenting 'we don't want to weaken that broad coalition by wrangling over illegality.' Instead, he appealed to council leaders to stay in office to defend jobs and services: better 'a dented shield rather than no shield at all' (*Guardian*, 2 January 1985). The effort to defuse the dispute within Labour's ranks failed, and the leader became the butt of loudly-declaimed denunciations from his left-wing critics.

In the event, non-compliance collapsed and the united front of left-wing councils fell apart when Ken Livingstone (to the fury of his allies) voted to set a rate in the GLC. As the deadline neared, other councils compromised leaving only Lambeth of the 16 rate-capped authorities (together with non-rate-capped

Liverpool) firm in defiance. In fact, the whole strategy was an elaborate but ill-conceived game of bluff as few councillors seriously intended to risk personal bankruptcy and surcharge. The outcome of the whole episode was more bad publicity for Labour and its leader: as one observer tartly commented, 'Far from creating a crisis for the government, Labour has manufactured a crisis of its own' (Lansley, 1985). An exasperated Kinnock had been unable to avert it. The cautious way in which he proceeded, and the fact that most of the running in devising and spearheading policy on the issue was made by local government leaders indicated how far he was from mastering the Party. His powerlessness was compounded by his embroilment in the controversy over the miners' strike, the most testing experience of his leadership so far.

The miners' strike was by far the most important industrial dispute in the years of Conservative Government from 1979 to 1992. It was an issue which for historical reasons ignited particularly deep passions within the Party and an unprecedented number of members were involved in activities designed to support the strikers. The miners' cause was overwhelmingly perceived by the rank and file as a just one and the strikers were acclaimed for their heroism and perseverance in resisting a reactionary and ruthless government. Left-wing union leaders were solidly behind the miners (at least verbally) and few on the right were prepared to publicly criticise them, whatever privately they might have thought. The NEC too – where votes were publicly recorded – stood four-square behind the NUM and passed a stream of motions (from none of which Kinnock dissented) expressing the Party's full solidarity.

From the start Kinnock (along with other senior frontbenchers) did not share this enthusiasm. He believed that industrial disputes were electorally damaging, and that militant trade union leaders like Scargill frightened the voters. He profoundly disagreed with the view, articulated by Scargill and his political allies, that the strike should be used to mobilise mass opposition to the Tories and lever them from power, though he was aware that it had considerable resonance throughout the movement. He was convinced that a disastrous mistake had been made in not calling for a ballot, which was required by union rules and successfully invoked in the two miners' strikes of the early 1970s. He was also under constant and unremitting pressure from the media and the Government to condemn Scargill's refusal to hold a ballot and to repudiate acts of violence on the picket line. But, knowing that any criticism of the miners whilst the strike continued would be vehemently resented, and extremely anxious to avoid receiving the blame for its defeat, he felt unable to do either. Caught between opposing pressures, Kinnock walked a tightrope. On the one hand he publicly espoused the miners' cause, but was noticeably reticent to debate the matter in Parliament, speak at miners' rallies or appear on picket lines. In his speech to the 1984 Conference he condemned violence but in a carefully-honed, qualified manner which perturbed many in a Conference ardent for the miners whilst not coming near to placating his critics in the media. To render his dilemma yet more painful, Conference, disregarding Kinnock's objections, went on to pass a number of resolutions condemning the use and behaviour of the police during the strike.[4]

Both the rate-capping issue and the miners' strike afforded vivid illustrations of the constraints and pressures to which Labour's leadership was subjected. Confronted by two serious challenges, in neither case was the national leadership able to determine Labour's response. However, once the lessons of the failure of the strike sank in, it was the leadership that benefited. The strike, as Heffernan and Marqusee (authors sympathetic to the far left) comment, was 'a watershed. The NUM's ultimate defeat led to a loss of confidence at all levels of the labour movement. It left the base of the Labour Party increasingly reliant on the leadership to win elections for it' (Heffernan and Marqusee, 1992: 61). Large numbers of people at all levels and in all sections of the movement lost faith in the viability and value of extra-parliamentary mobilisation, mass industrial action and a class-based political strategy. Whilst initially the strike retarded the 'realignment of the left' (which we discuss below) the bitterness and recrimination in its later stages accelerated it, easing the task of restoring leadership control.

In the longer term, nevertheless, the miners' dispute inflicted enduring damage on both the Party and the leader. In Kinnock's view, it was an immense diversion of energy, 'taking a year out of the job we should have been doing, renovating policy' and the episode confirmed the belief of many voters that Labour was little more (to use Kinnock's expression) than a 'union support group'.[5] The leader himself was the target of incessant obloquy at great cost to his public image. Almost universally, his handling of the situation was castigated – by the more radical sections of the left, or 'hard left' as they now came to be called, for whom it symbolised his willingness to betray every principle; by the less radical or 'soft left', who criticised his half-hearted support for the strike, by the other parties and more or less the entire press for his failure to denounce picket-line violence. His short-lived popularity of 1983 was dissipated, never, for any sustained length of time, to return. His need to temporise, to engage in intricate balancing acts, offered manifold opportunities which a hostile press exploited with alacrity to present him as a weak, indecisive leader at the mercy of a Party infested with left-wing militants.[6] Once these images had hardened, they became very difficult to remove.

PARTY ALIGNMENTS AND LEADERSHIP POWER 1985–7

By mid-1985 Kinnock recognised that the political context was altering fast: the end of the miners' strike had removed the pressure to maintain solidarity (and refrain from public criticism of Scargill) at all costs; the strategy of non-compliance over rate-capping was in total disarray and the left was fragmenting. Hence the tougher, more combative style of management which he displayed at the 1985 Party Conference over two fraught issues. A resolution was submitted to Conference calling for the reimbursement of the NUM for fines levied against it and for the reinstatement of all sacked miners. Kinnock regarded it as electorally suicidal but only obtained the NEC's backing – and by the narrowest margin – after the utmost pressure. Despite the likelihood of losing the Conference vote on reinstatement (which he did) he defied the mood of the hall and seized the opportunity to launch an impassioned critique of the NUM President's handling of the strike (Leapman, 1987: 57). But the speech that really captured the headlines was his onslaught on Militant. In a major tactical blunder, the Militant leaders of Liverpool City Council had just issued redundancy notices to all its employees which though designed as a ploy to intensify pressure on the Government instead angered the unions and many within its own workforce. Kinnock had been biding his time for an attack on the Trotskyist group and now struck in a devastating and very powerfully delivered speech to Conference:

> I'll tell what happens with impossible promises. You start with far-fetched resolutions. They are then pickled into a rigid dogma, a code, and you go through the years sticking to that, outdated, misplaced, irrelevant to the real needs, and you end in the grotesque chaos of a Labour council – a *Labour* council – hiring taxis to scuttle round a city handing out redundancy notices to its own workers. (Applause). . . . You can't play politics with people's jobs . . . (Applause and some boos).[7]

It was, according to the *Guardian*, 'The bravest and most important speech by a Labour Leader in over a generation' and one shadow cabinet member gleefully commented, 'with one speech [Kinnock] lanced a boil' (*Guardian*, 2 October 1985; *Observer*, 6 October 1985). What was perhaps less expected was the speech's reception from predominantly left-wing constituency delegates: most eagerly applauded and 'drowned the scattered boos almost completely' (*Guardian*, 2 October 1985). Whilst Kinnock was vilified by the hard left, much of the soft left welcomed the speech and the disciplinary action it clearly prefigured. The attack (in combination with the assault on Scargill) reflected his determination to manage the Party more firmly and was designed to project, to the wider public, an image of a strong leader who would have no truck with extremists and indeed the *Guardian* commented that 'Mr Kinnock has displayed the kind of leadership that the British people seem to like these days' (*Guardian*, 4 October 1985).[8] The attack upon Militant both testified to and further augmented his hold on the Party whilst the reaction to it from the rank and file suggested the beginnings of a sea-change in attitudes.

Party alignments and the weakening of impediments to change

The 1985 Party Conference was a turning point in Labour's transformation into a more tightly controlled Party. Prior to it, the leadership had made relatively little progress in its bid to change either organisation or (as we shall see) policy. Kinnock lacked the capacity to direct the Party's response to environmental challenges and was unable to prevent the adoption of strategies which he felt scarred its image. The key obstacles were the continued strength of the left and the institutional dispersal of power. With the end of the miners' strike, internal restraints began to relax as the power of the left receded. In fact, the left's hold on the Party after 1979 had always been slenderer than it appeared and by the early 1980s, the great surge forward of the 1970s – as the unions shifted to the left and a new generation of young, middle-class radicals filled the constituencies – had already ended. Like a catapult which has thrown its bolt, the onward momentum of the left drove it forward even after the initial motive-force was spent but only a range of contingent factors sustained it in the 1980s: union disillusion with the 1974–9 Government; the 1979 defeat for which the right was widely blamed; the SDP defections which both denuded and discredited their former allies who remained; and internal divisions and incompetent leadership amongst right-wing unions.

If contingent factors had helped the left, underlying ones were operating to their detriment. With the victory in 1979 of the right-wing Terry Duffy in the contest to succeed Hugh Scanlon as leader of the second largest union, the AUEW, the pendulum in the unions was already swinging back to the right and it was only a matter of time before the weight of the union was thrown against the left. In their uncompromising drive for constitutional reform the left seriously over-extended themselves. They deployed impressive tactical skill and organisational ability to force through, by fragile majorities, the constitutional changes for which there was no real consensus and the error was then compounded by Benn's decision to challenge Healey for the deputy leadership. Anger at the fresh bout of internal Party warfare this precipitated, coupled with deep resentment at Benn's efforts to mobilise the left within their ranks spurred the right-wing unions to rally their forces, with startling success (Minkin, 1991: 203). At the 1981 Party Conference no less than five left-wingers were swept from the NEC, to be followed by two more the next year – in its speed, an unprecedented change in the composition of the Executive – and the ousting of Benn and Eric Heffer as chairmen of the key Home Policy and Organisation committees by leadership loyalists. From this point on, the left had lost control of its main power base, although the right and the leadership were yet to regain it. If Benn's initiative united the right, it divided the left. Although most left-wing unions voted for Benn, several senior left-wing union leaders had strongly opposed his candidature (Minkin, 1991: 202) and relations between the union and political left grew more distant. A small group of anti-Bennite Tribunite MPs (most notably Neil Kinnock) refused to back Benn on the decisive second ballot – provoking mutual recrimination and prompting Bennite MPs to set up in December 1982 a new group, the Campaign Group, which widened and institutionalised the split on the left.

In the first two years of his leadership, Kinnock faced an Executive composed of roughly equal blocks of left and right, only backed by a small group of centrists in between. As it became evident that his political outlook was on most matters closest to the right, a centre–right bloc linking his supporters with the right was forged but its majority was too tenuous and unreliable to afford him with solid, and therefore authoritative, majorities. As David Blunkett later recalled, NEC meetings in these years were 'often traumatic . . . dramas . . . with Kinnock employing persuasion, cajoling, bullying and arm-twisting to get his way.'[9] But from late 1985 growing divisions on the left splintered the oppositional block. Initially a common disaffection with the leadership's lukewarm attitude to the miners' strike had held the left together but eventually it was to provoke the first public break when a call by Dennis Skinner and Benn for 'all-out industrial action' to aid the miners provoked a furious row between Skinner and Tom Sawyer, Deputy General Secretary of NUPE, the second largest left-wing union and formerly a leading Bennite.[10] The issue of reinstatement and reimbursement for the miners led to further acrimony among former allies when Meacher – a key Benn lieutenant in the 1981 contest and the Bennite deputy leadership candidate himself in 1983 – ensured by his vote that the NEC rejected (by 15 to 14) the NUM indemnity resolution at the 1985 conference.[11] Rows on the NEC reflected what was happening within the left at large. The soft and hard lefts came to differ on a wide range of policy, organisational and strategic matters, differences which were ventilated in a widely publicised article in *Tribune* penned (after consultations with Sawyer, Meacher and Blunkett) by its recently appointed editor, Nigel Williamson (the treasurer of the Benn campaign team in 1981). The article made clear that rifts within the left over specific issues in fact reflected more fundamental disagreements for whilst the hard left continued to regard the struggle against the right and the leadership as a priority, the soft left believed that a *modus vivendi* between left and right was essential to Labour's electoral health and that a shift to the left could best be achieved by constructing 'a majority centre–left coalition around the Party leader' rather than by opposing him. The article concluded by appealing for a 'realignment of the left' – a code for a break with erstwhile allies in the Bennite campaigns (*Tribune*, 4 Jan 1985). The old Bennite alliance finally fell apart over Militant. As the reality of Militant's rule in Liverpool was uncovered by a Party investigation in early 1986, the soft left reversed their earlier opposition to disciplinary action and, on the NEC, combined with the right to push through expulsions of leading Militants and reorganisations of Tendency-controlled local parties. The hard left denounced the expulsions as a right-wing purge and relations between the two sections of the left become further embittered.

By the close of 1985 a clear soft-left current had emerged. Amongst activists, it was represented by the LCC, in Parliament by the Tribune Group and it had the support of the *Tribune* weekly. Within the NEC it formed a distinctive bloc grouped around Blunkett, Sawyer and Meacher whilst within the wider labour movement many senior figures in left-wing unions like NUPE, the TGWU and the NUR were broadly sympathetic. For a time the soft left became a significant factor in the internal politics of the Party. As long as they maintained a minimal level of cohesiveness, as long as the right lacked the strength to reassert its traditional control over the Party, and as long as the hard left still posed a threat to the leadership, they were in a position of strategic strength. This Kinnock appreciated and he patiently worked to detach Blunkett, Sawyer, Meacher and others on the soft left from their former Bennite allies: the outcome was a slowly emerging coalition between the right and the soft left which, for the first time since the 1960s, afforded the leadership a firm basis of support in all key Party arenas.

Coalition requires compromise and concessions had to be made to the soft left. The most notable one was the maintenance of the non-nuclear defence policy adopted in 1981 and reaffirmed by an overwhelming majority at the 1984 Conference.[12] The right-wing majority in the Shadow Cabinet was profoundly unhappy with this and urged strongly that it be revoked[13] but Kinnock had not only championed unilateralism for years but was also convinced that it formed the only basis around which the Party could conceivably unite (Leapman, 1987: 149). The issue of nuclear weapons had long been a bone of contention between left and right and by the mid-1980s – with the right staging its come-back – the retention of a non-nuclear defence policy had become both sign and symbol that not all the left's gains of the previous years had yet been forfeited. Hence many members throughout the Party who were broadly on the soft left and who were prepared to compromise on most other issues were adamant against any retreat over unilateralism. 'There is now universal acceptance', the *Guardian* observed in 1985, 'that [Kinnock's] commitment on this issue has to be beyond question if he is to have the room for manoeuvre that he needs on other policy issues' (*Guardian*, 14 October 1985). Furthermore, as long as he stood by his unilateralist commitment, Kinnock was able to conserve his reputation as a man of the left. This stood him in good stead as it fostered a disposition in much of the soft left to give him the benefit of the doubt, and to stand by him as the most left-wing figure the Party was likely to have as leader. Faced with the resistance of the left as a whole, the struggle to change the Party would have been considerably tougher for a man, like Hattersley, with his roots on the right.[14]

Even with the retention of unilateralism and (as we shall see) concessions over public ownership in 1986 doubts began to be voiced within the soft left over the rapprochement. The feasibility of the soft left project rested on the assumption that, once liberated from his reliance on the right the leader would move back to the left. This proved incorrect and in September 1986 Williamson wrote that the strategy he had adumbrated in January of the previous year had been a 'spectacular failure' as the centre–right remained the dominant force (*Tribune*, 26 September 1986). It became increasingly evident that, far from being a prisoner of the right, Kinnock shared many of their views, although he could never rely on their total confidence. This presented the soft left with a strategic dilemma: should they continue to back the leader and hope, by providing him with a left–centre power base, to push him to the left – or oppose him as he moved to the right? Forced to make the choice, more and more opted for the former, partly because they were persuaded that Party unity was essential for electoral reasons, partly because of a growing enmity towards the hard left, partly because they themselves were shifting to the right.

As a result of the fissuring of the left and the rapprochement between the soft left and the right a pattern of concurrent pro-leadership majorities in all key Party institutions was restored. The reassertion of leadership control not only gave Kinnock command of Labour's official policy-making machinery – it enabled him to alter the institutional structure of power by neutralising the NEC's resistance to the transfer of responsibilities to the Shadow Cabinet and (even more important) to his own much enlarged Leader's Office. The Leader's Office was transformed into a major seat of power from which emerged, by early 1986 (as we shall see below), a powerful informal system of strategic decision-making.

PROGRAMMATIC CHANGE 1983-7

Kinnock had been bequeathed a radical programme with little appeal to the electorate. The magnitude of the 1983 defeat convinced him that Labour had to be returned to the political mainstream if it were to regain their confidence. There was broad consensus over reversing policy on opposition to council house sales and withdrawal from the European Community but beyond this neither the pattern of alignments nor the still radical temper within the Party suggested that a sharp swerve in the direction was politically feasible and, as a result, the pace of programmatic change in the first two years of the new leader's tenure was tardy.

Macro-economic policy

As we have seen, Keynesian economics had been at the centre of the left's economic strategy. The new Shadow Chancellor, Roy Hattersley – unlike his predecessor, Peter Shore – entertained doubts about the continued feasibility of Keynesianism and regarded the French Socialist Government's enforced U-turn in 1983 as a salutary warning of the price to be paid for ignoring external pressures (Hattersley, 1985; Hattersley, 1987a: 52). Party policy in the period 1979–83 had proposed a combination of devaluation, exchange controls and import controls as a way of tackling the anticipated threats of capital flight and currency

41

speculation and hence enabling it to reflate the economy. The new leadership was sceptical about the value of devaluation (Kinnock, 1986: 168); import controls ceased to be an option once Labour had reversed its policy on withdrawal from the EC; and exchange controls were also deemed impracticable on the grounds that the complex exchange control system dismantled by the Tories could not be easily reconstituted.[15] Did it then follow that a Keynesian course was not practicable? If not, what was to replace it? Rather than confront the problem, or construct an alternative macro-economic framework, Labour response was to place a more cautious and 'realistic' gloss on the established revisionist approach. Thus Hattersley stressed the need for 'a firm financial framework' and 'a rigorous pattern of priorities' and warned the shadow cabinet in March 1985 against any commitments that would expose Labour to charges of extravagance in public spending (Hattersley, 1987a: 60; *Guardian*, 1 March 1985). Initially, he encountered considerable resistance from colleagues unwilling to sacrifice the Party's social goals and in 1985 a policy document still promised 'a major programme of public investment' in housing, health and education. But resistance was overcome, hard and fast pledges to boost spending were generally avoided and by early 1987 the target of full employment was replaced by a commitment to cut unemployment by one million in two years.[16] The problem for Labour was that this indicated a lack of confidence in Keynesianism without actually adumbrating any alternative.

Inflation, incomes policy and the unions

There was no more intractable problem for Labour's policymakers than that of inflation for a range of reasons. Firstly, the Callaghan Government had been broken on the wheel of inflation. The electorate's vivid memories of the rampant inflation of the mid-1970s and of the collapse of pay policy in the Winter of Discontent were easily stirred. Failure to convince the voters that the Party had a convincing anti-inflation policy was, according to Hattersley, a major cause of the 1983 debacle (Hattersley, 1987a: 28). Secondly, critics argued persuasively that a future Labour Government was bound to be assailed by severe inflationary pressures. The unleashed expectations of shop floor unionism would almost immediately provoke a rash of wage claims; the lowering of unemployment – which headed the list of the Party's priorities – would revive the labour market power of the unions; and reflationary measures would stimulate demand-led pressure on prices. Thirdly, the financial markets were likely to impose a premium on any social democratic government as the speculative tidal wave which would almost inevitably follow its election would probably compel a Labour cabinet to jack up interest rates. Due to the mistrust of the City it would also experience considerably greater difficulty funding a payments deficit than the Tories and would then be under great pressure to curb the deficit by improving the competitiveness of British industry through containing labour costs.

Since the early 1970s, the established social democratic remedy for inflation had been an incomes policy and, indeed, within months of the election the Shadow Chancellor was insisting that, 'if we are to have growth without an unacceptable level of inflation, the unions and a Labour Government must come to a voluntary agreement about the overall level of money wages.' Without such an agreement 'our economic policy would be incredible and will be exposed as incredible' (*The Times*, 9 November 1983; Hattersley, 1987b: 241). But advocates of incomes policy faced a series of hurdles. Although their influence was waning, strident opposition could be expected from the hard left. Much more disturbing was the attitude of the unions for whilst a number of right-wing union leaders accepted the need for some form of incomes policy, many on the left did not and adamantly defended the principle of free collective bargaining.[17]

In 1985 the TUC–Labour Party Liaison Committee published a statement, *A New Partnership. A New Britain*, summing up progress in discussions between the two wings of the Labour movement. It was, in general, an anodyne document – the lowest common denominator of agreement between Labour and the unions (*Guardian*, 5 August 1985). 'Statutory norms and a Government-imposed wage restraint' were repudiated and the Party's support for a National Economic Assessment reaffirmed yet very little was said of the form this would take or the areas it would cover.[18] This certainly fell short of what Hattersley (and probably Kinnock) wanted. By 1986 the leadership had begun to reconsider its position. Even if union agreement could be obtained, was an incomes policy in fact feasible? Several amongst

Kinnock's and Hattersley's economic advisors argued that the institutional conditions for an effective incomes policy were absent in Britain: it required powerful central union and employer organisations able to implement and police a negotiated agreement, and a system of industry-wide collective bargaining. Neither existed. They concurred with Todd's view, articulated in 1986, that collective bargaining was now 'too decentralised, too close to the point of production . . . to be amenable to the sort of simple wage restraint arithmetic which has been the traditional basis of incomes policy in this country' (Minkin, 1991: 430). Even if an incomes policy were to be agreed, the electoral advantages no longer appeared obvious. Prior to 1983, the partnership between a Labour Government and the unions was presented as the keystone of the Party's corporatist economic strategy, a view which lingered until 1985. From 1986, Labour's new strategic advisers warned of the electoral perils of a commitment to erect corporatist structures since it would revive the spectre of union power at a time (they advised) when it should be distancing itself from, rather than advertising its links with, the unions. The upshot was that whilst Kinnock and Hattersley continued to press − under the umbrella of the NEA − for a broad economic package which contained a pledge over wages they no longer regarded it as a priority (Minkin, 1991: 430–31). Thus whilst the 1987 election Manifesto spoke vaguely about 'the concerted action' under the aegis of the National Economic Assessment a Labour government would take with employers and the unions 'to increase investment, contain inflation and achieve sustained recovery' none of the details were fleshed out.[19] In effect, Labour in 1987 was still a party in search of a policy on inflation.

However, a substantial shift did occur in the way Labour approached the wider question of the relations between capital, the unions and the state. Up to 1983, the Party had subscribed to what we have called social corporatism, a system of economic and social regulation in which business, the unions and the state would co-operate in shaping economic strategy around an axis formed by a partnership between the unions and a Labour Government. Even as late as 1985, Labour declared that the partnership would determine 'the nation's social and economic priorities', including 'investment, public spending, regional development and the distribution of income and wealth.'[20] But two factors prompted a major shift. Firstly, Labour's retreat from planning and intervention in the investment process (which we document below) meant that the private sector would remain primarily responsible for capital accumulation. Since it followed that a Labour Government would rely very heavily upon business confidence to raise investment levels, jeopardising it by pursuing a policy that would alienate business and impair its capacity to manage the economy seemed thoroughly unwise. The second factor concerned public opinion. The Party was now keen to assuage fears amongst the electorate – and indeed in business and the media – of a revival of union power if it returned to office and as a result, from 1986 references to partnership with the unions become scarce with pride of place now given to the task of creating 'a constructive partnership between public initiative and private enterprise.' The logic was taken a step further in the 1987 manifesto: the NEA was almost entirely disengaged from any larger planning or redistributory programme, ceased to be conceived as an instrument for granting the unions a role in the resource-allocation process and was relegated to acting as a mechanism of information-diffusion and co-ordination between the two sides of industry and the government.[21]

However, in the key policy area of industrial relations law, the strategic aim of relieving public anxieties was not achieved. The 1983 Manifesto had called for the repeal of all Tory industrial relations legislation but the consistent message of opinion research was that the legislation was welcomed by the bulk of the electorate and by the business community (as were most of the additional measures enacted between 1983 and 1987). This created a dilemma for Labour's leadership as existing industrial relations law was a matter of immense concern to the unions and they were not prepared to accept a total reversal of policy. Given that the left as a whole was sympathetic to union interests this meant that navigating any drastic alteration of policy through the NEC and Conference carried immense risks and Kinnock and his colleagues perforce had to proceed gingerly. Their compromise solution was to maintain the policy of repealing Conservative legislation but to couple this with a pledge that the unions would be legally obliged to hold ballots over strikes and for union executive elections – two of the most popular measures enacted by the Government and, on democratic grounds, the most awkward to challenge. Though only by throwing the whole weight of his authority behind the proposal was Kinnock able to overcome union objections (Leapman, 1987: 136–7; *Guardian*, 14 August 1986)[22] this policy shift was still too narrow and too nuanced to have any impact on public opinion, which continued to see Labour as subservient to union interests. As anticipated, the old Winter of Discontent newsreels were re-run during the 1987 election and popular fear of the unions stoked up. It was not until after a third election defeat that Kinnock felt strong enough to press for more drastic changes.

The market, planning and the state

In the early 1980s Labour espoused a highly interventionist industrial policy and, initially, this was maintained. The policy statement, *Investing in Britain*, criticised the City for sacrificing the needs of the domestic economy by pumping funds abroad rather than into productive investment at home. Resting on the premise that an active state intervening in the investment process was vital to the competitiveness of the British economy, it proposed the establishment of a National (later retitled British) Investment Bank (BIB) aimed at providing long-term finance (at preferential rates of interest) for industry, taking the form of equity or long-term loans.[23] As in other areas of policy, the real shift to the right occurs after 1985 with the policy statement, *New Industrial Strength for Britain*, (published in March 1987) marking a notable retreat from the Party's *dirigiste* approach. It was, for example, noticeably vaguer in its specification of the role of the BIB, with greater emphasis being placed on its purely facilitating function and less on the use of funds to procure compliance with government objectives. Trade union involvement and agreed business plans – envisaged in the original formula – were no longer required but simply advised and no indication was given as to the scale or sources of the BIB's resources.[24] Further, proposals for a National Planning Council and a Department of Planning were scrapped, their role to be transferred to an upgraded, but inevitably weaker NEDC.

The retreat from planning reflected a re-thinking about the relationship between the state and the market, spurred by a decay in the influence of the left, the replacement of radical economists by those from the mainstream as the Party's economic advisors and weakening confidence in the efficacy of interventionism – the first, tentative, response to the widely-disseminated new right critique. Thus in 1986 Kinnock wrote that, 'the market is potentially a powerful force for good. It can be a remarkable co-ordinating mechanism. [It] can stimulate innovation and productive efficiency,and provide an economic environment in which individuals can experiment' (Kinnock, 1986: 42). Unfettered market forces were castigated for their inefficiency in generating economic growth not for their inequity or exploitative character. The role of the state increasingly began to be presented as facilitating the operation of the market by stepping in to perform functions which it was unwilling or unable to discharge rather than as a source of alternative allocative criteria. Though this clearly prefigured one of the main themes of the Policy Review, the leadership still felt constrained to proceed carefully. To avoid treading too heavily on Party sensibilities, the leadership remained reluctant to say openly what it thought in private.

Social ownership and industrial democracy

In 1986, Labour published a detailed statement on public ownership entitled *Social Ownership*.[25] In some ways, the statement is a bit of a puzzle. We have, so far, charted a slow but steady movement of the Party away from the radicalism of the turn of the decade. *Social Ownership* appears to buck the trend, partly because it was written at all – as we have seen, little systematic consideration was given to the subject in the early 1980s – and partly because of the radicalism of many of its proposals. The solution to the puzzle is largely political. By 1986 Labour was facing a thorny problem over what to do with the privatised industries and utilities. The 1984 statement, *A Future That Works*, reaffirmed the policy, first adumbrated in 1982, that Labour would, in returning to the public sector privatised industries, pay compensation on the principle of 'no speculative gain'[26] but since then British Telecom had been privatised and British Gas was next in line with the almost certain prospect of a massive increase in the number of share-holders. In these circumstances Labour's policy, as it stood, seemed a certain vote-loser yet feelings ran high in the Party and within public sector unions over the issue and many were ready to pounce on any signs of backsliding. A tactical decision was made to set up a working party to consider the issue but to widen its remit to the whole question of public ownership – so as to mask the intention to offer full compensation to privatised industries restored to the public sector.[27] The two main authors of the report were John Smith and David Blunkett and this brings us to the second purpose of the exercise: to solder the alliance between the right and the soft left. The price of achieving both these aims was a more radical statement than originally anticipated so whilst the soft left agreed to drop existing policy on privatisation and agree to more generous compensation the right swallowed its reservations about an apparent commitment to a significant extension of the public sector (Thomas, 1986).

The statement claimed that, whilst old-style Morrisonian nationalisation was out-dated and defective, Clause 4 – common ownership – 'is as relevant today as it has ever been'. It argued that the concentration of ownership and control of industry and finance in the hands of a small minority was the source of vast inequalities of power and wealth 'incompatible with democracy and individual freedom for all' and that the private sector 'on its own and as currently organised' was incapable of achieving economic growth and full employment. Hence, it called for a 'fairer and more democratic society' in which wealth and power were more equally distributed.[28] Particular importance was attached to the proposal for the new state holding company, British Enterprise (BE) whose role, as initially envisaged, was an ambitious one. According to Kinnock, 'it will take the lead for the government in operations to restructure industry and rationalise production' (Kinnock, 1986: 113). It would operate as a public entrepreneur moving into sectors (either through acquiring equity, joint ventures or establishing new companies) of vital national interest, e.g. new technology. In BE-assisted firms management and workers (through their unions) would draw up business plans 'specifying the company's long-term strategy, and covering areas such as investment, research and development, marketing strategy and training.' BE would 'have the financial backing needed to fulfil its role' with funds to be provided by the state, the BIB and through the market – though no information was given as to the size of its budget and, hence, the scale of its operations.[29]

Social Ownership can be read in different ways. On the one hand it can be seen as an imaginative attempt to devise new forms of social ownership and control; it was innovative in insisting on the need for socially-owned industries to be more democratically organised and much more responsive to their consumers, whilst reaffirming the Party's commitment to enlarging the public sector. Thus the report stated clearly that 'the next Labour Government will embark upon an ambitious programme to move towards wider social ownership.'[30] Alternatively, the report could be presented as a major step forward in the modernisation of Labour with the main focus on the junking of nationalisation. Talk of 'social ownership' could be shrugged off as a sugaring of the pill. Given the character of the report as a compromise between the right and the soft left, this ambiguity was not surprising and it soon became evident that the compromise represented a temporary stage in a constantly shifting equilibrium of forces in which the balance was moving in favour of the right. The report was, as one senior Party official put it, 'softened' by the 1987 statement *New Industrial Strength for Britain*: for example the establishment of business plans in BE-assisted companies becomes an 'aim' rather than a requirement and the functions of the BE were more narrowly defined.[31] However, the Party still remained committed to restoring most privatised assets to the public sector, though on much improved terms, and, in this area, the really substantial and explicit shift had to await the Policy Review.

In contrast, there was a notable retreat from the radicalism of the early 1980s in the sphere of industrial democracy. The 1986 report, *People at Work: New Rights, New Responsibilities* sounded a tentative note and there were constant references to further discussions to work out the details. For instance, 'the size and scope of representation' – a critical question – would be 'open to joint discussion and agreement', changes would require the assent of management and Joint Union Councils, which in Labour's earlier policy would have been important centres of trade union shop floor power, disappeared from view. Indeed, the whole rationale for extending workplace rights was altered since workers' participation was now advocated as a method for rebuilding consensus and smoothing the process of industrial change through negotiation rather than management fiat, rather than as a method of enfranchising the workforce or modifying the balance of power between workers and employees.[32] Again, we can detect the influence of new strategic thinking with its sensitivity to any policy which could be interpreted as promoting the revival of trade union power but other considerations influenced the shift in policy. There were widespread doubts (even amongst its progenitors) about the feasibility of the proposals outlined in the 1982 document and – in a period of massive unemployment – interest in industrial democracy in both the Party and the unions dwindled. But the significance of the move is worth emphasising. Whilst, for more than a decade, the extension of democracy to industry had been a major principle of Party policy this principle was effectively discarded even before the Policy Review.

The return to revisionist social democracy?

The widely held view that in the years 1983 to 1987 changes were mostly matters of presentation (see, for example, Jenkins, 1987: 251–3) and that therefore the Policy Review constituted a sudden and massive reversal of existing policy (See, e.g., Crewe, 1992: 23–4) is clearly inaccurate. Labour's response in the 1979–83 period to the perceived failure of revisionist economic strategy, with its reliance on demand-side economics, was to advocate a much more interventionist approach. By 1987, much of this had been scrapped. The fate of industrial democracy illustrates the general pattern of policy change from 1983 to 1987: a gradual retreat from more ambitious schemes of reform aimed (albeit often loosely) at a recasting of the social order and a return to the revisionist preference for pragmatic and largely consensual reform signalling the abandonment of any sustained challenge to the power and privileges of business in favour of developing co-operation between the producer organisations and the state, with redistributive measures largely confined to the social sphere.

Yet whilst major incremental changes took place – over the EC, economic management and industrial questions – as Kinnock and his front-bench allies sought cautiously, sometimes stealthily, to wean the Party from the radicalism of the early 1980s, internal Party constraints prevented more sweeping policy innovations. As Kinnock later recalled, he was 'never sure the whole party was with me. I was always dragging it, inch by inch, advancing a little, fighting more, advancing. I had to choose my ground so carefully' (Hare, 1993: 236). The unions were in general prepared to afford steadfast political backing to Kinnock (Minkin, 1991: 409, 402) but assembling majorities at Conference often involved patient negotiation and complex bargaining. Right-wing unions like the Engineers usually saw eye to eye with the Party leadership but it often encountered difficulties with large left-of-centre ones, like the TGWU, NUPE and MSF. Thus, as we have seen, Kinnock had been thwarted over parliamentary selection, could only obtain relatively modest modifications in Party policy on labour law, made little progress in developing a credible anti-inflation policy and had virtually no hope, even by 1987, of securing a Conference majority to overturn unilateralism.

Further, the immensely damaging consequences of the civil war of the early 1980s had rammed home the message that, without internal cohesion, Labour could not hope to recover. As his biographer noted in 1987, Kinnock well understood 'the importance of keeping the Party behind him in everything he has done, both to safeguard his own position and to avoid more internal contention' (Leapman, 1987: 189) and he himself later recalled, 'to have changed all policies simultaneously [in that period] would have fractured the Party.'[33] The effect of this was to retard the progress of modernisation, in two ways. Firstly, as we have seen, the leader had to expend considerable efforts on consensus-building. By mid-1986, a new ruling coalition extending from the right to the soft left had been consolidated helping prevent the re-emergence of a united left – which would have threatened Labour's cohesion and Kinnock's leadership – and giving him a mastery over the NEC he was never to lose. But concession had to be made to maintain coalition cohesion and although the adhesion (never uncritical) of the soft left removed some impediments to change, in major areas of policy – public ownership and, in particular, defence – it effectively stalled it. Secondly, it entailed paying due regard to those values and ideological tenets which helped cement the Party. Thus state ownership of industry was rejected but replaced by 'social ownership' and policy shifts were often clothed in a language and symbolism designed to reassure a membership tutored into anticipating betrayal. Whilst this served to preserve internal unity, it did so at the expense of reducing the voters' awareness of moves designed to appeal to them and it rendered Labour incapable of responding in any systematic way to the sweeping institutional changes effected by the Thatcher Government – reflecting both the primacy given, in this period, to subduing the hard left and Kinnock's own talents and preoccupations as a party manager rather than as a policy thinker. The significance of the period in laying the groundwork for the Policy Review should not, however, be overlooked in that the process of piloting Labour back to the middle ground was already well underway whilst the leader had acquired a grip on the party machinery which was an indispensable precondition for any fundamental change of course.

3

LABOUR'S CAMPAIGN AND COMMUNICATIONS STRATEGY 1983–7

CAMPAIGNING AND COMMUNICATION: THE CONTEXT

In an age of party dealignment and electoral volatility the campaign strategies of parties – the assumptions they make about voting behaviour, the messages they seek to convey, the techniques they employ and so forth – will have a substantial impact upon electoral outcomes. Campaigning involves communication, that is 'a planned effort on behalf of a sender to influence some or all groups in a society with a certain message or set of messages' (Windahl, Signitzer and Olson, 1992: 19). Since the introduction of the mass media – newspapers, the radio and above all television – and the spread of new techniques of persuasion, derived from commercial advertising and marketing and first systematically used in the US, the communications system has altered tremendously. In 1955 the Conservatives became the first party to employ an advertising agency – a development scorned by Labour which, in 1959, explicitly repudiated modern media techniques and expertise (Rose, 1967: 63). But by the early 1960s Labour was exhibiting a keen interest in new methods of communication and in the 1964 election it recruited outside professionals to advise on communications methods, employed opinion research to identify target voters, strengthened its publicity department and used advertising to project its key election themes (Butler and King, 1965: 67–72; see also Rose, 1967). In addition, Wilson grasped the importance of television which he exploited in a masterly fashion.

However, this innovatory attitude languished in the following decade particularly after the NEC swung to the left. The left were traditionally hostile to American-style campaigning methods, partly because they disliked the commercial spirit it embodied, partly because it appeared to trivialise politics and substitute psychological manipulation for reasoned argument and partly because the information that opinion polling often produced – that left-wing policies were unpopular with the electorate – was not welcome. In the early 1980s control over the Party machine gave the left the opportunity to put into effect their own campaigning prescriptions. Labour organised a series of mass demonstrations and marches addressed by Foot and other senior figures in Liverpool, London and elsewhere over the issues of jobs and peace,[1] some of which – e.g. in Liverpool – attracted very large numbers of supporters. The Party also urged constituencies and branches to conduct local campaigning activities such as the holding of public meetings, the distribution of leaflets, doorstep canvassing and active involvement in the struggles of local communities over, for example, hospital closures and educational provision. However, much of this campaigning petered out by 1981 as most politicians and activists became embroiled in internal Party affairs. Furthermore, within many constituency parties grass-roots campaigning tended to be neglected in favour of 'resolutionary politics' that is the passing of resolutions as substitute forms of action. And, as we have seen, hardly any methodical preparations were made for the 1983 election campaign which thereby descended into chaos.

THE TRANSFORMATION IN LABOUR'S CAMPAIGNING AND COMMUNICATIONS

Along with many others, Kinnock was struck by the contrast between Labour's campaign and the sophistication and professionalism exhibited by the Tories and a total overhaul of its approach to campaign and communications was an early priority. A resolution on campaign strategy moved by David Basnett, leader of GMBATU, deplored the incompetence of the campaign and called for the establishment of a Campaign Strategy Committee to inject a more professional approach.[2] The Campaign Strategy Committee (CSC) was set up in October 1983, consisting of representatives from the Executive, the

Shadow Cabinet and senior trade unionists, and was charged with a wide range of campaigning and communications responsibilities.[3] However, the formation of the committee was motivated by political as much as campaigning considerations as Kinnock intended to use the new body to short-circuit the NEC and thereby reduce the role of its still influential left-wing contingent. Initially the CSC was a powerful committee, with control over organising campaigns, opinion research and party political broadcasts but its value diminished and its role contracted as Kinnock secured an Executive more to his liking and, with the passage of time, its main function came to be to legitimate decisions taken elsewhere – by Party officials, front-benchers and new ad hoc groups.[4]

After the setting up of the CSC the sense of urgency evident in the aftermath of the election was dissipated as Kinnock became increasingly distracted by the miners' strike and other internal Party problems. This left many of the organisational problems which had beset Labour for years still to be tackled. No one was responsible for devising and implementing an overall communications policy. Responsibility for campaigning was placed with the Organisation Department, that for communications with the Press Office. The former defined its task mainly as one of stimulating local party activity whilst the latter perceived its role largely as managing day-to-day press relations. Competing departments and sections maintained separate contacts with the press and there was no organisational structure to ensure that the Party spoke with one voice. There was poor co-ordination between key parts of the Party machinery: the Press Office at Walworth Road, the PLP and the Shadow Cabinet. Campaigning was hampered by lack of co-operation as no one acknowledged a final authority. And whilst the responsibility for initiating campaigning was shifting to the leader's office and the front bench, the bulk of organisational resources were located in Walworth Road under the aegis (formally at least) of the NEC.[5]

In 1985 Larry Whitty, Head of Research at the General and Municipal Workers' Union replaced Jim Mortimer as General Secretary and the process of institutional reform was resumed. All campaigning and communications functions were brought together within a single body, the newly-established Campaigns and Communications Directorate into whose hands control over the conduct of media relations was vested so that it could operate as the clearing-house for all contacts between the Party and the media. In October 1985, a further – and what transpired to be a crucial – appointment was made when the 32-year-old Peter Mandelson was selected as Director of Campaigns and Communications. Mandelson (the grandson of Herbert Morrison) had already gained experience as a TV producer and as a former aide to a Shadow Cabinet member as well as being a friend of Kinnock's key advisor, Charles Clarke (Hughes and Wintour, 1990: 13) and possessed a sharp appreciation of the realities of modern political communications. In a report to the CSC shortly after his appointment he urged an 'even greater disciplined communication and expertise in projecting key policies to target audiences' and called for:

- an agreed communications strategy;
- cohesive presentation of our message through the full range of media;
- publicity material which is better and is used more often;
- and proper use of outside professional support.[6]

Virtually his first initiative was to commission a report by a politically sympathetic advertising executive, Philip Gould, into the state of the Party's communications. Gould operated on the same wavelength as Mandelson and was convinced that the Party's election fortunes could be revived if – like the Tories – it was prepared to utilise modern communications and marketing methods (Hughes and Wintour, 1990: 50). His bulky 64-page report was a damning indictment. Public perceptions of the Party were highly negative. It was no longer seen to represent the majority: 'instead it is often associated with minorities' and it suffered from 'an old-fashioned cloth cap image.' Too much effort was dispensed on localised campaigning using outmoded techniques like leafleting; campaigning was too often geared to Party activists rather than the wider public. Use of advertising methods was rudimentary, messages were poorly co-ordinated and the work of the Press Office was too reactive (Hughes and Wintour, 1990: 50–51). Gould's key recommendation was the recruitment of a group of advisors from the world of advertising prepared to work for the Party on a voluntary or expenses-only basis. The group's role would be 'to draft strategy, conduct and interpret research, produce advertising and campaigning themes, and provide other communications support as necessary' (Hughes and Wintour, 1990: 51–2). Mandelson eagerly endorsed the proposal. He believed it vital for the Party to tap the skills of such professionals as creative designers and writers, advertising account directors and experienced qualitative researchers and planners. The NEC assented and he immediately placed upon a more organised footing the 'breakfast group' of volunteers initially set up by Robin Cook, to form what soon came to be known as the Shadow Communications Agency (SCA).[7]

The Agency was able to call upon an impressive array of talent, including a number of highly rated top advertising executives. Amongst its members were Chris Powell, Peter Herd, Alan Tilly and Paul Leeves from the BMP agency (which had run Ken Livingstone's GLC anti-abolition campaign), Deborah Mattinson (Gould's business partner and joint co-ordinator) and Colin Fisher. Initially, it also included volunteers from journalism and the academic world, but as the Agency became more institutionalised and cohesive, and developed a settled approach to campaigning and communications they began to feel out of step and drifted away. The SCA also worked closely with Bob Worcester and Brian Gosschalk (from MORI) but its key liaison was with officials from the leader's office, Kinnock's Press Secretary, Patricia Hewitt, and his chief of staff, Charles Clarke (Hughes and Wintour, 1990: 54–5).

The strategic community

By early 1986, a new strategy-making community had emerged. Its key participants were Mandelson, Philip Gould, Deborah Mattinson, Chris Powell and others from BMP, Patricia Hewitt, and Charles Clarke, with the latter two representing the Party leader. In the years 1986 and 1987, two rising politicians, Robin Cook and Bryan Gould, were, as successive holders of the post of Campaign Co-ordinator, also members. Hewitt, after serving as Kinnock's Press Secretary, became his policy co-ordinator and subsequently Deputy Director of the left-of-centre Institute for Public Policy Research but remained close to the leader. Sharp, intelligent and energetic, she soon became one of the Party's leading strategists as well as acquiring, after 1987, an increasing influence in the policy field. Although Mandelson was in theory accountable to the NEC, in practice he acted on behalf of the leader working closely with his aides, particularly with Clarke. A tough-minded, quick-thinking, no-nonsense figure, Clarke became the most influential figure in the Leader's Office and his approval of any measure almost invariably implied that of Kinnock himself. With Kinnock's solid backing, Mandelson extended the influence of the Campaigns and Communications Directorate within Walworth Road which thereby gained an increasing share of the Party's slim resources and came to supplant the much older Organisation and Policy Directorates as the most powerful body at Head Office. Mandelson and Hewitt became primarily responsible for formulating the Party's overall campaigning strategy and the meticulous planning of its election preparations.

The usual description of the SCA as a group of individual volunteers was a little misleading as a large chunk of its expertise and personnel came from current and former employees of the large and highly-regarded BMP Agency. Initially, some thought was given to actually hiring BMP as the Party's Agency, but a combination of cost and the reluctance of members of its board to see it too closely engaged with Labour prevented this from proceeding any further – to that extent the Shadow Agency was a matter of making a virtue of a necessity. Generally the degree of involvement of most SCA members varied according to the proximity of an election. One or two BMP people – such as Chris Powell, a top-ranking figure within the agency and brother of Mrs Thatcher's advisor Charles – had a considerable influence on the thinking and strategic approach of the SCA. Philip Gould and Deborah Mattinson's Agency (Gould Mattinson Associates) unlike the rest of the Shadow Agency, was awarded a contract by the Party. Formally their role was to liaise between the Agency and the NEC; in practice they worked to Mandelson and, there-fore, Kinnock. Gould and Mandelson were in close and regular contact, and it was through them that the Agency's ideas and proposals flowed into the Party's campaigns and communi-cations strategy-making.

The post of Campaign Co-ordinator, a newly invented one, had no official status in the Party's organisational structure and, hence, no formal powers. The importance it acquired was due primarily to the ability of the two men who occupied it from

1984 to 1987: Robin Cook, and after he lost his seat in the Shadow Cabinet in October 1986, Bryan Gould, both of whom were eager proponents of new communications techniques and gradually widened the span of their responsibilities. Gould became responsible for ensuring that Shadow Cabinet members carried out their allotted tasks and he acted as a leading spokesman of the Party on TV – a task that swelled in significance as his skill in executing it became evident.[8] However Cook and Gould were relatively transient members of the strategic team whose hub consisted of Mandelson and other senior officials in his directorate, the Shadow Agency and the Leader's Office.

The new strategic paradigm

It was from the strategy-making community (henceforth, 'Labour's strategists') that a new pattern of strategic thinking, arising from the pooled experience, understanding and professional expertise of its members, emerged. It consisted of a set of interlinked propositions and maxims about the nature of electoral conduct, campaigning and communications which can be organised into five main components.

The electoral model

To be able to order and make systematic use of information about the electorate, and hence to formulate strategic prescriptions requires a model of the electoral behaviour of floating voters. The new strategic thinking (or paradigm) incorporated a model developed by MORI[9] which saw this behaviour as a product of a triangle of factors: party image, leadership image and issues/policies. One senior Labour strategist defined a party image as a 'gestalt', a configuration of perceptions, feelings and values which summed up how the voter felt about a party. Was it sensible and trustworthy? Was it capable of managing the economy and running the country well?[10] A leadership image, similarly, encapsulated how voters perceived and felt about the leader(s), his/her personality, strengths and weaknesses. The final side of the triangle, referred to 'the perceived understanding and acceptance or consonance of the elector's ideas of the parties' stance on issues of importance or salience to the voter' (Worcester, 1991: 111).

Positioning

A central question facing all parties is whether it places more emphasis on accommodating or seeking to modify existing opinion. Here one can distinguish between the *programmatic* and the *positioning* party. For the programmatic party, 'policies are part of a settled long-range programme' and are selected not only on their merits and for their electoral appeal but because they derive from a party's value system and are 'elements in a long-range social purpose' (Epstein, 1980: 262). Traditionally, Labour has been a programmatic party though, as is inevitable in the real world of politics, a balance has always to be struck between party ideology and 'long-range social purpose' on the one hand and more pragmatic considerations on the other. The new strategic thinking, however, wished to go further than pragmatism holding that in the selection and ordering of policy commitments primacy should be given to *positioning*. Initially derived from the commercial world, the concept envisaged the voters as an electoral market and parties as 'sellers' seeking to extend market share by developing policy-products more closely attuned to 'consumer tastes' than those available from other competitors. It entailed researching the market to uncover which issues were of greatest concern to the voters, the spread of voters' opinions on these issues, the degree of proximity between aggregate voter opinion and the electorate's perceptions of where the parties stood and re-aligning of the Party's overall policy package as closely as possible to the views of the median floating voter on the most salient issues. As a rule, it was assumed that opinion on most matters tended to peak at the centre and therefore a vote-maximising strategy required occupying the middle-ground of politics.

Agenda-setting

The new strategic thinking viewed the belief systems of the majority of voters (especially those with loose allegiances) as heterogeneous and weakly integrated, containing a mix of values and policy preferences, some of which were more congruent with Tory principles, others with Labour ones.[11] As a result, on most issues, voters consistently preferred one or other of the main parties (e.g. Labour and health, the Conservatives and law and order); furthermore, preferences were not easily modified with the bulk of issues being 'owned' by one or other of the two parties.[12] Efforts to dislodge existing convictions were seen to be either pointless or even counter-productive since by raising the public prominence of issues which 'belonged' to the rival party one was likely to propel voters into their arms. The Party should, in the main, concentrate its communications effort on maximising the saliency of those matters where it was most in line with popular sentiment, such as health and education, and strive as far as possible to neutralise or exclude from the agenda issues such as industrial relations and defence, where it had few hopes of evoking a supportive response. It followed, as two key strategists observed, that 'competition between rival agenda-setting is at the heart of election campaigning' (Hewitt and Mandelson, 1989: 53).

Transmitting the message

The voters' agenda was seen as powerfully influenced by the issues which received most extensive coverage in the media (especially television). Hence controlling the agenda was largely a matter of projecting onto the screen as frequently as possible one's 'own' issues. It followed, as Gould recommended in his report, that there should be 'a shift in campaigning emphasis from grass roots opinion forming to influencing opinion through the mass media' (Hughes and Wintour, 1990: 52) which could best be attained by the professionalisation of communications, that is the use of specialists with an informed understanding of the practices, operating methods and news-values of media organisations.

The advertising mode of communication

The paradigm held that the most effective mode of communication was the affective or advertising one, where the communicator seeks to persuade the audience by appealing to its feelings or emotional condition. This entailed utilising audio-visual displays such as appropriate mood music and colour, stylised representations and a scrupulous regard for the dress and demeanour of Party spokespeople. The use of such techniques, it was held, was more likely to attract the attention of the audience (especially given the tendency to filter discrepant information), to evoke positive sentiments, to discourage the activation of critical faculties, thereby maximising the impact of the message.

Centralised control of communications

The new strategic thinking came to form the framework in which all strategic as well as tactical decisions were made, and increasingly influenced not only the presentation but the ordering and content of policy. It represented a major technical advance and was firmly supported by the leadership but to put it into effect required new arrangements for campaign decision-making. Although the NEC and its Campaign Strategy Committee were formally charged with overseeing all aspects of campaigning and communications, in practice both were shunted into the background, their functions transferred to new institutions and the informal networks they spawned. In October 1985 Whitty established what was variously called the General Secretary's Committee, the General Election Planning Committee and the Campaign Management Team (for convenience we shall use this last title or CMT) consisting of senior Party officials, representatives from the Leader's Office (Patricia Hewitt and Charles Clarke) and the Campaign Co-ordinator (Cook, and then Gould). It reported directly to Kinnock until the end of 1986 when the Leader's Committee of front-benchers, NEC members and trade union leaders was set up.[13] These committees were vested with the prime responsibility for preparing the general election campaign. Operating alongside this committee structure were informal mechanisms of campaign planning and implementation which, coupled with the new institutional arrangements, ensured that effective political control would be exercised not by the NEC but by the Leader's Office.[14] The establishment of this enclosed system of campaign decision-making allowed Party strategists to determine the allocation of campaign resources, to shape and transmit a standardised campaign message and to facilitate the disciplined implementation of campaign plans.

THE TRANSFORMATION OF LABOUR'S CAMPAIGNING AND COMMUNICATIONS STRATEGY

Applying the new thinking, strategists introduced the following key changes in 1986:

- the systematic use of opinion research to identify voter perceptions and preferences and to pre-test Party messages;
- the thorough utilisation of modern marketing techniques in designing and delivering the campaign message;
- the integrated transmission of campaign messages.

Opinion research

Whilst Labour had commissioned opinion polling for years far more systematic use was now made of it. Firstly, the two organisations responsible for gathering information, MORI and the Shadow Agency, were much more closely involved in the Party's campaigning structure than ever before (Butler and Kavanagh, 1988: 133). A polling sub-committee of the CSC was set up in April 1984 to analyse polling data and MORI and, after its creation, the Agency submitted regular reports to the full Committee. More significantly, senior figures from both MORI and the Agency were closely involved in the designing of all aspects of the Party's campaigns and communications strategy. In his post-election report, Worcester noted the wide range of MORI's responsibilities: 'undertaking omnibus "tracking" research as necessary, conducting "semantics" research, evaluating party political broadcasts via group discussions, conducting area surveys and by-election studies.'[15] Opinion research was far more thoroughly integrated into campaign strategy than in the past when the Party had accumulated masses of information – a fair amount replicating what was freely available from published polls – without a clear and precise idea of its uses, and with politicians spending far too much time mulling over shifts in voting behaviour, 'the least important thing polling can tell us', as Patricia Hewitt complained.[16]

Opinion research was employed to monitor movements in public thinking, attitudes to Party policies, perceptions of the parties and their leaders, and the pre-testing of campaign vocabulary, themes and concepts. Particular reliance was placed on qualitative research which took two forms: first, the establishment (in early 1986) of the National Panel Survey, a panel of voters 'questioned repeatedly over the next 12 months in order to detect shifts in voter attitudes' (Hewitt and Mandelson, 1989: 51); and second, the use of 'focus' (i.e. small discussion) groups to provide in-depth information about the motivations of target voters. Qualitative research was felt to be of especial value because it enabled the investigator to probe more deeply into the electorate's underlying attitudes, values and feelings. Conducting it came to be the Shadow Agency's responsibility and notably extended its influence: because qualitative research sought to explore mental and emotional undercurrents – to feel the electorate's pulse – political judgment and intuition was essential to sift through the findings and to discriminate between core and more superficial responses. Because it became the Agency's task not only to accumulate the information but also to draw out its inner meaning and significance it was increasingly able to shape the parameters of strategic debate.[17]

Designing and delivering the campaign message

In the past the Party had paid little attention to the vocabulary it used in deploying its case yet opinion research carried out for the Party in 1984 disclosed that voters absorbed less than 10 per cent of the information they received and were 'unlikely to retain much more than a fleeting impression' of most communications messages.[18] To surmount this problem, the Agency devoted considerable care to crafting Labour's message, that is constructing an effective 'campaign code' which, for purposes of exposition, we can divide into verbal and non-verbal forms.

Verbal code

'Language', a Conservative Communications Director has observed, 'is often a key determinant in winning the battle of ideas' (Bruce, 1992: 176). In September 1985, MORI had presented a report, commissioned by the NEC, which explored attitudes towards language and themes used in Labour's 'Jobs and Industry' campaign. Based on group discussions with target voters, it found widespread confusion and misunderstanding of such habitually used phrases as 'public ownership', 'social ownership', 'public enterprise', 'infrastructure' and 'market forces' with many of the words commonly used by Labour politicians (significantly, much less so with Tories) arousing bewilderment.[19] 'We must ensure', Mandelson insisted, 'that our message is simply encapsulated in memorable phrases and policies explained in terms people can understand', which entailed using market research to ensure that 'our language . . . is neither patronising nor over the heads of our potential supporters.'[20] The Agency emphasised the importance of a central organising theme which condensed the campaign message, lending it the force and simplicity vital to instilling it in the audience's mind, and front-benchers were urged to continually expound the theme by constant repetition and by drawing upon a common stock of (pre-tested) ideas, slogans and arguments.

Non-verbal code

The use of non-verbal symbolic forms derived from advertising amounted to a more substantial departure from traditional forms of campaign communication. The left, and elements of the right too, had traditionally fought shy of the 'Americanisation' or 'commercialisation' of campaigning in part because it implied a lack of faith in the ability of rational argument to persuade the public. With the left still in a position of influence in 1983 and with an intellectual leader, Michael Foot, in whom confidence in the persuasive powers of reasoning ran strong, the Party's campaign that year relied heavily upon traditional forms of discourse. Its total failure facilitated the adoption after 1985 of (what we have called) the advertising mode of communication. This involved creating product recognition through the use of trademarks and slogans; differentiating the product from others by creating a unique selling proposition; encouraging the audience to want the product by enveloping it in a set of favourable associations; committing the audience to the product and its associated promises by inducing it to identify with the adverts' symbolised meaning and ensuring that the audience recalls the product and its need for it by repeated messages (Jamieson and Campbell, 1988: 170).

All of these methods were, to varying degrees, employed. 'Style and packaging', one top strategist recalled, 'was crucially important in projecting the image of a modern party',[21] whilst in a memo to Larry Whitty, Mandelson urged the adoption of a new 'trademark' or emblem – the red rose – in order 'to reinforce the impression of an innovative party shedding old associations and image' (Mandelson, 1988). The use of core themes, embodying Labour's central message, were designed to form its 'unique selling proposition'. But the key technique borrowed from advertising was the use of (what we shall call) 'symbolic images'. A symbolic image aimed to transfer to or project upon Labour (or its leader) a desirable quality – like trustworthiness or modernity – by associating or juxtaposing the Party (or Kinnock) with objects, persons or scenes seen commonly to symbolise that quality. Thus one Party Political Broadcast described by Mandelson as 'warm and emotional' culminated 'in the 10 year-old star running into the safe hands of a bobby on the beat' (Mandelson, 1988). A confidential memo by Patricia Hewitt discussing the choice of locations for campaign appearances furnishes another illustration of the technique: 'We want places that are modern. . . . We do NOT want any closed factories, derelict housing sites, run-down hospitals . . . or other wrecks of Thatcher's Britain. We also want *people* – bright, attractive people presenting an image of the broader base Labour has to capture – *not* people who present an image of old fashioned Labour diehards.'[22] Similarly, the defence campaign – whose key object was to demonstrate that the Party stood for a virile defence – relied on 'the use of potent images and language that associate us with the building-up of our defences and them [the Tories] with running them down. This means showing the destroyer that has been cut, and the tank that will be built. . . .'[23]

The technique was extensively used during the election, when Labour's photo-opportunities often presented the leader at gleaming, high-tech factories to convey an image of a party at the cutting edge of the future. An outstanding example was the Party Election Broadcast that so impressed commentators that it was actually repeated and came to be dubbed 'Kinnock – the movie'. This:

> opened with a warplane streaking across the sky, switching to a seagull soaring effortlessly, backed by the muted strains of the Party's theme from Brahms' first symphony. Distant figures, soon revealed as Neil and Glenys Kinnock walked

hand in hand across a sunny headland, with Neil Kinnock voicing over his belief that the strong should help the weak.
(Butler and Kavanagh, 1988: 153–4)

The integrated transmission of the campaign message

Political communicators have available to them a variety of channels to transmit their messages: TV and radio, the press, party political broadcasts, advertising and a party's own organisations. Since obviously they will seek to utilise them all the important point is the overall mix. With the arrival of Mandelson and the Shadow Agency, the role of the constituency machinery was heavily down-graded in favour of the mass media, especially television, and maximum favourable TV coverage became the end to which much of Labour's campaigning was geared. As Patricia Hewitt explained in a memo to the Campaign Management Team in December 1985, '1987 will be an ENG [electronic news-gathering] election with news editors demanding – and getting – virtually instant responses to every key speech and statement' (quoted in Butler and Kavanagh, 1988: 60).

A key recommendation of the 1985 Gould report was that combined and co-ordinated use should be made of all communications outlets to convey the agreed message. 'Major speeches, events and PPBs should be followed up by supplementary speeches, a co-ordinated PR push and the use (where possible) of advertising and direct mail' (Hughes and Wintour, 1990: 52). In a confidential memo written in October 1986, Mandelson advised the Party:

to use our captive media (advertising and PPBs) for agenda setting purposes i.e. aggressive, personalised assaults on the Tories (especially ads) coupled with inspirational projection of our central messages and messengers. Using non-captive media to reinforce this agenda but also to fight back against opposition attacks on us. Use broadcasting to convey atmosphere, confidence and unity of the campaign through daily events.[24]

Whilst pursuing this approach proved, in practice, to be difficult, the concerted orchestration of its message became a pronounced feature of Labour's election campaign.[25]

THE LONG CAMPAIGN

We shall now examine how Labour's new approach to communications was applied firstly in pre-election campaigning and then in the actual election campaign. The notion of a long campaign was a new development whose origins actually lay within the period of left ascendancy prior to 1983 though campaigns then relied on traditional methods of communication (marches, demonstrations, public meetings and so forth) and were usually poorly organised and haphazardly implemented. In the wake of the 1983 defeat, there was a widespread demand for the leadership to take campaigning much more seriously. The first major initiative taken by the newly established Campaign Strategy Committee was a 'Save our Health Service' campaign to protest against NHS cuts but though there were one or two new developments (such as the use of a touring ambulance to attract local publicity) the campaign relied heavily on established (though rarely employed) techniques, such as local party campaigning against hospital closures, conferences, and the production of leaflets and posters. The first real change in campaigning style – one which predated the Mandelson regime – occurred with the launch of the Jobs and Industry campaign in 1985.

Jobs and Industry campaign

The campaign originated in a paper prepared by Head Office officials[26] and considerable effort throughout 1984 was invested in the planning and methodical organisation of the campaign which was finally launched in April 1985.[27] A significant innovation was the use of focus groups to provide in-depth explorations of economic attitudes.[28] These disclosed that Party was seen as the purveyor of tried, tired and discredited remedies. Calling for a boost to the economy through higher public spending fostered the image of Labour as 'the well meaning Party that prints money to solve each and every problem. Our very strength – that we care – becomes our greatest weakness'. Further, people were highly fatalistic about mass unemployment with Labour voters feeling powerless and in despair, whilst even amongst those with experience of unemployment, less than half blamed the government. In response, the campaign aimed to enhance the Party's economic credibility by dispelling the myth – as Kinnock put it – that Labour was a party 'solely concerned with redistribution and [by convincing] people that it was a "party of production" '[29]

Campaign strategists observed that: 'we can never rely on sympathetic media coverage, nor do we have the resources to mount a major advertising campaign. But we *do* have a unique resource: the Party membership and affiliated union membership.' In the past, Labour's constituency organisations had been largely inert and passive, except at election times. In fact, and almost entirely as a result of independent initiatives, many constituency organisations had – at around this time – flung themselves with considerable verve and commitment into campaigning on behalf of the miners, then engaged in their protracted dispute. This may well have influenced the thinking of Party strategists who now saw local parties, potentially at least, as valuable campaigning instruments. Thus CLP's were encouraged to organise local initiatives to promote the campaign in their area and campaign packs, videos and other briefing material of a much more professional quality than in the past were circulated to all constituency parties. They were urged to organise public meetings, involve themselves with trade union branches and local voluntary associations, issue press releases to local papers and raise the Party's presence in shopping centres, works canteens and wherever people assembled.[30] This was supplemented nationally by the Party organising or supporting rock concerts, gala nights, sports events and musical presentations at campaign road shows.[31]

Freedom and Fairness campaign

In assessing the Jobs and Industry campaign, the NEC noted that 'the potential for campaigning by local parties has barely been touched'.[32] Nor was it to be in the future. By the time the next campaign – Freedom and Fairness – was mounted, the transformation in Labour's approach to campaigning and communications was in full swing. One senior member of the new strategic community diagnosed two disabling defects of the Jobs and Industry campaign: it concentrated on grass-roots activities rather than 'disciplined communication via the mass media' and it 'lacked a strategic conception integrating style, language and message.'[33] It was these faults that the Freedom and Fairness campaign was designed to remedy.

In July 1985, the Party had commissioned qualitative research to ascertain the attitudes of targeted groups of voters to social policy and to the parties' stance on them and to test possible campaign themes, key phrases and slogans.[34] The research uncovered a complex and in some ways disturbing picture. Whilst social policy was generally seen as a plus for Labour, there were considerable doubts as to how it would fund new initiatives and about its ability to actually deliver the goods. Further, whilst most voters favoured higher spending on education there were widespread complaints about ' "scroungers" and the abuse of welfare benefits.' Respondents perceived the Party as 'caring' but also as 'unfashionable' and 'unprofessional', peddling out-of-date solutions and identified with a remote and impersonal state. At the same time, the research pointed to a mounting sense of distaste towards Thatcherite values, associating them with a trend towards a greedier, uncaring and more violent society.[35]

In line with the new strategic thinking, the major object of the campaign was 'to set the agenda for political debate' by focusing public attention on 'quality of life' issues, Labour's traditional strong suit. The Conservatives had projected themselves as the party of freedom and choice whilst depicting Labour as the party of the heavy-handed, bureaucratic state. Yet opinion research indicated that the values of the welfare state were widely shared and that the public would respond positively 'to a clear vision of what we are about'. Kinnock sought to capitalise on this and reclaim the value of freedom 'temporarily embezzled' by the new right, by promoting his vision of 'the enabling state': a state which nourished talent and opportunity by supplying the means – health, education, housing – for a freedom 'which is not nominal but real'.[36]

The campaign intensified efforts to develop a persuasive campaign code. A campaign message, the Agency argued, should incorporate three major elements: vision, programme and symbolic policies. The purpose of a vision was 'to spell out the kind of society which could result from a Labour Government'; that of a programme was to 'spell out the way in which the vision may be realised'; whilst that of a symbolic policy was 'to bring to life both the programme and the vision' by encapsulating the

Party's core values in policies offering voters tangible benefits (the example frequently given was Conservative policy on council house sales).[37] Kinnock instanced under-five provision and cervical cancer screening as such examples of the latter but they had little resonance, and the search for the winning symbolic policy was to prove highly elusive. The main innovation of the Freedom and Fairness campaign lay, however, in its use of audio-visual techniques. The campaign was launched 'amid the sort of razzmatazz commonly associated with the commercial advertising agencies' (*Guardian*, 23 April 1986). The PPB staged to coincide with it was, Hugo Young commented, 'a minor masterpiece . . . the world here briefly glimpsed was a promised land, where every house was new, every school a clean, well-lit place, and every surgery was equipped with a computer,' images designed to convey the notion of the high quality services Labour's enabling state would provide for all. 'Chaotic romanticism has given way to the hard-eyed exploitation of sentiment, a pretty child being the new jump-suited logo of socialist realism' (*Guardian*, 24 April 1986).

Investing in People

Qualitative research amongst target groups commissioned from MORI during the Jobs and Industry campaign told a dispiriting tale. Whilst voters were worried by high unemployment, the government continued to escape blame. 'The old doubts about the Party had not been dispelled: would inflation and taxes rise, how could Labour pay for its programme, would money be squandered, would the unions run the whole show, could Labour deliver?' Labour's response was to launch an economic campaign designed 'to appeal to uncommitted voters by projecting an image of unity, competence and modernity'.[38] The 'central logic' of the campaign was the notion of 'investing in people' (a phrase chosen after the pre-testing of a range of options in focus groups recruited from target voters).[39] By investing in people one strengthened the economy, promoted social cohesion and enhanced individual freedom. The impact of the campaign, however, was negligible, partly due to a lack of interest and commitment by the politicians but also to a muddle over policy. A central campaign pledge was to reduce unemployment by one million within the first two years of a Labour

Government but the Party retreated from the original plan to create new jobs mainly in the public sector because of a fear that it might be depicted as 'feather-bedding' and it was replaced by a new one promising expansion in the private sector.[40] It was an early example of policy being subordinated to communications imperatives, but the impression left was of a confused party, unsure of its touch.

The defence campaign: Modern Britain in a Modern World

Virtually everyone accepted that defence had cost Labour votes in 1983 but there was little enthusiasm within the Party leadership for campaigning, on the grounds that defence was a Tory issue. In July 1985 Robin Cook, the Campaign Co-ordinator (and a prominent unilateralist) sought to stir the Party into action. He rejected 'conventional marketing advice to play to our strengths and therefore downplay defence as an issue.' He adduced four reasons for this: (1) the electorate simply perceived Labour as a party of disarmament and was wholly unaware of its defence policy; (2) since the Party was not going to alter its stance it had no option but to alter public perception of it; (3) it was vital that Party activists be equipped with arguments to overcome the voters' anxieties; (4) the Conservatives would inevitably highlight the issue.[41] The NEC agreed to organise a campaign and was indeed instructed to do so by Conference in October 1985. But foot-dragging amongst senior officials in Walworth Road delayed its launch and by early 1986 anxious International Department officials were warning of 'damaging constituency unrest' and 'a deluge of resolutions' condemning the failure to implement the 1985 Conference resolution if a 'serious campaign' was not underway by September.[42] The campaign was finally mounted – perilously late in the day – at the end of 1986.

An internal paper, analysing available polling data, uncovered some encouraging signs. Only a minority felt that American nuclear bases, which the Party was committed to remove, made Britain a safer place and Labour's pledge to secure the withdrawal of Cruise missiles enjoyed majority support. However, for the most part Labour's defence policy had little appeal with substantial majorities opposing the other main planks – decommissioning Polaris, a non-nuclear defence policy and the withdrawal of NATO short-range nuclear weapons from Europe.[43] One can sum up the quantitative data by saying that it presented a worrying picture with nevertheless some gleams of hope. The results of the qualitative research conducted by the SCA (mainly amongst lapsed Labour Alliance voters) came as something of a shock. It painted a portrait in much darker, more sombre hues. Whilst defence was rated a low saliency issue it was found to rouse 'strong, atavistic feelings'. There was a high degree of ignorance which encouraged a search for 'simple solutions as a way of understanding a frightening issue'. The possession by Britain of nuclear weapons was not only seen as essential for effective deterrence, it was also associated with powerful sentiments of national pride. Labour was regarded as unreliable on defence, with widespread fears that it would deprive the country of the means to protect itself.[44]

Strategists recognised that defence could never be a vote-winner – hence the aim of the campaign was to reassure floating voters who were contemplating backing the Party by calming their anxieties about defence. In the past the thrust of its argument in favour of a non-nuclear approach were that reliance on nuclear weapons was immoral, and that abandoning Britain's nuclear deterrent would contribute to international disarmament. Strategists now proposed that the best way to propitiate the electorate was to shift the terrain and present the issue in terms of differences over the most effective means to achieve the agreed end of stronger defence. The main theme of the campaign would therefore be to project Labour as 'the Party that puts the defence of Britain first; that believes in strong, usable effective defence; that believes in spending more on the Royal Navy, the Airforce and the Army; that is a staunch and committed member of NATO' counterposed to the Tories as 'the party that saps our defences in order to pay for Trident and Cruise'.[45] This approach was approved and the overriding objective of persuading the electorate that 'a vote for Labour is also a vote for a strong defence policy' determined the language, style and themes of the 'Modern Britain in a Modern World' campaign launched in December 1986. The core message was 'either nuclear weapons or a modern defence force – we cannot pay for both' with the government charged with being 'disarmers by stealth'.[46]

Opinion polls commissioned by Labour to assess the impact

of the campaign were disappointing. The level of recognition of Labour's policy improved somewhat: 55 per cent of respondents now agreed that a Labour Government would strengthen Britain's conventional forces compared to 24 per cent prior to the campaign launch (though a majority continued to believe that the Party would take the UK out of NATO). But on the central issues of whether it was possible for Britain to have a strong defence without nuclear weapons the percentage concurring actually fell from 44 per cent to 38 per cent with the percentage dissenting rising from 45 per cent to 53 per cent.[47] Party strategists may have anticipated this and hoped to draw the sting from the issue. Matters were not helped by Kinnock's two ill-conceived and poorly handled trips to the US which, far from demonstrating, as intended, the statesmanlike qualities of the leader, both (quite predictably) exposed Kinnock to embarrassing snubs from the Reagan administration and contrasted starkly with Mrs Thatcher's triumphal procession through the Soviet Union. All did not augur well for the general election which could not long be delayed.[48]

Labour's pre-election collapse

In December 1986, a major Conservative Party strategy document declared: 'The Labour party leadership must be tied in with their extremists' (quoted in Butler and Kavanagh, 1988: 38). Two months earlier, the Conservatives had launched their highly effective 'loony left' offensive against Labour. Ministers in concert mounted virulent attacks against left-wing councils, with Environment Secretary Nicholas Ridley charging that the Town Hall had become 'an arena for aggressive political posing, disruption, wild accusation, threats and fear' (*Guardian*, 18 November 1986). The message was loudly, repeatedly and often skilfully echoed by the Tory tabloids as left-wing Labour councils in London were remorselessly pilloried. The *Mail on Sunday* charged that black bin liners had been banned in (the black) Bernie Grant's Haringey; the *Sun* headlined 'lefties *Baa Black Sheep*' on the grounds that the nursery rhyme was racist. Countless other examples were offered by the tabloids to demonstrate the stupidity, intolerance and capriciousness of Labour-run councils. Most of them were either wildly distorted or entirely fabricated (Media Research Group, 1987) though with a few accurate ones which added a seasoning of credibility. (The most widely-publicised was the suspension of the headteacher Maureen McGoldrick by the left-wing Brent council on unsubstantiated charges of racism.) The attacks reached a crescendo during the by-election for the safe Labour seat of Greenwich, where the local party had selected a member of the hard left (Deirdre Wood) as their candidate – and which was disastrously lost to the SDP. The effect on Labour of this sustained and high-volume campaign was devastating. Its standing in the polls plummeted and the steady improvement in its image in the years following the last election was reversed: 67 per cent perceived the Party as too extreme, 73 per cent as split and 55 per cent as lacking in economic competence (Hewitt and Mandelson, 1989: 49). Labour's own qualitative research conducted amongst undecided voters in March 1987 revealed that it was seen as a party in a disarray, its leader as a 'very nice bloke' but pushed about and bullied by extremists, the unions, immigrants and homosexuals. Many voters sympathetic to Labour's 'compassionate' policies would not vote for it 'because they are afraid of its extremists, and don't trust its leadership to hold them in check'.[49]

The leadership had few doubts about what had gone wrong. In a leaked letter Patricia Hewitt declared:

> It's obvious from our own polling, as well as from the doorstep that the 'London effect' is now very noticeable. The 'loony Labour left' is taking its toll; the gays and lesbians issue is costing us dear amongst the pensioners; and fear of extremism and higher taxes/rates is particularly prominent in the GLC area.
>
> (*Guardian*, 6 March 1987)

Labour's leaders would have preferred to have publicly and forcefully disassociated themselves from the London 'hard left' and were privately utterly dismayed by the crass behaviour of some Labour councils but political realities did not, at the time, permit them to do so. The issue re-awoke (as one close associate of the Party leader recalled) 'the fears which many potential voters still had about Labour extremism, divisions, unfitness for government and Kinnock's own leadership ability' (Butler and Kavanagh, 1988: 72). On the very brink of the election, the Party stood in real danger of being relegated to third place.

Whilst in public, its professed aim was to beat the Tories, in private its overriding object was the rather more modest one of retaining its status as HM Opposition.

The 1987 election: campaign strategy

In formulating and implementing its campaign strategy, Labour pursued two main aims: to secure control of the campaign agenda debate and to sway the uncommitted by posing the choice as one between Kinnock and Thatcher. The key strategic decision for the election campaign was the choice of agenda. Labour opted for a 'quality of life' agenda, that is the issues of health, schooling, jobs and pensions. The Conservatives were vulnerable – opinion research uncovered widespread anxiety about deteriorating public services and growing social divisions; it was seen as one of the main areas of demarcation between the two main parties; and, above all, it was Labour's best card – Labour was perceived as the party that 'cared', that was in touch with people's real needs and that had the best policies.[50] One final, and decisive, consideration influenced this choice – the evidence in early 1987 that weak Labour adherents were drifting in droves (especially after the disastrous Greenwich by-election) to the Alliance – opening up the doomsday scenario of third place. So a key strategic aim became to shore up the Party's support by accentuating those concerns traditionally close to the hearts of Labour voters.[51] As a result, mobilising public sympathy for the values and institutions of the welfare state became the spearhead of Labour's campaign. In the words of three key members of the Shadow Agency 'this portfolio became the nitty-gritty of our campaign'; it formed the Party's 'brand image'.[52] It constituted the major theme of the most celebrated features of Labour's campaign: Kinnock's Llandudno speech (the 'thousand years of Kinnocks') and the much-acclaimed Hudson 'Kinnock-the movie' election broadcast.

The decision to run a 'presidential' campaign was taken for both positive and negative reasons. There were more people (according to surveys) who were pro-Kinnock than were pro-Labour. Campaign strategists were convinced that careful planning – 'cheering crowds and roses everywhere you go' as Patricia Hewitt wrote in a memo to the leader – could generate a wave of enthusiasm. In Mandelson's words: 'His strength and character should come through television and therefore much else should be sacrificed to assist this. . . . Neil must represent an exciting and trustworthy new start for the nation. In conclusion. . . . FDR spliced with Camelot'.[53] Finally, highlighting Kinnock's qualities was designed to pre-empt the personal attack Party strategists had discovered that the Tories were planning. Personalising the campaign also enabled Labour to exploit Mrs Thatcher's perceived unpopularity. Mandelson wrote that people voted more against governments than for oppositions, that Labour's own recent record in government was not a glowing one, that it could only make modest promises, and above all that 'Thatcher is a sitting target to vote against'. He concluded that Labour should:

> set out to unite the country by polarising opinion between those who can afford the Tories and the rest of us who can't, those who profit from the status quo and the majority who need change. . . . Those who like Thatcher and those who can't stand any more of that boring, sanctimonious voice.[54]

This depiction of Mrs Thatcher's Government as heartless and selfish became the key theme of the Party's advertising campaign – summed up by one ad: 'if the Tories' had a soul they'd sell it'.

The 1987 election: the campaign

Labour's meticulously planned campaign strategy swung into action immediately the election was called with a drive and panache that caught the Conservatives by surprise. Within days, it was being praised for its efficiency and for the skill in which modern techniques were – in such stark contrast to 1983 – deployed. Labour's 'Kinnock – the movie' PEB (written by Colin Welland and produced by Hugh 'Chariots of Fire' Hudson) with its 'slick presentation of Neil Kinnock as a family man of humble origin, offering caring and effective leadership put heart into all of his followers and alarmed his opponents' (Butler and Kavanagh, 1988: 102). His opinion ratings soared. Labour's tightly organised plan enabled it, for much of the campaign, to set the running with its agenda – though, worryingly, the rise in its morale was not matched by any commensurate improvement in the polls.

The first major upset was over defence. As it happened the issue erupted rather earlier than the Tories had intended. On Sunday 24 May, in response to a question speculating about war between a non-nuclear Britain and nuclear armed forces Kinnock declared that 'in these circumstances the choice is posed . . . between exterminating everything you stand for and the flower of your youth, or using all the resources you have to make any occupation totally untenable' (Butler and Kavanagh, 1988: 103). In the middle of an election campaign this was a careless remark. The Tories saw an opening and pounced – as one cabinet minister put it 'when you're presented with an open goal, you tap the ball in' (*Observer*, 31 May 1987). Kinnock's words were taken out of context, distorted and remorselessly exploited. Mrs Thatcher summed up the main theme of the Tory offensive, amplified by most of the tabloids:

> So Labour's non-nuclear defence policy is in fact a policy for defeat, surrender, occupation and finally prolonged guer-rilla fighting . . . [Kinnock] has conceded that once this country has renounced its independent deterrent it would have no alternative but to surrender to a nuclear threat.
>
> (*Guardian*, 27 May 1987)

Or, in Dr Owen's succinct phrase, 'he wants Dad's Army back' (*Guardian*, 26 May 1987). In what was acclaimed by many as the most effective advert of the campaign, in the final days, a full-page picture appeared in the press of a soldier with his hands in the air and the simple caption 'Labour's policy on arms'. Labour's initial response was to ignore the issue in the hope that the voters would lose interest, and spokesmen were instructed not to discuss it in the media but the Party soon had to change tack. The high profile of the issue in the second week of the campaign was sustained by a well-timed warning from President Reagan that Labour's defence policy contained 'grievous errors' and he would 'try with all my might' to dissuade a Labour Government from implementing it (*Guardian*, 28 May 1987). It was impossible amidst the din of a campaign to explain that scenarios conjured up by the Party's opponents were utterly unreal, hence Labour appeared defensive and uncertain. The salience of the issue rose considerably and the Conservatives' already very considerable lead on the issue swelled even further (up 9 points to 48 per cent over Labour's 20 per cent, down 4 points) (*Guardian*, 29 May 1987). According to another poll 45 per cent of non-Labour voters gave defence as the main reason for spurning the Party, up 10 per cent in a fortnight. (*Observer*, 31 May 1987). A post-election poll revealed that defence was the second most important issue after unemployment (cited by 35 per cent) and twice as many Labour defectors mentioned the issue as Labour loyalists (Crewe, 1987b).[55]

Besides defence, the Tories (and their tabloid allies) concentrated their fire on two other Labour vulnerabilities: the 'loony left' and the tax/economic competence complex. Treasury ministers claimed that Labour's pledges would cost £35 billion (oddly, the same figure was used for the 1992 election – not even index-linked) entailing the levying of massively heavier taxation. Labour spokesmen appeared unprepared and issued contradictory messages leaving an impression of either amateurism or intended deception. The problem was that the Manifesto had been left (deliberately) so sparse that on many key issues detail was omitted and agreed positions had not been reached: as a result, several commitments were made by leading Labour campaigners which had never figured in the document (Butler and Kavanagh, 1988: 257). The Tories and their allies were quick to seize on this as proof of their opponent's incompetence. The *Mail*'s headline denounced 'Labour's Lies on Taxation' whilst the *Express* proclaimed 'Exposed: Labour's Tax Fiasco' (Butler and Kavanagh, 1988: 106).

The 1987 election result

In the final week before the election, Labour's campaign faltered as an exhausted campaign team appeared to run out of ideas. Even then, few were prepared for the result. Labour's share of the vote rose a mere 3.2 per cent to 30.8 per cent and it added 20 seats to reach a total of 229 – its second worst result since 1945. The one objective that was fully achieved was the winning of the battle of the opposition, as the gap between Labour and the Alliance widened from 2 points to 8 (Crewe, 1987a). Labour made significant gains amongst routine non-manual workers (up from 20 per cent to 26 per cent) and foremen and technicians (up from 28 per cent to 36 per cent) but of the two largest social classes it gained a mere 2 per cent of the salariat's vote (from 13 per cent to 15 per cent) and actually slipped back marginally within the working class (from 49 per cent to 48 per cent). To place this in historical perspective, it is interesting to measure these figures against the 1970 result, the last time the Party won over 40 per cent of the vote (although it lost the election).

	Salariat	Routine non-manual	Petty bourgeoisie	Foremen & technicians	Working class
1970	29	41	19	56	61
1987	15	26	16	36	48

Source: Heath *et al.*, 1991: 68–9

Labour's share of the working-class vote remained discouragingly low in the south and amongst home-owners (both growing groups) and highest in those sections (like council house-owners, union members, public sector workers and workers in manufacturing industry) which were shrinking. Crewe concluded that it had:

> come to represent a declining segment of the working class . . . while failing to attract the affluent and expanding working class of the new estates and new service economy of the South. It was a party neither of one class nor one nation; it was a regional class party.
>
> (Crewe, 1987a)

Further, whilst Labour had succeeded in pushing to the foreground the issue of the NHS and was the preferred party on most social policy issues, it had failed to excise its image of extremism. What appeared to matter most was the satisfaction a plurality of the electorate felt with the state of the economy and their own rising standards of living (Crewe,1987b).

Despite the unprecedented vigour and professionalism of Labour's campaign, its total vote had crept up only slightly and the Tory majority was hardly dented: in the circumstances, the electorate's judgement of the Party was as unambiguously negative as ever.

4

A PALER SHADE OF PINK: THE POLICY REVIEW

THE AFTERMATH OF THE ELECTION

With high hopes raised by the quality and professionalism of the campaign, the outcome was, in the Party's own words, a 'devastatingly disappointing result': not because Labour lost the election – few regarded winning as a realistic scenario – but because, in comparison with the wretchedly mismanaged campaign of 1983, the advance was so weak.[1] Why had Labour lost so conclusively in 1987? What factors inhibited people from voting for the Party? Shortly after the 1987 election, a report entitled *Labour and Britain in the 1990s* was produced by a team comprising Mandelson, Philip Gould, Deborah Mattinson, Roger Jowell (Director of British Social and Community Planning Research), Paul Ormerod (Director of the Henley Centre for Forecasting) and Lord (Andrew) McIntosh from IFF Research Limited[2] (Hughes and Wintour, 1990: 60). In the following discussion, the report has been supplemented by interviews with leading strategists, Shadow Agency reports written in 1987, Party documents and other relevant material. The diagnosis of Labour's predicament had two purposes: to analyse the nature of the problem but also to prepare opinion within the Party for the sweeping changes of policy that the authors believed were essential.

Broadly speaking, whilst Party strategists employed the same triangular analysis of electoral behaviour as used earlier, that is issues, leader image and party image, far more attention was given to the questions of values, perceived economic competence and trustworthiness in exploring the mental picture the voters held of the Party. Strategists distinguished between

81

habitual voting, derived from class and party identification and non-habitual forms of voting. A large slice of the Labour electorate comprised habitual voters but their numbers were falling because of a range of major social trends. The era of the Party's strength – roughly the generation from the 1930s to the 1960s – had been the age of 'Fordist' production, with its huge industrial plants organising masses of workers engaged in repetitive, alienating tasks and often living in nearby socially homogeneous council estates. These conditions gave rise to high levels of unionisation, a strong sense of class identity and solidarity and allegiance to the Labour Party as the party of the working class. But the age of Fordism was passing, employment in heavy and the extractive industries rapidly falling and being replaced by geographically more dispersed, smaller-scale light industries, with employees engaged in a much more varied range of tasks. Further, industrial employment was shrinking fast whereas the size of the service sector was expanding rapidly. At the same time, economic and technological trends, encouraged by government policy, were giving rise to an increasingly differentiated working class. In 1979 the Conservatives had gained the allegiance of a large segment of the working class, largely skilled workers residing in the South and Midlands, many of whom subsequently benefited from income tax cuts, rising real wages and enhanced social status – often taking advantage of council house sales to purchase their own homes at discounted prices, and realising quick capital gains by buying deliberately underpriced privatised shares. Most of these subsequently remained loyal to their new allegiance, increasingly identifying with the Tories as a party which shared their aspirations and protected their interests.

Labour and Britain in the 1990s calculated that about 6 per cent of the 13 per cent loss of support since 1964 could be accounted for by social structural change.[3] Part of the rest was due to the sense that the Party was out of touch with the new pattern of values and aspirations engendered by social and economic changes. Collectivist values withered with, in Leadbeater's words:

> the loss of trust in the state's ability to act as the guardian of collective social interests; the decay of traditional sources of solidarity and common identity forged through work; the

growth in the importance of individual choice in consumption, the revolt against centralising sameness, the pursuit of
diversity.

(Leadbeater, 1988: 17)

Experience of participation in a mass consumption economy
with its wide range of goods and services that most people could
afford, the growth in individual purchasing power and the
exposure of the bulk of the population to sophisticated television advertising all contributed to the emergence of the citizen
as consumer, characterised by a more individualistic and mater-
ialistic set of attitudes, neatly encapsulated (in the view of one
leading strategist) by the observation of a participant in a focus
group, 'we want videos, not visions.'[4] Many were, or hoped to be,
upwardly mobile with ambitions to purchase private health and
medicine. This fostered a sense – in the words of one strategist –
that 'empowerment came through purchasing' and increasing
numbers of people became convinced that they could advance
themselves most effectively by the exertion of their own individual efforts and not by collective action and hence found the
Thatcherite invocation of individual virtues attractive. Labour,
in contrast, was perceived as old-fashioned and incapable of
understanding the hopes and aspirations of ordinary people:
there was 'a general sense that Labour's "not for me" – either
because Labour had changed or because "I've left that behind." '[5] Rather than advancing their interests it was seen as
preferring to give priority to those of minorities (especially
'immigrants' and gays), the poor and the failures in life.

Given that most floating voters defined their interests in terms
of individual betterment, clearly they would opt for that party
most likely to protect and improve their standard of living.
Here, according to strategists, was another crucial source of
weakness. Many felt estranged by the Party's collectivist stance
on issues such as tax, industrial relations and nationalisation and
although they affirmed that increasing public expenditure and
reducing unemployment was more important for the country
than cutting taxation and and inflation, when asked what
mattered most to them personally they tended to rate these
latter goals more highly. Questions of specific policies, however,
mattered less than views as to which party was better capable of
managing the economy and even those voters who favoured

Labour's position on individual issues had considerably more confidence in the Conservatives. Thus during the election campaign no less than 56 per cent of voters feared an economic crisis if Labour triumphed.[6] Furthermore, for all its efforts to brush up its image it was still regarded as divided, vulnerable to an extremist take-over, subservient to the unions, and above all untrustworthy with a widespread lack of confidence in its ability to deliver its promises and in the calibre of its leader.

THE ESTABLISHMENT OF THE POLICY REVIEW

Previously its leadership had supposed that electoral losses had been caused largely by short-term, political – and therefore reversible – factors. Now it had to confront the prospect of relentless attrition set in motion by powerful social and cultural forces – unless it took drastic action, so when Tom Sawyer, the Deputy General Secretary of NUPE, a close ally of Neil Kinnock and chairman of the Home Policy sub-commitee of the National Executive proposed a wide-ranging reappraisal of policy the initiative was welcomed by Kinnock and, indeed – bar the hard left – throughout the Party. Hence the Policy Review. Yet if the soft left and the leadership both welcomed the initiative, they conceived it in quite different ways, though this was not evident at the time. The soft left wanted an open-minded, critical scrutiny of Labour's programme, with no preconceived notions as to what the final outcome would be. The leadership and the increasingly influential strategic community saw the purpose of the Review as adapting the Party to the new social, economic and cultural realities of Britain in the 1990s, as they defined them, which, they believed, entailed a considerable lightening of the Party's traditional ideological freight. The revisionist project of the 1950s, in a similar way, reflected the desire of the then leader, Hugh Gaitskell, and his entourage to adapt Party doctrine and programme to the new social and economic physiognomy of the post-war era. However, it was ideology-driven in that the revisionists were equipped – especially by Crosland's *Future of Socialism* – with a coherent analysis of society, a conception of the type of social order they wanted and a programme which indicated how this could be built. In contrast, the Policy Review was conceived by the inner leadership (that is Kinnock, his closest colleagues, aides and advisors) primarily as a strategic exercise. They concluded from their diagnosis of the Party's predicament that it must be repositioned to bring it more into line with current beliefs, values and aspirations, that voters must be convinced that it was capable of managing the economy and bettering individual living standards and above all that it was responsible and trustworthy. This demanded excising unpopular commitments and replacing them by ones more acceptable to the public at large. However, because the Policy Review was unveiled as an open-minded enterprise, and because its power base still rested on the alliance with the soft left, the leadership was not in a position to enforce its version until the second half of 1989. Hence there were two distinct phases to the Policy Review.

In the first phase, two reports were published.[7] The object of *Social Justice and Economic Efficiency*, presented to Conference in 1988, was to produce a statement of values, goals and major policy themes. It was the least influential and soon forgotten. The detailed elaboration of policy was left to the second phase; its report, by far the bulkiest, was entitled *Meet the Challenge, Make the Change*. Submitted to the 1989 Conference it included several substantial policy departures, but not the more ruthless expunging of existing policy that the leadership wanted; and it contained a number of ambiguous formulations which reflected underlying disagreements. From the perspective of the Party's electoral strategy, policy innovation had proceeded too slowly, with too many compromises and without the really radical departures that would impress mass and elite opinion. The original function of the third phase was to finalise any outstanding policy issues and then concentrate on the promotion of the new programme. But the growing power and confidence of the leadership enabled it to use two further reports, *Looking to the Future* (1990) and *Opportunity Britain* (1991) to place its stamp more emphatically on the Party's programme.[8]

THE POLICY REVIEW

The market and public ownership

Labour has traditionally been associated with the belief that a large publicly owned sector and a substantial measure of state intervention were required for the more rational and efficient

organisation of economic life. However, by the late 1980s, collectivist economic ideas were under sustained attack from the new
right. Protected from market pressures and lacking the spur of
the profit motive, nationalised industries were alleged to be
inevitably poorly run, wasteful and unresponsive to consumer
demand. The free market was seen as by far the most efficient
way to organise economic life and any type of state involvement,
whether direct ownership, indicative planning, industrial policy
or demand-management, was held to prevent the most productive use of resources since profit-seeking entrepreneurs were
the best judge of commercial opportunities. The rise of neo-
liberalism was not confined to Britain (and the US) but permeated governments and economic and business establishments
throughout Western Europe and by the late 1980s had also been
embraced by social democratic governments in France, Spain
and to some degree even in Norway and Sweden (see, e.g., Hall,
1987; Lafferty, 1990; Pontusson, 1992).

In what was widely construed as a dramatic change in
Labour's thinking, *Meet the Challenge, Make the Change* responded
to the altered climate of opinion by commending the market as
the best mechanism for allocating most goods and services:

> in very many areas of the economy the market and compe-
> tition are essential in meeting the demands of the con-
> sumer, promoting efficiency and stimulating innovation,
> and often the best means of securing all the myriad, in-
> cremental changes which are needed to take the economy
> forward.[9]

Such fulsome approval for the market was unique in a major
Labour policy statement and it represented a repudiation of the
proposition often found in Party statements that the market was
inherently flawed. However, in practical terms, the change was
by no means as fundamental as was generally claimed. As we
have seen, revisionism accepted the market and price signals as
the most effective way of co-ordinating the economy whilst
denunciations of the market in the past were usually confined to
the realm of rhetoric and rarely affected actual policy-making in
government. Furthermore, outside the shrinking bounds of the
hard left, few within the Party now queried the principle of
the market. Thus it was Michael Meacher, a leading figure

on the soft left, who argued that there was 'no socialist objection to the technical conception of a market' and called for the 'taboo' over the market 'to be exorcised once and for all' (*Tribune*, 4 December 1987). Commentators on the Policy Review would have profited if they had reflected on the observation of Harold Wilson's *eminence grise* Harold (later Lord) Lever that:

> Labour's leadership . . . knows as well as any businessman that an engine which runs on profit cannot be made to run faster without extra fuel. . . . For their part businessmen should show less sensitivity and more sense. It is time they realised that a ringing political slogan is often used as a sop to party diehards or as an anaesthetic while doctrinal surgery is being carried out.
>
> (Quoted in Panitch, 1989: 342)

Nevertheless, it was significant that Labour no longer felt that an anaesthetic was needed – that instead it ought to make an explicit and unambiguous acknowledgement that markets were indispensable and in many respects beneficial – because it calculated that to free itself from its image as the party of centralised planning and heavy-handed state interference, and for its economic philosophy to have any credibility, a public profession of its belief in the market was vital.

Meet the Challenge, Make the Change also repudiated state ownership but struck an equivocal note in its avowal of support for *social* ownership. 'Our ideal', it declared, 'is an economy in which enterprises are owned and managed by their employees – or, where appropriate, by consumers or local communities – and thereby serve the wider interests of their consumers and the community'.[10] However, the few tangible proposals for the expansion of social ownership in the report hardly lived up to this: for example, the law would be changed to encourage ESOPs (Employee Share Ownership Plans) and the status of the limited liability company would be reviewed to render it more responsive to its employees and customers. This reflected a lack of consensus with Gould, Blunkett (the co-author of the much more radical 1986 statement on *Social Ownership*) and others on the soft left favouring social ownership but with the inner leadership opposed to any significant modifications in the status quo. The disagreement extended to the more tangible and controversial issue of the future of the privatised industries. *Meet the Challenge, Make the Change* argued that the utilities, as essential services of vital importance to both economic and social wellbeing, ought to be owned by the community but then immediately added that since private owners would have to be reimbursed by paying 'a fair market price' returning privatised assets to the public domain would be too expensive. It then proposed securing a majority shareholding in British Telecom by boosting the public's stake from 49 per cent to 51 per cent. Water, which the Government was in the process of privatising, would however be 'an early candidate for a return to some form of public ownership'; elsewhere voting control would be established but without necessarily buying the equity. The report also suggested that regulation might achieve many of the goals public ownership was supposed to accomplish and proposed powerful new Regulatory Commissions but whether this would rule out public ownership of the utilities in the future was left unclear.[11]

Ambiguities were removed in the second phase of the Review as a shift in the internal balance of forces strengthened the hand of the leadership. In *Looking to the Future* references to social ownership vanished and only water was earmarked for return to public ownership. Beyond this, and in contrast to the earlier report, there were no indications that the existing structure of ownership was regarded as undesirable. By the time the 1992 election manifesto was written, reference to public ownership of water was replaced by a call only for public *control*[12] and it did not contain a single pledge to extend public ownership. For the first time in its history, Labour ceased to regard any modification to property relationships as a significant object of political endeavour and beyond the margins of the hard left, there appeared to be little pressure in Labour's ranks to reinstate a commitment to public ownership. As things stand, any future Labour government would preside over a mixed economy with a much smaller public sector than its predecessor had left behind. In an earlier clash over public ownership Bevan had defined the debate as being 'between those who want the mainsprings of economic power transferred to the community and those who believe that private enterprise should still remain supreme but that its worst characteristics should be modified by liberal ideas of justice and equality' (quoted in Greenleaf, 1983: 470). With the completion of the Policy Review the debate was firmly resolved with the victory of the latter.

The developmental state

Whilst the indispensability of the market was not a matter of dispute, a real debate did occur – quietly, since the main protagonists were on the front bench – over the question of 'the governance of the market', that is the respective roles of the state and the market, between the proponents of what we shall call the 'enabling' and the 'developmental' state. Although it did not raise matters of high principle, it did involve weighty differences in policy. The main advocates of the developmental state were Gould, co-convenor of the Economic PRG and Shadow Industry Secretary until October 1989 and the team of economists he assembled, the Industrial Strategy Group (Industrial Strategy Group, 1989) and it enjoyed the sympathy of the soft left. Proponents of the enabling state included Kinnock, the majority of the front bench and the right in general. Since in analysing the disagreement (which extended to macro-economic policy) we shall concentrate on what separated the protagonists it is important at the outset to note that both rejected the *dirigiste* system of planning espoused earlier in the decade and accepted the continuation of a market-based economy.

Meet the Challenge, Make the Change reflected an attempt to accommodate both 'developmental' and 'enabling' schools of thought but in this section we shall concentrate on those passages which are consistent with the former.[13] Conceptions of the role of the state in economic life are largely a function of analyses of market failure. Advocates of the developmental state (for convenience, we call them the interventionists) acknowledged that the market was, in Gould's words, 'an immensely effective and valuable means of allocating scarce resources, meeting consumer preferences, encouraging efficiency and rewarding innovation' but one that suffered from inherent limitations. It was:

> often irrational, inefficient, too short-term, too narrow, too fragmented, to be entrusted with providing the basic decencies of life to those with little purchasing power, or with making the necessary investment in long-term projects to

benefit the community as a whole, or with protecting the environment for future generations.

(*New Statesman and Society*, 3 May 1991)

Whilst the private firm, under the spur of the market, might be internally efficient, there was no guarantee that its pursuit of its own ends would benefit the community as a whole: thus multinationals often impaired the economic welfare of the country, as they concentrated investment in locations which maximised the return on investment irrespective of the loss of jobs or the depleting of the resource-base of peripheral areas. Further, whilst markets were very effective in coping with incremental change they were considerably less able to anticipate and adapt to fundamental change 'involving *quantum leaps* in product, process or structure' (Cowling, 1989: 12, 11; emphasis in original).

The pre-1983 approach to industrial intervention had proposed an extensive and intricate planning framework. In contrast, the developmental approach was strategic and sectoral, avoiding operational detail and targeted on 'those parts of the economy where intervention is going to have its most significant potential impact on the dynamism of the economy as a whole' (Cowling, 1989: 14). It entailed a '*pro-active* rather than a *reactive* role' for the state for only the state 'can provide the longer-term perspective, the organising and co-ordinating capacity and in some cases the resources to ensure that we make the essential provision for success' (Cowling, 1989: 13; Gould, 1989a: 8). The centre-piece was a Medium Term Industrial Strategy, to be administered by a strengthened Department of Trade and Industry (modelled on the Japanese Ministry of International Trade (MITI)) and intended to act as a 'a powerhouse dedicated to raising the quality and quantity of investment in British industry'. The Department would be equipped with sufficient resources for long-term commitment of funds and with 'the powers to intervene decisively in crucial sectors of the economy in terms of the provision of finance, new product and process initiatives and the ability to bargain with the transnationals.'[14] Lack of competitiveness was due above all, *Meet the Challenge, Make the Change* explained, to the 'fixation with the short-term' which lay at the root of chronic under-investment, the neglect of R&D, training and new technology. 'If short-termism', the report continued, 'is the disease, then it is the City which is the source of the infection'. This analysis was developed in a more sustained way in an earlier draft entitled *Supply-Side Socialism* which saw 'the concentration of power and wealth in the City of London' as 'the major cause of Britain's economic problems'. The acute sensitivity of manufacturing industry to the daily fluctuations of share prices and the ever-present fear of hostile take-over bids forced the sacrifice of long-term needs – such as research and development – on the altar of short-term profitability. The strategic importance of the financial markets had, in addition, furnished finance with so abundant a power that macro-economic policy under all governments 'has been dominated by City values and run in the interests of those who hold assets rather than those who produce.'[15]

It followed, then, that that the developmental state needed to acquire a substantial measure of control over finance and investment. Such control, Zysman has argued in an influential study, is vital if 'the player state' (his terminology for the developmental state) was to influence the strategies of the corporate sector (Zysman, 1983: 76). The interventionists concurred with this analysis and *Meet the Challenge, Make the Change* proposed the setting up of two new institutions, British Technology Enterprise (BTE) and the British Investment Bank (BIB) to provide long-term industrial investment. BTE (aided by regional enterprise boards) would concentrate on stimulating new technologies, either by establishing new companies or in partnership with established ones. It would be allowed to evaluate proposals against 'alternative commercial' criteria though not to bail out lame ducks. The BIB would act as a source of long-term investment capital and would co-ordinate the operations of newly formed regional and local investment banks. The central aim of these interventionist tools would be '"the creation of winners" as a result of the continuing and careful nurturing of strategic industries and enterprises' (Cowling, 1989: 14). *Supply-Side Socialism* proposed that the core of the BIB's funding should come from special bonds directed at the financial institutions with the aim of freeing 'vast sums for investment for relatively little outlay'. If insufficient bonds were sold, the paper added, the threat to remove fiscal privileges would be employed to induce financial institutions to purchase more.[16] However, in *Meet the Challenge, Make the Change* this passage was removed and little was said about the size or source of funding for these two new interventionist bodies indicating that opposition was watering down the interventionists' case. The pursuit of a developmental strategy would inevitably precipitate conflict with the City – which Gould for one anticipated with some equanimity: 'the attempt to gain the confidence of the financial establishment is not only futile but not even desirable. The only condition on which it can ever be attempted is the abandonment of our programme' (Gould, 1989a: 85). Whether others in the Party were prepared to pursue this logic was another matter.

The enabling state

Kinnock and the right as a whole were not satisfied by the industrial package produced by Gould's team. Gould was regarded as an impediment to the adoption of a more market-oriented approach and in the Shadow Cabinet reshuffle of October 1989 he was replaced by Gordon Brown, receiving in return the consolation prize of the Environment portfolio. This left the way free for the leadership to disengage Labour from some of the more radical and interventionist ideas pushed by Gould (*Guardian*, 18 April 1990) and by the time the manifesto appeared in 1992, the Gould-sponsored strategy of the developmental state had been replaced by the less interventionist approach of the 'enabling state'.

Exponents of the enabling state agreed that the market possessed significant defects. Left to itself, it neglected investment in science and technology, training, and infrastructure, and it took too little account of the needs of the environment and of peripheral areas but these were imperfections, not deep and endemic flaws. In contrast to the interventionists, the enablers firmly believed that decisions over investment opportunities were best left to private corporations who were motivated to make sound commercial decisions by their search for profitable outlets. The belief held by socialists and, to a lesser degree, by revisionists that a perennial tension existed between the interests of business and that of the community at large was largely abandoned and, indeed, the public interest was actually defined in terms of ensuring 'a fully competitive market' (Blair, 1991). The proper domain of state intervention was seen as accomplishing those tasks which the market was either unable or unwilling to discharge. This approach we shall label 'functional intervention'. It entailed co-operation between government and industry to meet clearly defined goals such as improving skills, encouraging long-term investment and securing balanced regional growth.[17] Thus Brown's revised industrial policy proposed increased capital allowances, new tax incentives, tax credits for R&D spending, the release of local authority capital receipts and special employment measures to help small firms – all measures which would have been perfectly acceptable to the pre-Thatcherite Conservative Party. Education and training were declared to be the new 'commanding heights' of the economy and the 'skills revolution' the key to industrial success. Hence Labour proposed an expanded training programme and an obligation by employers to spend at least 0.5 per cent of payroll on training. The underlying philosophy was – in a conscious echo of a slogan used by the German Social Democrats in their Bad Godesberg programme – 'Business where appropriate: government where necessary'.[18]

As we have seen, in the first phase of the Policy Review the main cause of low levels of investment was diagnosed as City-inspired short-termism. But by late 1989 senior members of Labour's economic policy-making community (such as John Eatwell, Kinnock's influential economic advisor and John Smith the Shadow Chancellor) wanted the City to be placated, partly for pragmatic reasons – to avoid an outflow of capital and a sterling crisis that the leadership feared would upset an incoming Labour Government, if not, indeed, its election prospects[19] – but also because such a view was more consonant with their own thinking. Labour's economic policy-makers had little confidence in the capacity of the state to prod or cajole industry into increasing manufacturing investment, still less to provide that investment itself. In Kinnock's words, 'the government has neither the means nor the judgement to make large-scale manufacturing investment' (*Guardian*, 2 May 1990). Earlier plans for an enhanced state role in the investment process were largely dropped, and the National (or British) Investment Bank was relegated to the relatively minor role of providing funds for growing high-tech industries and small and medium firms in the regions. *Looking to the Future* claimed that the NIB 'would help bridge the gap for long-term funding' but since it would operate 'at arm's length from government and on strictly commercial

93

lines' (previous references to 'alternative commercial criteria' vanish) and would raise its own funds 'in the same way as other banks' it is by no means clear how it would do so. Similarly, only passing reference was made to British Technology Enterprise, previously envisaged as a formidable instrument of industrial intervention. In the manifesto, references to the NIB and BTE were very brief and they were presented as devices to foster closer working relations with industry rather than as part of an industrial strategy.[20] This completed the process by which the industrial strategy urged by the exponents of the developmental state was progressively dismantled.

Although both the scope and magnitude of Labour's industrial policy were scaled down, the claims made for it were not. The Party continued to argue that its supply-side strategy was the key to industrial recovery, despite the fact that only a small sum was committed to it. Precisely how was never really explained.[21] Indeed Zysman's analysis suggests that an approach focused mainly on training and investment allowances and which did not seek to influence directly the investment process was unlikely to have much effect (Zysman, 1983). Voters may well have sensed this gap between the modesty of Labour's proposals and the remarkable effects they were supposed to have, since they did not appear to make any impression whatsoever on public opinion (see Chapter 8, p. 187).

Employment, inflation and the unions

Revisionist social democracy had never shown much interest in notions of a developmental state, and the shift away from pro-active interventionism in the second phase of the Policy Review could be interpreted as a return to the traditional emphasis on demand-management. However, Keynesian economics by the 1980s had ceased to represent mainstream wisdom and had been subjected to an apparently powerful critique by the new right. Manipulating aggregate demand to encourage higher output and more jobs, it was argued, would only provoke a steep inflationary spiral and a rapid deterioration in the balance of payments. High public spending would swell the budget deficit, fuel an inflationary growth in the money supply and push up interest rates; and by damaging business confidence it would lower both output and employment. This critique had come to be widely accepted amongst influential opinion-formers, much of the press, industry, the City, the Treasury, the Bank of England, as well as the West's central banks, the IMF and the international financial community. Influential figures within the Labour Party, whilst not prepared to swallow the whole of this analysis, believed it had some validity but divisions amongst economic policy-makers resulted in a cursory treatment of macro-economic policy in *Meet the Challenge, Make the Change*. Bryan Gould was a staunch Keynesian and was able to secure the incorporation in the economic section of the report of a call to end reliance on 'high interest rates and an uncompetitive currency' with the implication that devaluation would be used to boost international competitiveness, but beyond this nothing was said of any consequence.[22] With Gould's removal, those more sceptical of Keynesianism – Smith, Brown and Eatwell – controlled economic policy-making. They no longer believed that the sustained growth in output needed to produce full employment could be achieved by demand management, feared that a major infusion of demand would indeed stimulate an inflationary spiral and fierce speculative pressure on sterling and felt that, in the changed realities of an integrated global economy, the state now had a much diminished capacity to shape its economic environment. They concluded that a future Labour Government had no option but to rely primarily on the willingness of the private sector to raise investment and output and that the major contribution macro-economic policy could make was to create the conditions in which business would have the confidence to invest. As a result, the foremost object of policy ceased to be full employment and growth but, as *Looking to the Future* explained, 'a monetary framework which will provide long-term exchange rate and interest rate stability'.[23] This in turn required an effective anti-inflationary strategy. The revisionist recipe since the early 1970s had been to seek a broad arrangement with the unions to exchange wage moderation for social concessions in a loose neo-corporatist structure. As we have seen, prior to 1987 Labour relied mainly upon the National Economic Assessment to counter inflation, though with declining enthusiasm. By the second phase of the Policy Review, it was further downgraded and *Opportunity Britain*, which contained the fullest discussion of inflation, envisaged the NEA primarily as a co-ordinating and opinion-forming body, in which 'the social partners' would discuss 'Britain's economic prospects and the competing claims on national output, taking account of the need for investment, exports and public spending'. In other words, the exercise was mainly designed to induce the unions to alter their bargaining strategy by pointing out the implications for national economic objectives and welfare spending of given levels of pay increases.[24]

The majority of unions remained resistant to anything more ambitious. When the leaders of the GMB and the UCW, John Edmonds and Alan Tuffin, proposed instituting 'synchronised wage bargaining', that is a more co-ordinated approach to pay determination, it was interpreted as a move towards a voluntary incomes policy and met with a very cool reception from both left-wing unions like MSF and the TGWU and the right-wing craft union the Engineers (see e.g., the *Guardian*, 7 May 1991 and 12 June 1991). Critics of the unions often bemoaned their adhesion to old-fashioned class attitudes – but in reality the problem was not that they acted as class organisations but that they were (for the most part) *unwilling or unable to do so*. A considerable body of research into the governing experience of social democratic parties has shown that 'social democratic parties are more capable of altering the distribution system and maintaining growth with full employment when they are linked with powerful and centralised trade union movements' (Esping-Andersen and van Kersbergen, 1992: 202). Such a strategy requires the unions to deploy their industrial strength as political leverage by seeking to trade wage restraint for extended welfare programmes, full employment and enhanced influence over public policy formation within the contours of corporatist arrangements. The feasibility of such a strategy presupposes unions which are both sufficiently centralised to deliver wage restraint and, above all, which define their purposes as labour movement organisations representing 'the interests of an encompassing working class' (Lehmbruch, 1984: 77). This is a role which most British unions have been reluctant or incapable of filling.

Furthermore, by the late 1980s, the Party leadership had largely lost interest in nationally negotiated pay restraint and neo-corporatist machinery. Some economic policy-makers, like Eatwell, no longer regarded incomes policy as feasible, given the increasing fragmentation of the wage bargaining process, the weakness of central authority within the unions and the employers' own preference, in their search for greater flexibility and control, for decentralised pay systems. Corporatist strategies – with their echoes of 'beer and sandwiches at No. 10' – were also inconsistent with the Party's definition of its strategic needs, hence the leadership was not inclined to cede the unions the additional influence entailed by a new social contract (Minkin, 1991: 475–6). Finally, policy-makers had found what they believed could act as a replacement for an incomes policy. A confidential paper had argued in January 1989: 'On inflation, we could solve a large number of our problems at a stroke by declaring that it is our intention to join the EMS [Economic and Monetary System] . . . it would transform the perception of how serious our economic policy really is.'[25] During the first phase of the Policy Review, Labour had been very wary about membership of the Exchange Rate Mechanism (ERM). *Meet the Challenge, Make the Change* listed a series of conditions which would have to be met before a Labour Government would agree to entry: less reliance on interest rate adjustments and more on central bank co-operation, a trade policy which contributed to balance of payments stability for all EC members, and a co-ordinated EC-wide growth policy. This reflected Gould's grave reservations about the ERM's deflationary bias, but policy began to shift after his removal from the industry portfolio. John Smith, increasingly the dominant voice in the formulation of Labour's economic policies, was much more favourably disposed towards the ERM. *Looking to the Future* promised entry 'at the earliest opportunity' once the conditions had been met but in reality these had already been dropped. Smith enthusiastically described the case for ERM membership as 'overwhelming'[26] and, indeed, the Government was condemned for its tardiness in joining. The manifesto pledged Labour to 'maintain the value of the pound' within the ERM[27] and the leadership's positive attitude towards the Mechanism – which helped precipitate Gould's resignation from the Shadow Cabinet after the election – was to survive until Black Wednesday in September 1992.

There were a number of reasons why Labour's policy-makers found the ERM appealing. Firstly, they were all too aware of the dangers of a flight from sterling if Labour triumphed at the polls. Membership of the ERM was seen as doubly useful in that it would afford some protection against speculation whilst also reassuring the money markets of Labour's fiscal rectitude. Indeed, with the City and the press overwhelmingly in favour of ERM entry, the Party's stance did win some plaudits. Secondly, ERM membership would contribute to the monetary stability seen as vital for higher investment. Thirdly, it furnished Labour with what it hoped would be perceived as a credible and electorally convincing counter-inflation strategy through the mechanism of a fixed – and high – exchange rate. Thus in April 1992 Eatwell, as Kinnock's chief economic advisor, attacked 'the proponents of devaluation' (who included, behind the scenes, Bryan Gould) who 'perpetuate the exclusively macro-economic approach which had done such damage to British economic policy thinking' and who failed to grasp that not only would devaluation's competitive benefits soon be lost but that it would actually force interest rates up (*Observer*, 8 March 1992; on Labour's opposition to devaluation, see also Kinnock's speech to industrialists, the *Guardian*, 1 March 1992). A fixed exchange rate regime in contrast would, as John Smith explained in an interview with the *Independent on Sunday*, depress inflationary expectations by denying employers the option of a competitive devaluation if they succumbed to pay claims too easily. If they conceded inflationary demands, they would price themselves out of markets with the result – as Smith pointed out – that 'there would be unemployment, wouldn't there?' (*Independent on Sunday*, 6 May 1990). In short, not only had the fight against inflation supplanted full employment as Labour's prime economic goal but it intended to use the prospect of job losses – created by the commitment to a fixed currency regime – as a means to achieve that goal. This represented a major departure from the revisionist model, a point to which we shall return.

The search for an alternative anti-inflationary strategy may have reassured those unions for whom the preservation of free collective bargaining was an overriding principle but in practice it signified a substantial shift in the way the Party's inner leadership viewed organised labour and capital. In the early 1980s, the left's espousal of a Party–union partnership in government reflected their conception of the unions as an integral part of a wider labour movement which was the main vehicle for achieving progressive social change as well as the institutional protector of the interests of the mass of wage and salary earners, whilst business was viewed as a vested interest representing the wealthy and privileged. Labour's swing to the right led to a radically different conception of both business and the unions. Having abandoned an interventionist industrial strategy and lost confidence in the viability of Keynesian demand management, the leadership concluded that economic growth depended on the level of confidence within industry. It followed that government's main tasks should be to help provide those inputs (like a skilled workforce) that the market alone could not produce and to establish a stable and predictable economic environment. Given that it was upon its ability to manage the economy that government was above all judged by the voters and given further that Labour in office would rely heavily on economic growth to achieve its social aims, it was but a logical step to view business as its natural partner in government. From the same perspective, the interests of unions seeking higher pay for their members and (in the case of public service unions) more social spending did not fit easily into the Party's definition of the nation's needs and thus came to be viewed as pressure groups promoting partial interests.

Strategy concerns pointed Labour in the same direction. Strategists were convinced that the identification in the public eye with the unions was an electoral handicap, were aware that it was common practice for the media to portray the Party as dominated by union 'barons' and 'bosses' and therefore concluded that it was vital that it should demonstrate that such views were unfounded. As it happened, the leadership's economic and strategic goals could at least in the immediate term be reconciled with the policies of the majority of unions over the issue of pay policy. This was less true, however, of the other major area of entrenched union concern, industrial relations law.

Since 1979 successive phases of legislation have transformed the legal framework in which unions operated, subjecting them to a battery of restrictions and penalties that has drastically curtailed their freedom of action and every step had been warmly received both by mass and elite opinion. Prior to the 1987 election Labour was pledged to repeal the bulk of Tory legislation and to return to the unions the collective immunities which had traditionally afforded protection against civil actions in the Courts. Kinnock, along with Party strategists, regarded this policy as a major vote-loser and was determined to discard it. However, not only did several powerful unions, including the

TGWU and MSF, object forcefully to this, so too did Michael Meacher, co-convenor of the People at Work PRG, front-bench spokesman on Employment and, like Gould, a leading member of the soft left. On what was widely seen as the critical issues, he supported (with the backing of the leading experts on his group, Lords McCarthy and Wedderburn) a substantial widening of the boundaries of legally permissible sympathy (secondary) action and protection for unions against prosecution and fines in civil actions. Kinnock, in contrast, was convinced that a commitment to extend the rights of unions to engage in secondary action (and organise picketing) would be ruthlessly and profitably exploited by Labour's opponents (Hughes and Wintour, 1990: 149). Fraught discussions within the Policy Review group and the NEC culminated in a compromise in which, on balance, Meacher emerged the victor but the triumph cost him his job.

Kinnock was furious that he had been thwarted[28] believing it essential that Labour should not be seen as 'giving way' to the unions and, indeed, viewing a commitment to maintain much of the Tories' legislation as a useful signal to the public that the Party could not be cowed by union barons. Kinnock pushed aside the People at Work group and in October 1989 replaced Meacher with the more amenable Tony Blair who, in collaboration with the Leader's Office and working closely with sympathetic TUC officials (Minkin, 1991: 471) set about securing agreement with the unions to a sweeping revision of Labour's long-held position on labour law, including tight restrictions on picketing and secondary action, and the abolition of the closed shop. Given the importance to the unions of such matters, this meant protracted and difficult bargaining sessions, especially with left-of-centre unions.[29] In fact, many union leaders recognised that Tory labour laws were popular, not least amongst their own members and they were equally aware of their own diminished status, as union membership had shrunk massively since 1979. But most important of all, and whatever their own views, virtually all key union leaders were prepared, if pressurised enough, to accommodate to what the Party leadership regarded as an electorally vital adjustment of policy (Minkin, 1991, 468–73). In Ron Todd's words, 'if we don't win the return of a Labour Government we can wave goodbye to all that is good in Labour's proposals' (*Independent*, 2 October 1990). With the publication of *Looking to the Future* the leadership's triumph became evident. On the controversial issues of sympathy action and picketing the Party now adopted more restrictive and stringent formulae than ever before. On the highly sensitive question of enforcement Labour proposed the creation of a new Industrial Court, but emphasised that the unions would continue to be liable to fines and damages. The upshot was that, by the conclusion of the Policy Review, the Party was committed to retaining most of the Conservative legislation on the statute book and the manifesto, in line with its electoral strategy, was able to assure voters that 'there will be no return to the trade union legislation of the 1970s. . . . There will be no mass or flying pickets.'[30]

Social democratic values and the welfare state

Revisionism had identified two central aspirations for the Labour Party: social welfare, or the relief of social distress; and equality, that is more equal access to social resources such as education, health and housing. The indispensable instrument to meet these aspirations was the welfare state which allowed for protection against the market by collectively providing vital services and transfer benefits as far as possible on the basis of need. To what extent were these values still realisable? Quantitative opinion surveys conveyed the message that most voters were willing to pay more in taxes in return for better public services but Labour's policy-makers were unconvinced. In 1987, the Party commissioned the Shadow Communications Agency to undertake qualitative research into public attitudes towards social spending and taxation. The findings made disturbing reading. Most voters welcomed what they perceived as a substantial reduction of taxation under the Tories – and expressed apprehension that a Labour Government would reverse the process. Poverty was not seen as a major social problem and there was considerable resistance to the use of the tax system as a way to redistribute wealth (Hughes and Wintour, 1990: 137–9). Put in a nutshell the message was that the voters did not want and saw no need to pay more in taxes but feared that this was precisely what Labour would make them do.

Broadly speaking, Labour could respond either by seeking to mobilise support for its traditional values by expounding the economic, social and moral case for welfare spending and progressive taxation or by accommodating to existing opinion. It opted for the latter. Thus Kinnock emphasised that a Labour Government would maintain a tight rein on public spending (*Guardian*, 9 May 1989) whilst the Shadow Chancellor endlessly repeated the injunction that 'we can't spend what we haven't earned. We intend to earn it before we spend it. That will be the guiding light of the next Labour Government's economic policy' (*Guardian*, 2 October 1989). Whilst Labour was prepared to borrow to finance public investment (e.g. on training and R&D) social spending would have to be paid for out of current revenue. If the money was not there, then social ambitions would be scaled down – indeed, Smith envisaged only a 'modest increase' at most in public spending as a proportion of GDP (*Independent on Sunday*, 6 May 1990).

By the same token, the Party strove to assuage fears about Labour's tax plans by emphasising that, for all but a small minority, there would be no net increase in taxation. Tax had been a major weakness for Labour in the 1987 election, hence Smith sought to shed Labour's image as the high-tax party stifling enterprise and denying merit its due reward. The key features of the new policy, as they emerged in 1990, were no return to high marginal rates of income tax with an upper limit of 50 per cent and a lower one of below 20 per cent with a series of graduated bands in between, and the abolition of the upper limit on National Insurance contributions (which meant an effective top rate of direct tax of 59 per cent). Exact figures as to rates and bands, Smith made clear, would have to await a Labour budget but, he insisted, 87 per cent of taxpayers would not lose from the changes and many would gain. It was expected that this policy would release sufficient additional revenue to fund increases in child benefits and pensions (the only specific pledges that survived the Smith–Beckett pruning). Beyond that, expanded public services would have to be financed from the increments of economic growth. But whilst Smith and Margaret Beckett were diligent in weeding out spending pledges in Policy Review reports, critics were quick to seize on an evident flaw in Labour's case. Time and again its spokesmen lacerated the Tories for their miserly indifference to the public services. But was Labour prepared to spend more? And if both higher taxes and increased borrowing were ruled out, how long would it take before economic growth delivered fresh resources? Reflecting this dilemma, the 1992 manifesto was full of pledges to improve services, but all but pensions and child benefits were covered by the rider – only to be redeemed when resources allow. Much depended then upon the ability of a Labour Government to accelerate the rate of economic growth but, as we have seen, the Party committed itself (via the ERM) to restrictive fiscal and monetary policies so it was difficult to see how this could be achieved.

Revisionism and post-revisionism

By what values, then, did Labour now profess to stand? The document *Democratic Socialist Aims and Values*, written largely by Hattersley, was intended to define Labour's ideological identity and lay down guidelines for the Policy Review. It declared that 'the true purpose of democratic socialism and, therefore, the true aim of the Labour party, is the creation of a genuinely free society in which the fundamental objective of government is the protection and extension of individual liberty.'[31] It then proceeded to argue that freedom was real only to the extent that it could be exercised and this entailed access to a good education, a comprehensive health service and employment.[32] In essence, the document reaffirmed the Croslandite creed that visualised Labour's mission as the promotion of equality to be attained primarily through publicly funded and freely available services. Hattersley appeared to regard the Policy Review as having given effect to this creed when he declared that, 'The Labour Party as it now stands is ideologically the Labour Party I have wanted to see throughout my life' (*New Statesman and Society*, 26 July 1991).[33] Similarly, Martin Smith concluded an account of the Policy Review with the claim that the Party had moved into 'the tradition of European Social Democracy. . . . Labour's social democracy is based on the commitment to welfare and state intervention as a means of creating a society with greater social equality' (Smith, 1992: 223, 224). This interpretation both misconstrues the logic underpinning the Policy Review whilst underplaying the differences between revisionism and what we shall call post-revisionist social democracy.

The Policy Review sought to address the new institutional order created by Thatcherism and the problems which were plaguing the Keynesian welfare state. As we have seen, by the end of the process it not only erased from its programme such traditional socialist planks as public ownership, planning and a steeply redistributive tax system but also no longer viewed the central aims of Croslandite revisionism, full employment and the pursuit of equality, as viable largely because the conditions which Crosland believed had rendered them so no longer obtained.

Dismissing the traditional socialist belief that power ultimately derived from control over the means of production, Crosland had claimed that democratic government, holding the reigns of political power, could always prevail against private economic power. 'Acting mainly through the budget . . . the government . . . can . . . determine within broad limits the division of total output between consumption, investment, exports and social expenditure' and also by using indirect tax and monetary, legislative and physical controls was able to 'severely limit . . . the autonomy of business decisions'. 'Political authority', he concluded, 'has emerged as the final arbiter of economic life' (Crosland, 1964: 7–8, 29). The transfer of economic power from management to labour also contributed greatly to the dissolution of business hegemony. This, Crosland accepted, was largely contingent on full employment which ensured that whoever governed 'organised workers will remain the effective power in industry' but he was confident that, for electoral reasons, no government would seriously challenge full employment. He therefore concluded that the economic power of capital had been very substantially curtailed (Crosland, 1964: 12–13, 28). At the same time, the motivation, attitudes and behaviour of business had been greatly modified. The aggressive and ruthless pursuit of profit had been replaced by a sensitivity to public opinion and a sense of social responsibility which, coupled with the awareness by business of its loss of power, rendered any fears of strident opposition by the City and industry to a Labour Government thoroughly implausible (Crosland, 1964: 15–19).

It was evident to Labour's policy-makers a generation later that none of these conditions held. The further evolution of capitalism had caused the reversal of the trends Crosland observed (and whose significance he had tended to exaggerate) and had greatly magnified the power of capital. In particular, the globalisation of capitalism had created an environment far less conducive to social democratic policies: capital and currency movements had been freed throughout most of the Western world as governments pursued policies of liberalisation and deregulation; the computerisation of the financial markets had greatly increased the speed at which capital and currency changed hands; and the currency markets themselves had expanded so hugely that whereas in the early 1970s, over 90 per cent of transactions had been linked to trade, this figure had, by the middle of the next decade, fallen to under 10 per cent, exposing all currencies to highly speculative movements. In this new political economy of massive currency and capital flows and instantaneous communication the capacity of the money markets to punish governments pursuing 'unsound' policies has been shown to be awesome.

Given the logic of Crosland's own argument, it was not surprising that the effect of the reappearance of mass unemployment was to tilt the balance of power between organised labour and capital decisively in favour of the latter – a fact that the Conservative Government exploited and compounded with its highly popular offensive against the unions. At the same time, and within the context of an enervated labour movement, it was evident that his portrayal of business attitudes and goals no longer had any validity. In the words of a *Financial Times* journalist, 'Companies are not in business for social purposes, they are not even in business to make products, they are in business to make profits' (Leadbeater, 1987: 4). The drive to maximise profits had bred in business a determination to regain full control over the labour process and a much more hostile attitude to unions, Keynesian policies, government intervention and public expenditure. Labour's leaders also had no illusions about both the ability and willingness of the City to challenge the policies of any government that failed to conform to the tenets of financial orthodoxy and, as we have seen, went to considerable lengths to allay the financial institutions' mistrust of their intentions. Thus whilst the revisionist model affirmed the capacity of the state to steer the market, and hence adjust private economic interests to the needs of society at large and thereby secure the basic social democratic goals of higher growth, full employment and an expanding welfare state, post-revisionism, appreciating the new realities of power, took a much more sanguine view of what could be achieved. Ultimately, it believed, it was only the private sector that could create the conditions for full employment, growth and therefore the wherewithal to finance improved public services. In short, post-revisionism regarded the central Croslandite proposition, that democratic government had the ability to prevail over the power of business, as false.

A prominent Swedish social democrat had described the dilemma of social democracy as 'how to abolish the negative effects of the capitalist system without, at the same time, injuring the laws and mechanisms of the system itself' (Tilton, 1990: 234). The dilemma was initially resolved in Britain by the Keynesian welfare state. In its historic compromise with capitalism, revisionist social democracy abandoned any effort to radically redistribute power or wealth whilst conserving the aims of widening social opportunities and narrowing disparities in income, status and access to collective goods. The compromise ceased to be perceived as acceptable by the business and financial community both in Britain and abroad causing a crisis of social democracy which was in this sense more political than economic in character. Labour's response to this crisis, as articulated by the Policy Review, was to renegotiate the compromise in conditions and upon terms much more favourable to capitalism. It now agreed that full employment could no longer be achieved by macro-economic policy without risking unacceptable levels of inflation and serious payments imbalances, that there were now tight fiscal limits to the expansion of welfare spending, that high levels of direct taxation were economically damaging and that increases in public borrowing would alarm the financial markets, and hence could not be contemplated. Finally (and notwithstanding the criticism after the election that they were too bold) its tax and spending plans would have made little impression upon the pronounced widening of income inequalities since 1979. By 1990, Labour was pledged to maintain sterling at its existing (grossly over-valued) rate, and (as ERM rules stipulated) to use interest rate policy to protect that rate. In other words, Labour was prepared to divest itself of the ability to use exchange rate and monetary policy as instruments of macro-economic strategy in order to secure its goal of monetary stability hence locking itself into a deflationary regime which – if carried through – would have made it extremely difficult to boost output and reduce unemployment: not least because there was no guarantee that wage bargainers would trade-off more modest pay demands against jobs, in particular if others lost the jobs whilst they benefited from higher pay. Not surprisingly, the National Institute of Economic and Social Research reached the conclusion, after a detailed review of Labour's policies, that 'the economic policy differences between the two major parties are narrower now than they have been for about twenty years' (*National Institute Economic Review*, 1990: 52). Given the extent to which the Conservative party had moved to the right during this period, nothing attests to the scale of the transformation Labour had undergone more than this convergence. Having abandoned full employment, a redistributive fiscal policy and, hence, the pursuit of equality, revisionist aspirations had contracted to post-revisionism's more modest aims of abating social distress, extending individual opportunity and incremental improvements to the public services (see, e.g., Gordon Brown, 'A New Popular Socialism', *Guardian*, 30 September 1991).

5

ORGANISATIONAL MODERNISATION

This period witnessed not only a process of programmatic but also of organisational modernisation. The central concern of this chapter is Labour's metamorphosis into a more centralised and disciplined party, with power firmly located within its inner parliamentary circle. The process of organisational change was a complex one. It was in part the outcome of goals consciously pursued by the leadership as Kinnock, convinced that Labour would never earn the confidence of the voters unless it was seen to be a respectable, orderly and united party, strove to tame the left, prune the influence of the extra-parliamentary party and, as far as possible, the unions and ensure that he had the power to respond swiftly and effectively to environmental pressures. However, not all organisational reforms were set in motion by the leadership, reflected its priorities or had intended and predictable consequences. Some had been long debated, were subject to extensive consultation exercises and were widely approved, such as altering the composition of Conference and introducing a more effective system of policy formation. Furthermore Kinnock always had to operate within the Party's procedures and seek the support of other power-holders, especially the unions, which often involved adjusting his goals. With these qualifications, the main pattern that unfolds in these years is a steady accretion of leadership power accomplished by the extension of central control and (paradoxically at first glance) the direct enfranchisement of members.

THE PROCESS OF CENTRALISATION

Control of the policy process 1983–92

In this period, leadership control was extended over two key internal party functions, policy formation and parliamentary selection. Control over policy was achieved through a combination of institutional and political methods. The first step, taken in the early years of the Kinnock leadership, was reform of the machinery of policy formation. Formal policy-making arrangements always have an impact upon outcomes as by allocating policy-making tasks they structure the distribution of power and determine the composition of the policy-making community. Constitutionally the power of leadership was checked by the institutional dispersal of rights and responsibilities, and was further constricted in the 1970s by the emergence of the NEC as an autonomous power and policy-forming base and by tension between the unions and the parliamentary leadership. As we have seen, between 1979 and 1983 the front bench had been sidelined and policy was developed via the NEC and the Liaison Committee, affording the major say to politicians whose power base lay in the extra-parliamentary party. In the wake of the disastrous 1983 election campaign, Geoff Bish, the Party's Research Secretary, compiled a powerful indictment of the procedures used:[1]

- The existence of two separate – and often antagonistic – centres responsible for policy development, the NEC and the Shadow Cabinet, had caused 'confusion, lack of mutual commitment and distrust', which became all too evident to voters.
- The Party had been overburdened with policies (culminating in the exceptionally long and detailed 1983 Manifesto) due in large part to efforts to tie the hands of the parliamentary leadership by detailed and binding commitments. As a result, hostages were offered to fortune, Labour's communication channels were clogged up and it failed to transmit clearly its key policies.
- Until too late, no effort had been made to assess public attitudes to the Party's messages, and opinion research was either wholly ignored or fed in at too late a stage. Policy formation had become 'almost wholly an internal process. An objective is identified, a problem perceived, a pressure group

109

exerts pressure, a resolution is received. The Party then works out in detail what needs to be done. The electors come into the picture, in any serious way, only at a later stage – when the policy is presented to them to take or leave as they wish. Our problem now is they are increasingly choosing to leave it.'

Kinnock acted quickly to implement Bish's reform proposals in December 1983. The NEC's network of sub-committees and study groups with their large number of co-opted advisors was wound up and replaced by a limited number of NEC–Shadow Cabinet joint policy committees consisting of an equal number of members from the two bodies plus a few additional trade unionists and advisors. Their reports were to be submitted to both the NEC and to the Shadow Cabinet for amendment and approval with any outstanding disagreements to be ironed out by a Policy Co-ordinating Committee consisting of senior representatives from the two bodies. This accorded the front bench (for the first time in Labour's history) an institutionalised role in the Party's policy-making machinery. The ostensible purpose was to establish a process of joint policy determination between the representatives of the parliamentary and extra-parliamentary parties. But this merely masked Kinnock's real intention which was to disable the NEC as a rival source of power and policy and transform it into an adjunct of the parliamentary leadership. Steps were taken to ensure that the joint policy committees were in practice dominated by front-benchers. The size of the Executive's research staff was reduced and the responsibilities of those who remained altered as, rather than operating as secretaries of study groups providing a specifically NEC policy input, they increasingly worked closely with researchers from the front-bench and the Leader's Office within a policy process under the aegis of the Shadow Cabinet. By 1986 responsibility for policy innovation had largely passed to the leader and senior Shadow Cabinet colleagues (Minkin, 1991: 409). Reflecting their waning status and the paucity of their tasks, the Home Policy and International committees (which once suffered from unmanageably large agendas) now met less and less frequently and were involved in policy formulation only at a late stage. The growing prominence of front-benchers on the Executive plus the holding of the committee chairs by leadership loyalists ensured that for the most part these bodies did little more than rubber-stamp decisions made elsewhere.[2] Finally, the criteria for policy selection altered as Party strategists and communications specialists came, in early 1986, to occupy key vantage points in the Party machine and were increasingly able to ensure that policy proposals were tested against their compatibility with existing public opinion. In the early 1970s, Richard Crossman had urged that the NEC become 'the battering-ram of change' and this was precisely the function it performed during the following decade. By installing a more easily managed system of policy-making Kinnock took a major stride towards ending the NEC's capacity to do so again and to act as a rival to the parliamentary leadership.

However, the centralisation of the policy-making system followed an irregular path as political developments interwove with institutional ones. Thus, in the first phase of the Policy Review from 1987 to 1989, leadership control over policy-making slackened, with the various PRGs enjoying considerable latitude in the shaping of policy. This was due to a number of factors: the grip secured by the leadership after 1985 had rested on two contingent political conditions, the proximity of an election and the support afforded by the soft left. After 1987, the first factor ceased to operate whilst the soft left took the opportunity to assert its influence. Furthermore, the initial conception of the Review envisaged it as an open and consensual exercise[3] whilst widespread disaffection with his leadership during the eighteen or so months after the election – reflecting both his own and the Party's low standing in the polls and his mishandling of a number of major problems[4] – undermined Kinnock's position.

In 1989 the tide turned as mounting economic and political difficulties eliminated the Government's lead and the leader's morale and standing revived. Dissatisfied with the flow of policy on key issues which failed to conform to the ruling strategic imperatives, Kinnock instigated procedural changes that eased the constraints that the organisation of the Review had imposed on him. Most of the PRG's were disbanded and responsibility for drafting the later Policy Review reports (*Looking to the Future* and *Opportunity Britain*) was vested in smaller groups in which the influence of senior front-benchers and leadership aides was paramount.[5] The work was overseen by the Leader's Office with a top strategist and senior Kinnock advisor, Patricia Hewitt, charged with drafting both the third and fourth Policy Review reports. Along with the reshuffle of Shadow Cabinet port- folios in October 1989, this placed policy-making, in the more sensitive areas, in the hands of 'reliable' front-benchers whilst Sawyer, chairman of the Home Policy Committee and an increasingly weighty figure within the inner leadership circle, played an important role in mustering support for the leader- ship.

Behind the scenes, management of the policy agenda by the leadership became more active. A significant role was played by the expanding stratum of 'political technicians' – policy and political advisors attached to the front bench and to the Leader's Office. Unlike Head Office officials, whom they increasingly out-numbered, they were not employed by or under the auth- ority of the NEC but were selected and paid (mainly from their allocation of the publicly provided 'Short' fund supplemented by contributions from the unions) by members of the Shadow Cabinet and the Leader to whom their primary loyalty was due, and upon whom the retention of their posts and their future careers was dependent. Some performed an important facilitat- ing role as members of the Policy Review secretariat; others were primarily political in-fighters and deal-makers who helped organise support for the leadership.[6]

Furthermore, like his predecessors, Kinnock used his power of appointment to tighten control. Whilst the Shadow Cabinet was elected by the PLP the allocation of portfolios was a preroga- tive of the leader and though some figures, due to their political weight, could lay claim to a senior position (e.g. Hattersley) this still left Kinnock with considerable discretion to advance the careers of some and retard those of others. Also there were more places waiting to be filled: the leader constantly expanded the size of the front bench and by 1990, 83 out of 229 members occupied front bench positions. Reinstating the more disciplinarian strand in Party tradition, he demanded that loyalty to PLP decisions extend to all holders of shadow posts, however minor. Thus in October 1988, Anne Clwyd, a junior front-bencher, was sacked for voting (along with 34 others) against the Government's defence estimates in defiance of a PLP decision – though in line with official Party policy – whilst a little later, Clare Short felt obliged to resign as a junior front-bencher over differences over the Prevention of Terrorism Act (*Guardian*, 7 December 1988).

However, far more effective and pervasive as an instrument of control was media management. The leadership, inevitably, enjoyed a much easier access to the (friendlier) press than its critics – and such papers as the *Guardian* and the *Independent* were not only the major source of information for Party members but also editorially more sympathetic to the Labour right rather than to those further to the left. Further, as we have seen, as part of the drive to improve the calibre of the Party's communications, senior communications officials had established close working relations with a number of political journalists, especially on the broadsheets. As well as being used to project the Party's message to the outside world this network was employed to influence the internal politics of the Party as briefings and leaks to selected and favoured journalists were used in a systematic way to isolate and discredit those who queried the official line.[7] Victims at various stages included prominent soft leftists such as Michael Meacher and Bryan Gould. Thus in the summer and autumn of 1989 stories began to circulate in the press about Meacher's poor judgement and unsuitability as front bench employment spokesman. Similarly Bryan Gould found himself at the receiving end of unflattering reports with the phrase 'a Gould gaffe' – suggesting that he was prone to rash and ill-considered statements – making a mysteriously frequent appearance in the press. In both cases the source of the reports was the Party's Communications Department and, shortly after, as we have seen, the two were assigned less controversial portfolios.[8] A striking example of the use of briefings to impugn dissenters was afforded in the early stages of the Gulf war. Largely for electoral reasons, the leadership pursued a bipartisan line, to which not only the hard left but also many on the soft left objected, including several members of the Shadow Cabinet. Some communicated their misgivings to the leader but the least discreet was John Prescott. He immediately became the butt of highly damaging press reports, his conduct being described by one 'senior Kinnock aide' as 'treacherous' 'self-indulgent' and motivated solely by ambition and it was intimated that he had destroyed his prospects of a place in a Labour cabinet. Similarly, the Supper Club (a loose association of leading soft leftists whose existence was for the first time publicised) was dubbed a conspiracy against the leader (*Observer*, 10 February 1991).

Labour's electoral credibility was seen to pivot on its ability to reassure anxious voters that it was a moderate, respectable party and any sign that the left retained influence or that left-wing policies were being espoused would simply confirm the voters' fears. As a result, open and critical debate over policy was increasingly stifled, particularly as the election neared. A good example of this was provided by the shift of policy over ERM membership where Labour swung from scepticism to unqualified support on a crucial issue of policy with minimal discussion and once the decision was made, critics like Gould and Prescott came under considerable pressure to desist from any questioning of the official line. Yet Labour faced a genuine dilemma. It operated in a communications setting where it was subject to a far more relentless and antagonistic scrutiny than its competitors. The articulation of policy disagreements rendered it vulnerable to attempts by the Tory press to revive the image of a dissension-riven organisation whilst even television habitually described such disagreements in terms of 'splits' and 'squabbling'. Ironically, journalists, TV producers and newspaper executives working in a political culture commonly portrayed as pluralist seemed to endorse norms which treated debate and dissent as unnatural and evidence of political malfunctioning. To survive in such an environment, the pressure upon Labour to act in a cohesive and staunchly disciplined fashion was intense.

Control of the selection process

Since the late 1960s – and largely in response to the rising influence of the left on the NEC – central control over the parliamentary selection process had been progressively relaxed. Under Kinnock, this process was reversed. A seminal event was the Greenwich by-election in February 1987. when, despite Head Office pressure, the local party insisted upon selecting a candidate associated with the 'loony left', as a result of which (the leadership felt) not only was a safe Labour seat lost to the SDP but its national standing suffered grievously. The leadership was determined to prevent a recurrence by tightening regulation of the selection of by-election candidates. A new rule introduced in

1988 stipulated that, where a by-election was due to be held, the Executive could require the CLP 'to select a nominee or one of a number of nominees the NEC may submit to it.' To give effect to the rule, the Executive established a 'Parliamentary Selection Panel' comprising five NEC members empowered to interview possible candidates, set the short list to be submitted to the constituency GC, and, if circumstances warranted, determine an alternative procedure.[9]

The new procedure was soon activated. In May 1989 a by-election was called for the Labour stronghold of Vauxhall due to Stuart Holland's resignation. It was a strongly left-wing constituency in an area with a large black population. The candidate who emerged with by far the largest number of nominations was Martha Osamoor, a controversial hard left black community worker from Hackney – precisely the type of candidate the leadership judged as unsuitable to contest a by-election. When the Parliamentary panel assembled it excluded from the short-list both Osamoor and – more contentiously – Russell Profitt (also black), who had served already as a parliamentary candidate, but worked for hard-left administered Brent Council and was connected with the left-wing Black Sections movement. Vauxhall rejected the short-list submitted by the NEC, whose response, in turn, was to impose Kate Hoey as candidate. The local party refused to participate in the election which was, nevertheless, safely won.

As the parliamentary session wore on, the possibility arose that a by-election might be called in a constituency where a parliamentary candidate had already been selected. Kinnock personally intervened at the NEC to urge that the Executive's By-election Panel be empowered to unseat a selected candidate and, if need be, impose a new one. Unlike the earlier extension of NEC powers – to which only the hard left had dissented – members of the soft left objected and the change was approved by only 16 votes to 10.[10] The following year this power was invoked for the by-election in the safe Tory seat of Eastbourne (which the Liberal Democrats won, though it returned to the Tories in the general election). The reason for the NEC's decision to withdraw endorsement of the sitting candidate appears to have been that he was on record as favouring non-payment of the poll tax[11] and he was replaced by Charlotte Atkins, a soft leftist. In another controversial by-election decision the following year, the NEC excluded Ken Capstick, vice-chairman of the Yorkshire Miners and a Scargill ally, from the short-list for the safe Labour seat of Hemsworth – despite the fact that he had received the largest number of nominations – apparently because it was feared that his selection would have endangered Labour's chances of winning the simultaneous by-election for the marginal Langbaurgh seat. What was becoming a familiar pattern then ensued: the constituency party, in protest, rejected the official short-list and the NEC by-election panel riposted by imposing Derek Enright, a former MEP, who was comfortably elected.[12]

This determination to ensure, by organisational means if need be, that constituencies acted in what the NEC considered to be the overall interests of the Party occasionally led to forceful intervention in routine selections. In the stringent disciplinary regime of the 1950s and early 1960s, the NEC as a matter of course would clamp down on constituencies which sought to remove sitting MPs or select far left candidates, but this became much rarer as left-wing influence grew (Shaw, 1988). As we have seen, Foot's attempt to prevent the endorsement of Peter Tatchell was thwarted by the NEC and, in the mid-1980s, several Militant Tendency candidates were selected and three won election to Parliament. As the NEC swung back to the right, the earlier pattern revived. We shall confine ourselves to the most controversial case which best illustrates the leadership's motivations – the aborted attempt to deselect Frank Field, the MP for Birkenhead. Field was a highly regarded chairman of the House of Commons Select Committee on Social Services. Self-willed, and often abrasive in manner, he had alienated left-wingers in his constituency and in December 1989, though securing a majority amongst individual members he was narrowly deselected in favour of Paul Davies, a left-wing local TGWU official who had attracted the bulk of the trade union vote. Amidst a blaze of publicity, Field announced that, unless the NEC declared the contest void, he would resign and contest the seat as an independent. The leadership was desperate to avert Field's threat to resign and fight a by-election: given the universal sympathy Field could command from the press, such a contest would have severely embarrassed the Party.[13] An investigation into the Birkenhead selection was able to find grounds to invalidate the first ballot – though no clear evidence emerged that any serious irregularities had taken place – and the NEC ordered that the contest be re-run which concluded in the MP's narrow victory.

There were two main reasons for this extension of central control. The first was a shift in the pattern of electioneering which had transformed by-elections into highly-publicised media events of national significance: paradoxically, Labour – unlike the Conservatives – did not seem able to shrug off a poor result. The second consideration was fear of the tabloids. The disastrous Greenwich by-election convinced the leadership that it could not risk a by-election (especially in a Labour seat) where the candidate could be with any credibility portrayed as extreme or where (as with Field) the issue of extremism resurfaced.

DIRECT ENFRANCHISEMENT

The second aspect of organisational modernisation was the extension of membership rights, via the spread of individual balloting (one member one vote, or OMOV). The intention was twofold, to extend democracy and to curtail the influence of activists by enfranchising the more moderate rank and file members. Kinnock's first attempt at reform was, as we have seen, a hurried and ill-contrived measure which was rejected by Conference in 1984. With the next round of reselections soon beckoning, he raised the matter again in 1987. His preferred solution was the introduction of OMOV but he soon realised that opposition from the majority of unions would prevent its passage. Whereas earlier OMOV had been seen as solely directed against constituency activists, there was now a growing suspicion – not least because of the way OMOV was presented by Party modernisers in press briefings – that it was also designed to reduce the union input into the Party. As a result, the generally loyalist union, the GMB, reversed its earlier backing for OMOV eliminating any possibility that it could secure a Conference majority. Rather than risking a defeat, Kinnock opted for a compromise, the creation of a local electoral college. Under this arrangement, the unions were assigned up to 40 per cent of the total vote, depending on the degree of union representation at GC level, whilst the rest of the vote was to be cast by individually balloted rank and file members – hence removing the power to select a candidate from activist-run CLP

General Committees. With the backing of all unions outside the hard right (who preferred a straight OMOV system) the college was overwhelmingly adopted by Conference by 4,545,000 votes to 1,608,000 (*Guardian*, 29 September 1987). Though involving more members in the selection process, the electoral college was cumbersome, difficult to operate and open to manipulation.[14] Its blemishes were so obvious that the NEC voted to discontinue it in 1990 and the Party was plunged into serious controversy, between supporters and opponents of OMOV, which was not to be resolved until 1993.[15]

Kinnock was, however, determined to extend OMOV to other areas of Party life. As long as the unions were not affected, little opposition was encountered, except from the largely powerless hard left. In its guidelines for the leadership and deputy leadership elections of 1988, the NEC encouraged constituencies to use direct membership balloting. The consequences were encouraging, as evidence suggested a strong correlation between the use of OMOV and support for Kinnock and Hattersley (*Guardian*, 8 October 1988). The following year the NEC recommended that the method be applied to voting for its own constituency section. This also appeared to be having the desired effect, as Livingstone was toppled from his seat – to the obvious delight of the leader – and as a result the NEC, in February 1990, made direct membership balloting mandatory.[16] When this came into effect in autumn 1991 a right-winger (Gerald Kaufman) was elected to the constituency section of the NEC for the first time in 15 years. The results the two years after were even more dramatic: in 1992 Dennis Skinner, a popular hard leftist, lost his seat and three more right-wingers were elected – Brown, Blair and (by now the former leader) Kinnock himself. In 1993 the last surviving representative of the hard left, and once the most powerful figure on the NEC, Tony Benn, was replaced by Harriet Harman; and with four seats (Kaufman had resigned) the right now had more members on the constituency section than at any time since the 1940s. In fact, the conclusion many drew – that OMOV was the sole reason for this swing to the right – is probably an over-simplification in that it assumed that members vote only along left–right lines. Although little evidence exists, it seems probable that other considerations have always played a part – for instance a strong media profile. Both Bryan Gould in 1987 and John Prescott in

1989 received much favourable TV coverage in the months preceding their election to the NEC and the same applied to Brown and Blair, two accomplished and regular television performers.[17] Nevertheless, it is clear that the introduction of direct balloting has harmed the hard left (whose representatives on the NEC were the only members to consistently oppose it).[18]

The enfranchisement of ordinary members enabled far more members to participate in decision-making, it rendered the Party more representative by curtailing the role of activists, and it reduced the scope for manipulative stratagems like packing GCs and multiple voting. Yet, paradoxically, it is also likely to contribute towards oligarchical control. The pluralist theory of mass voluntary associations explains why. It contends that voluntary organisations, like trade unions and social democratic parties, notwithstanding their democratic rules and institutional forms, contain within them endemic oligarchical tendencies arising from the command leadership exercises over the machinery, communications, information, and funds, coupled with low levels of participation amongst the rank and file. However, the theory further suggests that these tendencies can be counterbalanced by the existence of autonomous ancillary or intermediary organisations which can operate as centres of opposition, alternative sources of communication, agencies for mobilising the rank and file and suppliers of candidates to challenge senior office-holders. Such organisations can survive only where graded authority systems assign significant functions and allow a measure of discretion to lower-level units and where concerted dissent is legitimated by associational rules and norms (Lipset *et al.*, 1956; Martin, 1968; Edelstein, 1967).

From this perspective, the effect of the displacement of the GC becomes clearer. The extension of OMOV to parliamentary selection will almost certainly – as the leadership intended – reduce the accountability of MPs to their CLPs, because Constituency General Committees were the only institutional mechanism available to monitor and hence exercise some informed supervision over the behaviour of MPs. Further, under the old system, left ginger groups were able to promote candidates by publicising slates (which organised voting more efficiently) and disseminating supportive information in sympathetic weeklies which circulated amongst activists (e.g. *Tribune*, *Labour Briefing*) or by the use of their own internal communication channels (internal bulletins and membership mailings) which, in turn, could only penetrate their audience effectively when the electorate was restricted to activists. In future, the new and larger 'selectorate' will be much more difficult for left-wing ginger groups to mobilise whilst the importance of television exposure in gaining a high profile is bound to profit establishment candidates holding senior front bench positions. (In addition, the leadership can exercise a degree of control on who appears on TV through its nomination of spokesmen). It is no coincidence that by 1993 the NEC contained an unprecedented proportion of Shadow Cabinet members (six out of seven, with Kinnock as the remaining member). The consequences may well be far-reaching. Since the early 1950s, a predominantly left-wing constituency section had been the indispensable launching pad for left bids to gain a majority on the Executive and hence check the power of the leadership. By the same token, a leadership whose grip over the NEC cannot be seriously contested and thereby is able to utilise the powers allotted to both parliamentary and extra-parliamentary institutions can afford to ignore the rank and file and wields a formidable measure of control over all aspects of Party activities.

The extension of individual balloting should also be placed within the context of other organisational changes. These include ending the selection of constituency delegates to Conference by the GC in favour of election by the membership as a whole; substituting local subscription collection by a centralised computer system, the effect of which was to weaken personal links between activists (who generally acted as collectors) and those members who rarely attended meetings; and the replacement of the independent-minded *Labour Weekly* with the more tightly controlled *Labour Party News*. We can sum up the general pattern of change by saying that the opportunities and incentives for institutionalised horizontal communication are being diminished and replaced by the growth of direct vertical communication between the centre and the rank and file. In consequence, traditional forms of representative democracy – which allowed at best (not by any means always achieved) for decisions to be taken via a process of discussion and mutual learning at regular meetings between Party members – are being supplanted by a type of direct democracy where the only connection is between the individual member and Head Office.

Whereas representative democracy allows for the acquisition of political skills and can encourage a critical response, the individual member under direct democracy is more likely to be in a position where he or she can only respond to questions set and an agenda framed by the Party's central authorities. The effect is likely to be the atrophying of constituency-wide organisation, Labour's main locus for local mobilisation and co-ordination. However, the crucial role played by the unions as powerful, organised and constitutionally autonomous bodies represents a major barrier to a fully oligarchical system. Insofar as critical voices remain entrenched within the unions, then potent organised impediments to domination by the parliamentary elite will remain. For this reason – combined with electoral ones – reform of the Party–union relationship was a priority for the modernisers in the aftermath of the 1992 election.

The last substantial changes under the Kinnock leadership consisted of a shift in the distribution of Conference votes and radical alterations in the policy-making process. The two sets of reforms were presented by the leadership as the completion of organisational modernisation, transforming Labour into 'a modern, credible party with a broad-based internal democracy reducing the influence of trade unions and party activists' (*Independent*, 23 May 1990). In fact, their genesis was more complex, the intentions more varied and the consequences less obvious than this suggests. For years Conference had urged, and NEC study groups had considered, proposals to reduce the union vote in favour of the constituencies. Though major unions like the TGWU, the GMWU and the AEU all appeared to be sympathetic to some rebalancing, the matter was stalled, with the leadership exhibiting little interest in reform. Whenever Conference adopted motions (for instance on defence spending) which the leadership opposed, it was not unusual for official 'sources' to deny their legitimacy by referring to the 'undemocratic' block vote. In fact the system survived for so long because, on the whole, it rendered party management far easier. However, by the end of the 1980s the leadership came to favour diminishing the union vote, for a range of reasons: progress towards OMOV had lessened the danger of augmenting the power of left-wing activists; few were opposed to the idea and, above all, it fitted in with the strategic object of countering accusations that the Party was under the heel of the unions. The

NEC's recommendation, approved with little opposition at the 1990 Conference, increased the CLP vote from 9 per cent to 30 per cent with the possibility of further gains if constituency membership increased significantly.[19]

The second major change involved a recasting of established policy-making procedures. Conference as a forum for policy deliberation and decision-taking suffered from a range of defects. The process of compositing often produced clumsy and unwieldy resolutions, the manner in which the final agenda was set, hours before Conference assembled, virtually precluded considered constituency debate and the agenda itself was far too heavily encumbered. The quality of debate from the floor was generally low, and platform speeches were usually public relations exercises in rhetoric aimed at the voters, rather than contributions to the debate. As a result, a groundswell of criticism built up and after considerable internal gestation the NEC produced a report, endorsed by the 1990 Conference, recommending a new policy-making tier. It proposed the creation of a Policy Forum, with a membership drawn from all sections of the Party (including the NEC, the Shadow Cabinet, CLPs, the unions, women's, youth and ethnic minority organisations, councillors and Euro-MPs) and Policy Commissions (with the power to co-opt advisors) drawn from the Forum, charged with studying particular policy areas. The intention was to tie the work of these bodies into a rolling programme to be considered by the NEC, the Shadow Cabinet and Conference for final approval.[20] Mounting anxieties about both the cost and the future conduct of the new policy-making organs led the NEC to halve the original size of the Policy Forum (to around one hundred) and to amend the scheme so as to strengthen the oversight of the NEC–Shadow Cabinet Joint Policy Committee.[21] Few within the Party in practice knew what the effects of the new policy-making and decision-making processes would be – whether they would improve the quality of policy-formulation, extend democratic participation or operate in practice as a 'dignified' aspect of Labour's constitution legitimating the concentration of power in the hands of the parliamentary elite, and it will be some time before a judgment can be made.[22]

By 1992, the structure of power in the Labour Party had undergone a profound change. The highly pluralistic, deeply polarised Party characterised by the institutionalised dispersal of powers and weak central authority had been replaced by a powerful central authority exercising tight control over all aspects of organisational life. Not only was this a crucial aspect of the transformation process, it was the necessary condition for the radical overhaul of its programme and strategy and one that will not easily be reversed.

6

LABOUR'S CAMPAIGN AND COMMUNICATIONS STRATEGY 1987–92

In this chapter, after briefly examining the decision-making structure, we shall examine the contours of Labour's strategy, chart its campaigning activities in the pre-election period, then consider its election campaign strategy and its outcome. We shall then explore a number of problems and issues raised by the conduct of the campaign. Chapter 8 will explore in more depth the assumptions and principles of the new strategic paradigm which underpinned electioneering in both the 1987 and 1992 elections.

THE DECISION-MAKING STRUCTURE

In terms of organisation, processes and the composition of its strategic decision-making community, Labour's approach to electoral strategy, campaigning and communications did not differ substantially from the 1986–7 period. Formally-speaking, overall responsibility for campaigning and communications was vested in Labour's Campaign Strategy Committee (CSC) and the Communications sub-committee of the NEC, though in practice these were little more than a facade. From mid-1988 a General Election Planning Group (GEPG, later renamed the Campaign Management Team) was established 'to oversee all campaigning activity up until the general election.' This was to report to the CSC and the Leaders's Committee (see below). The committee was composed of senior Head Office officials, representatives from the Leader's Office and the Campaign Co-ordinator, Jack Cunningham. It was later joined by Philip Gould and Patricia Hewitt from the SCA and Lord (Clive) Hollick.[1]

The GEPG in fact did not function as intended and the key

campaigning committee became Jack Cunningham's Thursday Meeting consisting of the Campaign Co-ordinator, top Party officials and leading members of the SCA. It was formally responsible for the projection side of the campaign plus oversight of the campaign schedule (the 'Grid') but eventually became the key committee responsible for setting the general direction of the campaign. There were several other bodies charged with developing various aspects of the campaign including weekly meetings of the SCA. In January 1992 the CSC was replaced by a Leader's Committee, the body normally set up to exercise general political oversight over the campaign proper, and the structure of decision-making was revamped to prepare for the conduct of the campaign.

Strategic objectives

Applying the interpretive framework of the new strategic paradigm, Party strategists derived from their analysis of Labour's defeat in 1987 (see pp. 59–62 above) three overriding objectives: policy must be thoroughly revised to reposition the Party closer to public opinion; voters must be convinced that Labour could be trusted to manage the economy; and the Party's image must be revamped. Repositioning the Party was, as we have seen, the function of the Policy Review with particular emphasis given to neutralising the main vote-losing issues: high taxes, a weak defence posture, nationalisation and excessive trade union power.[2] By late 1989 on each of these issues Labour's position had been transformed as it came to accept the retention of nuclear weapons, privatisation, the bulk of the Tories' trade union legislation and the market economy. The Policy Review also aspired to meet the second strategic objective, matching Tory ratings on economic competence, not only by modifying the substance of policy but also by earning the respect of influential opinion-formers and hence appearing credible to the voters. Boosting Labour's image entailed convincing the electorate that it was at least as capable as its rivals of running the country: that it had a competent and reliable set of leaders, that it was united and well-led, that it could deliver the goods and, most vital of all, was worthy of the voters' trust. Image-building was, as we have seen, partly a matter of reforming the Party itself, and partly of improved presentation.

Party strategists were aware, of course, that Kinnock's un-popularity remained a problem. The response was two-fold. Firstly, efforts were made to project Kinnock as a tough and capable leader and, secondly, considerable exposure was given to the Party's collective leadership, with John Smith, Gordon Brown, Tony Blair and Margaret Beckett increasingly pushed to the fore as exemplars of a youthful, dynamic and capable team. However, efforts to give a brighter gloss to Kinnock's image were upset by such incidents as his hesitations over defence policy as well as by incessant Tory and tabloid assaults on his general competence, and the problem was never remedied.

LONG-TERM CAMPAIGNING 1987–91
(1) FORMAT: CONTROLLING THE AGENDA

As we have seen, Labour's central campaigning object was to obtain command of the agenda. By the late 1980s, a range of techniques to achieve this were regularly deployed:

- Spin doctoring. This was defined by Brendan Bruce, a former Conservative Director of Communication as 'a flexible technique that can be used not only to "fix" the results of events (speeches, interviews, debates and so on) after the event, but also to manage expectations of an event yet to take place' (Bruce, 1992: 141). Spin doctoring was Mandelson's forte. On the assumption that it was the quality press that helped set TV's agenda, he expended a considerable amount of energy seeking to put his gloss on the news. 'He wheedles journalists, cajoles them, takes them into his confidence, spurns them, adapts his tone to their's. . . . Then if they fail to present the party his way, he bullies, pesters and harries them' (*Independent*, 1 July 1989). He displayed considerable skill in enhancing Labour's capacity to disseminate its message in the more friendly broadsheets (*Guardian*, *Independent*, *Observer*) and he established a close relationship with key political journalists (e.g. Patrick Wintour – dubbed Mandelson's amanuensis, Colin Hughes, Andrew Grice) supplying them with reliable inside information (denied to others) in return for which their stories often bore the Mandelson spin.
- Keeping the Party in the news by issuing a steady stream of

policy and campaigning documents (hence the constant relaunches of the Policy Review).

- Placing the government on the defensive by releasing leaked documents and plying the media with statistics on matters which were both newsworthy and would embarrass the Government – such as information on house repossessions and hospital waiting lists, the state of school buildings and teacher shortages. The Party invested considerable resources in this as part of the continuing struggle for airtime – to induce the broadcasting media to cover *their* issues by supplying them with copy.

- More effective presentation of Conference. In the past, Party Conferences tended to be sources of political embarrassment and poor publicity. The control the leadership now wielded over Conference – combined with the willingness of delegates to perform their allotted roles – enabled Labour's strategists to convert it into a media event. Telegenic front-benchers were given the prime spots to catch TV news bulletins. Great care (in terms of colour, ambience, etc.) was devoted to the set. The whole operation was now aimed at securing maximum favourable media coverage; in Mandelson's words: 'Totally unashamedly, we have used the Conference to project the Party to make an impact on the public' (*Guardian*, 6 December 1990).

Given both the enmity of most of the press and the reliance of the majority of the population on TV as a source of news, influencing television news output was Labour's top priority. A notable feature of its new professionalism was its thorough understanding of the processes of broadcasting news production. In Mandelson words: 'TV is putting tremendous pressure on us . . . to turn out strong visuals so that they have interesting pictures for their news bulletins . . . to have that special exclusive shot, that interesting angle that their rivals don't have' (*Tribune*, 29 January 1989). This meant organising 'pseudo-events' and 'photo-calls' to deliver 'newsworthy' items for TV news bulletins. For example, as part of Labour's environment campaign, Ann Taylor appeared standing on the banks of river Don in Yorkshire, pointing to a river turned orange due to industrial pollution (*Guardian*, 27 February 1989). Further TV exposure was concentrated on the more adroit and telegenic front-benchers: those who were able to exude an air of competence and furnish the crisp 'sound-bites' on news bulletins that TV demanded. John Smith, Gordon Brown, Robin Cook and Tony Blair all proved particularly adept at this.

At the same time, Party officials intervened much more forcefully than in the past to influence news output. This extended well beyond traditional complaints about fairness and balance to encompass (as one ITV journalist referring to both main parties commented) 'detailed critiques of how the programmes were being made, how discussions were being organised, and even how individual items were being structured.' He instanced the following: a reporter preparing an item received a call from a Labour politician 'checking that she had understood the Party line in the story she was writing for transmission in a few minutes time'; an official upbraided ITN's political editor over 'the length and pace of a panning shot which had travelled from Neil Kinnock to Roy Hattersley'; the Party complained to the BBC over devoting too much time to Tory attacks on its tax policies; after the 'Jenny's ear' broadcast (see below) a Party unit run by an ex-TV news producer 'tried with some success to interest the popular regional news programmes in pre-researched programmes about sick children on waiting lists.' Both parties urged broadcasters to use their own pictures of events and rallies and tried to shape the terms on which interviews were granted (Tait, 1992). Whether or not Labour benefited, it could well be that its informed persistence in seeking to shape the TV news agenda reduced the advantage that a determined government secured in exploiting its much greater power to pressurise the broadcasters.

There are however limits to the extent that any party – however skilled – can control the political agenda. Not only were broadcasters ever-watchful; the communications setting was in constant flux. No one could predict what issues might suddenly erupt – a leakage in a nuclear reactor, an unexpectedly poor set of trade figures, the outbreak of serious civil disturbances and so forth. This put a premium on the capacity of politicians to cope with the unexpected: to size up the situation, to respond rapidly and effectively either to neutralise a weakness or capitalise upon an opportunity. On the whole, Labour's spokesmen proved quite adroit at exploiting political openings, but never managing to outweigh the Tories' two immense assets. To an unprecedented extent the Tories were backed by friendly tabloids willing to orchestrate and amplify whatever 'spin' the government placed on events. And with a single-mindedness never before seen, the government used all the advantages of office to flood the news agenda. (This will be discussed below.) In consequence, Labour's attempt to mould the agenda was an uphill struggle against stiff odds.

LONG-TERM CAMPAIGNING 1987–91
(2): CONTENT

Labour's approach to campaigning over the long term was shaped both by its overall strategy and by the political exigencies at any one time, particularly the state of the economy, government policy initiatives (e.g. the poll tax) and changing public sentiment. Labour campaigners distinguished between issues and themes. By issues they meant the major areas of public policy – health, tax and so forth; by themes, the specific points or arguments which they sought to communicate. They also divided themes into three categories: attack, positive and defensive. Attack themes were designed to exploit weaknesses in the Government's record and to exploit signs of public disenchantment; positive themes consisted of efforts to highlight Labour's strengths and promote its policies and values; whilst defensive themes sought to minimise its own vulnerabilities. In this section we shall explore the type of appeal Labour made in its main campaign initiatives and then examine briefly its targeting strategy.

The Quality of Life campaign

Labour's first major campaign launched in the summer of 1988 emanated from an influential SCA report based mainly on qualitative research.[3] Its key findings were that, though the Conservatives had convinced many people that, under their guidance, society now offered more choice and freedom, this was balanced by a feeling of collective loss: the social fabric was deteriorating with more division, more greed, more violence and less neighbourliness, compounded by growing anxieties about environmental despoilation. It also drew attention to a recent MORI 'values survey' which appeared to suggest that the majority of voters were still attached to collectivist values. Kinnock was impressed by the report. Given that 'a majority of voters hold values that can fairly be described as essentially socialist' he wrote, the theme that 'Labour values your values' should infuse all the Party's campaigning efforts. Grounded in the 'quality of life' agenda (a combination of social and environmental concerns) it should 'act as a motif for our general appeal to the people of this country.'[4] The theme figured prominently in Kinnock's powerful speech to the 1988 Party Conference in which he decried 'the fracturing of our society,' and 'the grabbing "loadsamoney" ethic' but thereafter only episodically came to life.[5] In fact, it was the environmental side of the 'quality of life' agenda which was pushed most vigorously. Partly in response to Mrs Thatcher's own attempt to seize the initiative on the question, in February 1989 Labour launched a week-long campaign berating the Government for its neglect of the environment. This campaign went into higher gear after the astonishing (if fleeting) success of the Greens in the June Euro-elections. In a paper to the Campaign Strategy Committee Mandelson urged a new campaigning strategy to raise Labour's environmental profile in order to attract the green vote.[6] Though Mandelson's call 'to dramatically step up our activity on the issue' was accepted, the environment did not survive for long as a campaigning priority. As the public's interest in the issue subsided, so did Labour's. This reflected its primarily reactive, poll-led approach to the public agenda. Unlike the German Greens or the green wing of the German Social Democratic Party, Labour was less interested in reshaping opinion or propelling new issues onto the agenda than in reflecting and turning to its advantage existing public concerns. From late 1989 onwards, these were overwhelmingly traditional social and economic ones.

The economic agenda: the attacking message

Party strategists always regarded the economy as lying at the centre of the political battlefield. The precise content of the campaign attack varied with economic circumstances, Government policies and public concerns. In 1988 and 1989 the main issues were the rapid rise in inflation and the massive balance of payments deficit shortly to be followed by the Government's 'one club response' – the jacking-up of interest and mortgage rates. In September 1988, Mandelson argued for a sustained offensive on the Government's handling of the economy and proposed two main themes. The first was mortgages. 'Home ownership has been an important symbol in the Tories' appeal and we need to make the costs of home ownership a key focus for discontent with the Government.' Hence Party spokesmen constantly hammered away at 'mortgage misery'. The second was the trade deficit to be used as a symbol of Tory economic mismanagement.[7] These were the leitmotifs of Labour's attack on the Tories in 1988–9. As tightening monetary policy provoked rising unemployment, a mounting toll of company bankruptcies, an alarming growth in mortgage arrears and a collapse in investment, these issues were highlighted. The Tories, through their slavish adherence to free market dogmas, were lambasted for presiding over the dismantling of Britain's economic base. A further target supplied by the Government was the poll tax. Labour sought to exploit its unpopularity by organising various initiatives (though it kept well away from the Militant-led mass protests) and by the end of 1990 it was riding the crest of a massive wave of indignation with the tax.

The economic agenda: the positive and defensive message

In September 1988, the SCA had identified the lack of confidence in its ability to manage the economy as the chief impediment to Labour voting and, despite the recession, the polls continued to register a substantial Conservative lead. Kinnock concluded that 'winning the economic competence argument is clearly therefore a vital task'.[8] The Party sought to close the gap with the presentation of a practical economic message 'which will be understood in terms of the personal benefit and enduring prosperity it will bring'.[9] Economic revival demanded the fuller and more efficient utilisation of the country's main resource, the skills of its workforce, and government-sponsored expansion of investment and R&D. Labour also strove to dissipate public fears (and counter incessant Tory and press attacks) of its alleged high tax plans and to convince opinion-leaders (e.g. economic journalists in the quality papers and on TV, and business leaders) that Labour had developed a sound and 'responsible' economic strategy. Considerable effort was expended on consulting industrialists and the Smith–Brown 'prawn cocktail offensive' turned Labour's two senior economic spokesmen into regular visitors to the City. Finally, it sported an economic team – Smith, Brown, Blair and Beckett – able to convey an aura of authority, expertise and prudence. Smith, in particular – with his air of the canny, shrewd and utterly reliable Scottish solicitor (or bank manager) – increasingly became a key figure in Labour's exposition of its economic case.

The social agenda

The key issues here were health and education. Labour, of course, knew that health was its strongest campaign card and it sought to keep the issue on the boil as much as possible; thus new health campaigns were constantly being launched. Its strategy was dual-pronged: firstly, it sought to publicise the deterioration in the health service (ward closures, shortages in medical staff, unacceptably high waiting lists, etc.) due to under-funding. Secondly, after the enactment of the Government's NHS reforms, it charged the Government with 'creeping privati-sation' – an accusation it pressed with increasing and unstinting energy as both the opinion polls and the Monmouth by-election (adroitly turned into a referendum on the NHS) suggested it was striking home. Health was the only one of 'Labour's issues' with the capacity to really stir the emotions and the unceasing flow of stories about the strains within the Health Service pro-vided Labour with a ready supply of ammunition (as did the well-publicised opposition of the medical profession to the NHS reforms). Focusing on education and training had a number of advantages. Opinion research indicated that education had emerged as a high saliency issue with mounting dissatisfaction over educational standards and inadequate resources. Voters rated Labour more highly on education and the Tory reforms appeared not to be bearing fruit – affording Labour an oppor-tunity to 'brand' quality education as 'its' issue (though with less success than it had hoped).

Labour's electoral targets

Strategists targeted particular groups within the electorate but this proceeded in a highly empirical fashion. Quantitative and (especially) qualitative data were inspected to detect shifts in patterns of partisan preferences, opinion and values in order to locate those segments of the population potentially most receptive to Labour's case. In designating its target voters, Labour used both political and demographic criteria . Politically, targets were defined in terms of the direction and intensity of partisan preferences; demographically by using the A–E classification system. The nature of the target varied considerably over time. There was, for example, an important shift in Party thinking after the Green upsurge at the 1989 European elections. In a long strategy paper, Mandelson saw Green voters as an 'important target category of voters for Labour' profiling them as 'youthful, middle class, well-informed, southernly, formerly Alliance-supporting and disproportionately female'.[10]

A year or two later, the environment had slid down the agenda and much less was heard of a distinctive bloc of Green voters. Another rather larger section of the population received more sustained attention: women. In 1988 SCA research showed that while the 'gender gap' persisted with many women alienated by Labour's strongly male image, women were far more likely to share Labour values.[11] Two major strategic decisions followed. Firstly, in the policy sphere, much higher priority was given to issues like child care, child benefits and pensions and the Party launched its 'Labour values your values' campaign to appeal specifically to women; secondly, in the presentational sphere female MPs were featured much more prominently and the language and imagery used in Party communications was adjusted to render it more appealing to women (*New Statesman*, 25 November 1988). In practice, women did not figure for long as a separate and distinct audience for Labour's messages as strategists increasingly tended to place greater reliance on political criteria. Demographic analysis was largely confined to identifying the social attributes (in terms of A–E grading, housing, regional residence) of priority groups in the electorate defined in terms of their orientations to the various parties. Thus in 1990 the focus was switched to disenchanted former Tories now turning to Labour. Using cluster analysis, NOP portrayed these as disproportionately young, male, C1/C2 voters, primarily motivated by pecuniary issues and alienated from the Tories chiefly because of the cost of credit and high mortgage and poll tax payments (i.e. 'Essex Man'). As the election drew near, the target vote was again redefined with this time the emphasis placed on weakly attached Liberal Democrats, former non-voters and the undecided generally who were disproportionately Southern, middle-class, home-owners and mainly driven by economic concerns.

The variations in Labour's thinking about its target audience indicates a weakness in its approach. It was almost wholly poll-driven and appeared not to be influenced by any rigorous social analysis. The effect was to deprive strategists of those discriminating instruments which may have enabled them to distinguish between rather superficial and ephemeral movements of opinion and more deeply-embedded attitudinal and social cleavage patterns; this would have helped differentiate between groups whose members were bound together by a sense of identity and perhaps by a sense of common interest and those which were merely statistical artifacts. For instance, because the polls in 1989 registered a massive upsurge in concern over environmental matters and because the Greens won a quite unexpected triumph, the 'Green vote' became a great object of interest.[12] Did the Green vote, as a distinct group ever exist? Whether it did or not, next year it was forgotten and was displaced as priority target by the instrumental southern C1/C2 voter. Further, no systematic effort was made to channel particular messages to specific target groups. One of the reasons, one suspects, why Labour strategists never made a great deal of progress with targeting was because the leadership did not think in these strategic terms. An interesting comparison is with the Conservatives in 1979 who clearly focused their income tax and council house sales policies on skilled workers disaffected because of compressed differentials and increased taxation.

THE NEAR-TERM CAMPAIGN

At the forefront of Labour's attack strategy was the Prime Minister. Senior ministerial resignations (Nigel Lawson, the Chancellor of the Exchequer and Sir Geoffrey Howe, the Leader of the House) supplied useful opportunities for concerted Labour assaults on her capricious, insensitive and autocratic rule. Thatcherism as ideology was portrayed as representing dogma-driven policies, extremism, confrontation and even (in one Kinnock speech) 'social engineering'. As such it played a crucial part in Labour's decision to position itself as a middle-of-the-road, pragmatic and consensually oriented party seeking to replace the rule of ideology with practical common sense as it, in effect, relied upon disillusion with the government to catapult it into office. This was thrown into confusion by Mrs Thatcher's summary ejection and the arrival of the far more mollifying, quietly spoken and (it transpired) very popular John Major who soon cancelled Labour's lead. Critics within the leadership circle including Bryan Gould, David Blunkett and even Roy Hattersley who, in the interests of party unity had in the past articulated their reservations discretely now voiced them (for a while) in public. But their call for a more positive and adventurous strategy was rejected. Instead the Party opted to portray Major as 'son of Thatcher': one-third on the basis of polling and two-thirds on Kinnock's intuition, one former Party strategist recalled. However, this depiction of the new PM was so unconvincing that Labour decided to shift ground and to attack him as a 'ditherer'. The spin was successful to the extent that charges of 'dithering' were, for a time, frequently heard on the wavelengths but it made no impression on public perceptions (at least at the time). Furthermore, Major's entry into No. 10 had, for Labour, the unfortunate effect of resuscitating the problem of leadership. This problem had been largely neutralised in 1989–90 less by any improvement in Kinnock's standing than by Mrs Thatcher's unpopularity. With her removal, the spotlight was once more on Labour's leader.

With the onset of the Major premiership, the run-up to the election effectively began. Labour's prime campaigning objectives in the near-term were firstly to induce the Conservatives to delay an election as long as possible so that they would eventually find themselves boxed-in, and secondly to enter the election campaign with an edge over its opponents. Both these objectives were achieved but the real significance of these pre-election months was the Party's failure to capitalise on the recession to secure a solid lead. Nevertheless, 1992 opened with a feeling of optimism in the Labour camp. Frosty economic statistics kept the 'green shoots' of recovery which the Chancellor had promised stubbornly underground whilst Labour held a small but steady lead in the polls. It had prepared a glossy document entitled *Made in Britain* aimed at presenting itself as the party of industrial modernisation, to bolster its economic credibility. But this fell immediately into oblivion as instead it found itself the butt of a relentless Tory/tabloid cannonade over taxation.

In November 1991 Conservative strategists produced a paper entitled *The Near Term Campaign*. This advised the Government to exploit all the advantages of incumbency – the issuing of ministerial statements, control of parliamentary time and so forth – to swamp the news (Butler and Kavanagh, 1992: 80–81). Conservative spokesmen were to hammer away at key Labour vulnerabilities, especially tax and leadership. Labour's spending plans were costed at £35 billion (displaying, for Conservative campaigners, an uncharacteristic lack of imagination – the same figure as in the 1987 election) which very conveniently was calculated to mean the easily remembered sum of £1,000 extra a year – later increased by another £250 – for the average (which seems to have been widely understood as each) taxpayer. This was Labour's 'Tax Bombshell' the theme for the near-term offensive launched in January 1992 (Butler and Kavanagh, 1992: 84). Posters, TV ministerial interviews and a rash of press coverage were orchestrated to broadcast this theme, which filled the television news bulletins for much of January. As one Tory strategist recalled, never before had a general election been preceded by so intense a period of campaigning. 'Labour votes to tax the poor', the *Daily Mail* informed its readers; 'Road to Ruin', the *Daily Express* announced; 'Labour to squeeze the back-bone of Britain', according to the *Sun*. More temperately the respected Institute of Fiscal Studies agreed with Labour's own calculation that four out of five families would gain, and only 9 per cent (those earning over £30,000) would lose, but this information made no impression (Newton, 1992: 145).

Labour's campaigners seem to have been caught unaware by the ferocity of the Tory onslaught. Although very predictable, no attempt had been made to 'inoculate' – to use an American campaigning term – the electorate. 'At times it was so bad', according to one Party source 'that some members of the shadow cabinet were not on speaking terms. Basic lines of defence had not been prepared' (*Guardian*, 13 February 1992). Labour reacted very defensively, notably with what came to be known as 'the Luigi wobble' when Kinnock (without consulting Smith) decided to resurrect a neglected safety device from the Policy Review – that tax increases would be phased in to limit their impact on personal incomes. Smith disagreed and the public exposure of disagreements and equivocations on a crucial issue – 'Labour's tax shambles' in tabloid parlance – appeared to demonstrate once more Labour's lack of economic competence (McSmith, 1993: pp 180–91). 'Gallup reported an increase in the Conservative lead over Labour as the party best able to deal with taxes from 4 per cent to 18 per cent between November 1991 and January 1992' (Butler and Kavanagh, 1992: 85). Ironically, after 13 years of Conservative Government public attention was concentrated on dissecting Labour's policies. This was in part a result of the agenda-setting capacity of the press and the incumbent party. But the fact that such issues as the decay of the public services and the level of social benefits were so totally marginalised was in part due to the lameness of Labour's response. As the *Guardian* pointed out, 'far from banging the drum to make Britain a fairer and more equal society, Labour seemed stuck yesterday explaining the modesty of its tax proposals' (*Guardian*, 7 January 1992).

Labour was beginning to pay the price for its 'play-safe strategy' which had always held that it was sounder to concentrate on establishing its prudence and moderation rather than risk sailing into more controversial waters – a strategy which, as Hugo Young commented 'seemed to father a terribly apologetic demeanour' (*Guardian*, 30 January 1992). This immediate pre-election period was of crucial importance as probably the last opportunity for either party to achieve any significant opinion change before real debate was smothered in the smoke of the election itself.[13] The Tories were able to rehearse some of their key arguments whilst no clear and confident messages emanated from the Labour camp. They were satisfied that their goal had been achieved: and one senior Conservative figure commented that the near term campaign had contributed substantially to the final outcome.

THE ELECTION CAMPAIGN STRATEGY

Election planning

In September 1991 BMP, on behalf of the SCA, prepared a document simply entitled *SCA Presentation* which, though formally designed to provide an advertising strategy, in practice supplied much of the thinking behind the Party's strategy for the forthcoming election. It sought to answer three questions: who is the target market? What is the key to their voting behaviour? How do we influence them?

The target market

Using NOP data it identified two groups as Labour's target market: new recruits to Labour and the 'undecided not unfavourable'. Compared to committed Labour supporters these groups were – in demographic terms – disproportionately ABC 1, more likely to be home-owners and much more likely to live in the South.

The key to their voting behaviour

The report argued that the attachment of these new recruits was fragile. 'The demographic structure of these voters represents those who got most 'stung' by Thatcherism, but whose political allegiance almost by necessity follows the cost of their debt.' But since the control of this debt, via interest rates and inflation, largely lay in the hands of the Government, these voters 'are likely to return to the Conservatives at a General Election'. Furthermore, three major blocks stood in the way of Labour voting – apprehension (not least amongst C2 and DE voters) that the Party would raise taxes for everyone, entrenched misgivings about its capacity to manage the economy – and hence protect living standards – and lack of confidence in its ability to run the country.

How do we influence them?

Firstly, the tax issue had to be neutralised. The SCA recommended that Labour broaden the issue so that voters understood that what mattered was the money left in people's pockets after VAT, the poll tax and interest charges as well as income tax. Further it should warn that the Tories intended to push up VAT for all (this was the rationale for Labour's 'VATMAN' poster) whilst emphasising that it would not levy any further taxes beyond those already pledged. This would enable Labour to guard its flank. Leading the attack should be health. Sentiments of fear and indignation over the NHS were common amongst Labour's target groups. Mobilising opinion over health would have the dual function of motivating apathetic and disillusioned voters whilst at the same time deterring those who might be tempted to return to the Tories. But the really crucial problem was to tackle doubts about economic competence. The authors of the report were impressed by Harold Wilson's strategy to win the competence argument in 1963–4 by contrasting backward-looking Tories with modernising Labour (the 'white heat' of technology). Adjusting to circumstances, Labour should try and replicate Wilson's success by projecting itself as the modernising party, whilst depicting the Tories as the party which still peddled the old (and according to polling evidence) increasingly unpopular dogmas of privatisation. This strategy would work only to the extent that Labour presented 'a resonant solution'. This entailed an analysis of the problem, 'a credible territory' and a vision, that is a distinctive profile. A common complaint of respondents in opinion research was that 'we don't make anything anymore': this should be the analysis; conversely, Labour held a lead as the party that will build Britain's industrial strength: its credible territory. Its policies on promoting technology and R&D should enable it to position itself as the party of modernisation: 'Made in Britain' and 'Modernisation not Privatisation' should constitute its vision.

The campaign appeal.

The final campaign strategy was based to a considerable extent on the SCA report. The Party chose three core themes to be rammed home throughout the campaign: 'Made in Britain', 'Modernisation not Privatisation' and 'Opportunity Britain'. The message of the first was that Labour would back British industry and British workers to rebuild the manufacturing base and recapture world markets; the second that whilst the Tories would privatise, Labour would guarantee a free, modern and efficient NHS and education system; the third that Labour would tackle poverty (especially child poverty) to ensure opportunity to all. In practice, the third theme was very much a subsidiary one: the core issues were the economy, health and education. The central campaign message was to be 'It's time for a change, it's time for Labour' – a motif that had constantly recurred in the Party's opinion polling. Labour's attacking themes were the obvious ones: mismanagement of the economy, unemployment, bankruptcies, repossessions, the poll tax and threatened privatisations; whilst the Party would need to protect itself against attacks over tax, competence and trust, Kinnock and extremism.[14] The style of Labour's campaign was to be generally a positive one. Kinnock was to be presented as 'The Prime Minister in Waiting' offering vision and hope and presiding over an energetic and talented team. Counter-productive mud-slinging was to be eschewed and an 'urgent, positive, attractive, confident' tone was to be cultivated conveying the idea of a Party eager and well-qualified to assume the burdens of office.[15]

Labour was aware that it was operating in a two-and-a-half party system. The strategy towards the Liberal Democrats was to avoid any direct attacks, where possible to foster the impression that the two parties were on the same side, with the Tories isolated, and to stress the three issues seen as of particular concern to Liberal Democratic supporters – constitutional reform, the environment and education (linked to childcare) – identified as 'the key issue for LibDems/floaters – *especially women*'.[16] Labour's objects were to entice Liberal Democrats sympathetic to Labour's agenda to switch allegiance whilst on the other (and mainly through ratchetting fears about the NHS) to induce anxious Tories to desert to Ashdown's party.

The general election campaign

For a variety of reasons – the budget, the continuing Tory assault on Labour's tax plans, the anticipated rash of poor economic statistics – Party strategists scheduled the economy as the first major campaigning issue. Key objectives here were to neutralise the tax issue, expose the Government's record on the economy and achieve at least parity on economic competence.[17] Breaking with precedent, an 'alternative budget' was unveiled, with the aims of furnishing a detailed rebuttal of Tory allegations, publicising Labour's own 'prudent and practical' proposals and, not least, placing Smith in the limelight. Great care was taken with the format of the alternative budget to convey the almost subliminal suggestion that, in his authoritative demeanour, his command of detail and his tone of sombre realism, Smith was the 'real' chancellor.

With the polls indicating a narrow Labour lead, the Party then moved to publicise its 'own agenda', spearheaded, of course, by health. Since health was seen as the main lever for prising away voters from the Tories and rallying the floaters the object was to pull well ahead by stoking fears of privatisation.[18] The issue, however, came to be overshadowed by the controversial PEB on 'Jennifer's ear'. The only broadcast produced in-house by BMP, it was described by one Labour insider as 'the first real piece of political advertising – even the famous Neil and Glenys film [a reference to 'Kinnock, the movie' from the 1987 campaign] was more of a promotional video' (*Observer*, 12 March 1992). It compared two young girls, both suffering from a painful ear complaint. One had to suffer for a year awaiting treatment from the NHS whilst the other was from a richer family able to afford immediate private treatment. There were no words, just soft music. Debate took place on whether it was too emotive to show – in trials some members in focus groups were left in tears. Undoubtedly a sophisticated and compelling broadcast, we will never know whether it would have achieved its purpose if discussion had not been so totally side-tracked by 'the war of Jenny's ear'. Labour had – carelessly – intimated that the PEB was based on a true life story and, shortly after, the name of the real 'Jennifer' was revealed. Much recrimination, and masses of news coverage followed about who had leaked the name. It transpired that, although her father was a Labour sympathiser, her mother was a Conservative, and her grandfather was a former Conservative mayor who, well before the election, had told Tory Central Office precisely what Labour was planning. One senior Labour politician later ruefully admitted 'we had walked into a trap'.

The right wing tabloids seized the opportunity to jab remorselessly at the key Tory theme of Kinnock's credibility. The *Sun* proclaimed 'are liars fit to govern?', the *Express* slammed 'THE BIG LIE' with the other tabloids in tow (Butler and Kavanagh, 1992: 203). In an anxious attempt to resurrect the health issue, Labour then compounded its embarrassment by releasing a shoddily researched dossier claiming to present other cases, but this was so inaccurate that it had to be withdrawn. This was a gift to the tabloids, who exploited it to drive home the familiar Tory campaign themes: 'LABOUR'S NEW HEALTH FIASCO' (*Daily Mail*), 'LABOUR BLUNDERS ON AND ON' (*Daily Express*),

'NEIL IN PANIC' (*Sun*), 'LABOUR'S OWN GOALS ON NHS
. . . a shambles' (*Star*). Opinions differed in the Party on the
impact of the row. Some felt that the PEB had achieved its
objective in that the agenda was dominated by health for several
days and it spawned a whole host of 'Jenny stories' in the local
media. On the other hand, as the Party's General Secretary
concluded, not only did it blur Labour's message, but it prevented the Party from gaining 'the high moral ground . . . and
looked not a little grubby.'[19]

In fact, the effect of a mixture of poor research, lack of co-
ordination, mishandling and simple bad luck was probably more
serious than this. The issue was important less for itself than
because it was used, by the Tories and their press allies, as a
tangible (and therefore easily grasped) illustration of their
charges against Labour: dishonest, sleazy, totally unfitted to
govern and led by a man with neither the moral nor intellectual
stature to be Prime Minister. Further, the episode totally
diverted attention from the points Labour wished to make:
'Jennifer Bennett and her glue ear received more coverage than
housing, transport, pensions, law and order, defence, foreign
affairs and Europe – indeed, than several of these put together'
(Butler and Kavanagh, 1992: 164). The message of recent election campaigns is that fear-based negative campaigning is highly
effective and the confiscation from Labour of its only 'fear card'
left it with no emotional voltage to combat the Conservatives
own remorseless appeals to fear. Further, health was the centre-
piece of Labour's attack strategy scheduled mid-campaign to
seize the initiative; with the blunting of the issue, the attack lost
all momentum. Not surprisingly, the broadcast, rather than
providing lift-off, caused 'a serious crisis in the campaign.'[20]

The controversy also stalled the next step of the campaign
over education. However, the Liberal Democrats' own initiative
over education (pledging a one pence increase in income tax to
fund improvements in education) had the effect of largely pre-
empting it as a Labour issue. The apparent surge in support for
that party in the final week of the campaign led to a change in
Labour's own strategy, the decision to introduce the topic of
electoral reform. The intention was to signal that Labour was a
listening, consensus-minded party, to reassure doubters that it
was 'safe' and to woo Liberal Democrat voters. For a variety of
reasons (including Kinnock's unwillingness to express his own

views clearly) the issue backfired. But it is worth noting that Labour played the card at probably the worst moment in terms of its credibility, in the heat of an election campaign – something that could easily have been foreseen.

Party strategists believed that the final week would be the decisive one. The final stage of the campaign was designed 'to consolidate the economic and social message and to give the impression of a "take-off and a bandwagon for Labour."' Hence the Sheffield 'mega-rally' and the 'endorsements strategy' – whereby an impressive list of eminent celebrities would publicly back Labour to dispel lingering doubts about its capacity to govern.[21] The huge, elaborately organised and packed Sheffield rally was held in a triumphal and overcharged atmosphere, since the polls had just suggested – inaccurately – that Labour had at last leapt ahead. Carried away by the excitement, Kinnock exclaimed on the stage – like a revivalist soul singer from the Deep South – 'Well all ri, well all ri' – confirming every prejudice so many felt about him. Huge flags billowing in the background and the loudly cheering audience gave the rally its nickname – Labour's Nuremberg. The harmful effects of Labour's Sheffield rally were probably not as great as imagined at the time. More relevant here is the decision to hold it in the first place (against the advice of several senior Walworth Road officials: it seems that the initiative came from the Leader's Office). In terms of money and effort it was a considerable drain on Labour's resources and it is unclear precisely why using them in such a way should have been considered a priority.

The Conservative campaign may have been less professionally organised than Labour's but it was far more successful in beating away relentlessly at its key messages, most notably over tax, economic competence and Kinnock's leadership. Labour strategists clearly miscalculated in believing that abolishing the NIC ceiling would have far less of a political impact than income tax (*Guardian*, 7 January 1992). They underestimated the extent to which attitudes to tax were – as the the SCA had in fact pointed out with some prescience in their September 1991 report – a matter 'of where [voters] see themselves aspiring to as much as where they are currently'. The original intention to re-impose NICs at £25,000 rather than £22,000 *might* have made a significant symbolic as well as practical difference. Labour was far too defensive and sluggish in responding to the Tory pre-election tax offensive and by the election campaign itself, attitudes had probably crystallised. Indeed (as friendly economic journalists had urged for some time) it would have been advisable for Labour to have been more discreet (or disingenuous?) over its tax intentions: the Tories had felt under no obligation in 1979 to publicise their intention to double VAT, nor did they ever hint at their own intention to tackle the massive budget deficit by both sharp spending cuts and heavy tax rises if they were returned to office as was revealed the following year.

Party strategists had, in addition, not prepared adequately (for reasons that we shall explore in the next chapter) for the tone and style of the Conservative offensive. O'Shaughnessy has observed that 'political marketing relies for its success on the provocation of *negative* emotional sensations' (O'Shaughnessy, 1990: 67; emphasis added). A fear-arousal strategy entails a communicator stimulating the emotional conditions of fear and insecurity and then suggesting a way in which the alleged threat can be averted, and hence the anxiety so created can be released. The ability of fear appeals to effect attitude change is enhanced to the extent that the issue is a highly salient one, the source of the threat is clearly identified and its nature convincingly presented (Hovland *et al.*, 1953: 61–2). The combination of tax, the unions and race (the issues) Labour (the source) and the tabloids (presentation) enabled the Conservatives to meet the conditions, and in both the 1987 and 1992 elections, fear-arousal was a central component in Tory campaigns. Thus one sympathetic chronicler of the 1987 Conservative campaign noted the emphasis on 'the "fear issues" – fear of strikes and secondary picketing . . . fear for personal safety with Labour's attitude to law and order and the police, fear of inflation with Labour's proposals to increase public spending, fear of increased taxation' (Tyler, 1987: 197). Similarly in 1992 fear was the Conservatives' key strategic concept. (O'Shaughnessy, 1993). Fear of tax rises and of a new 'Winter of Discontent' had by then become the staple diet of Tory campaigning but inciting fear can bring particularly rich political dividends when it exploits deeply ingrained emotional feelings and when the object is a stigmatised 'out-group' – as abundantly demonstrated by the highly successful 'Willie Horton' advert in the 1988 American presidential elections.[22] Contacts between the American republicans and the Conservatives were close (Butler and Kavanagh, 1992: 79) and so it was not surprising that, in the final week of the 1992 campaign 'the fear card was . . . played relentlessly on immigration' (Berry, 1992: 567). In an obviously carefully timed speech, Kenneth Baker, then Home Secretary, warned voters about the consequences of Labour's stance on his Asylum Bill and the tabloids followed the cue (totally ignoring the distinction between asylum-seekers and immigrants). The *Daily Express* headlined 'Bakers Migrant Flood Warning', the *Daily Mail* exclaimed 'migrant madness' and the *Sun* warned of the 'human tide' Labour would let in, with the common theme being of masses of immigrants flooding the country if Labour triumphed (McKie, 1992). 'Roughly half the electorate', Billig and Golding commented, 'were exposed to lurid 'fear' stories, playing at racist feelings at the latest stage of the campaign' (Billig and Golding, 1992).[23] Given that the questions of race were seen as a 'Tory issue' to be avoided as much as possible, Labour had not devised a strategic response to this onslaught though, as we shall suggest below, more fundamental matters were involved.[24]

THE FOURTH DEFEAT

Until the last moment, the polls indicated that Labour would scrape together enough seats to form a minority government. But the polls were wrong, the Party only pushed up its share of the vote by 3.6 per cent to 34.4 per cent (though scoring rather better in terms of seats) and Major retained power with a majority of 21. The result, its fourth successive defeat, was an horrific shock to Labour. Despite the salience of the tax issue, the Party performed best amongst ABs (professional and managerial) gaining 10 per cent compared to 1987 and 2 per cent to 1979. Similarly, amongst the DEs (semi-skilled and unskilled) the rise was 8 per cent since 1987, 2 per cent since 1979. However, amongst C1s (clerical workers) and C2s (skilled manual) the increase was only 4 per cent and in both cases down on 1979 – an election in which Labour had sustained particularly heavy losses amongst C2s. There were positive features – gains were made where previously Labour had lost most ground such as in the South, amongst working-class owner-occupiers and private sector workers. But these were modest consolations (Crewe, 1992b: 5; figures from Harris/ITN exit polls).

The context seemed ideal, with the country mired deep into a recession and an endless stream of poor economic statistics. But Labour's two strongest issues failed to galvanise the electorate. Amongst those who saw it as a major issue, the majority preferring it on unemployment fell and whilst the prominence of the health issue rose, its lead was considerably less than in 1987 – which may have been a fall-out of 'Jennifer's ear'. Significantly, far more voters chose to believe the Tories' line on Labour's tax plans than Labour's own, with 62 per cent convinced that Labour would raise income tax and considerably larger numbers feeling that they would be worse off if government changed hands. No progress had been made in the key object of eradicating its deficit on economic competence as the Conservatives led by 53 per cent to 35 per cent as the party most trusted to handle the economy (Crewe, 1992: 7–8; figures cited from NOP and Harris exit polls).

What had gone wrong? In this final section of the chapter, we shall consider two of the controversies debated within the Party in the immediate aftermath of the general election, the role of the Shadow Agency and of the Kinnock leadership.

Designing the strategy: the role of the SCA

Almost immediately after the election, critics within Walworth Road, the NEC and the Shadow Cabinet – most notably soft left members such as John Prescott, Bryan Gould and David Blunkett – claimed that the Shadow Agency had exercised a disproportionate influence in the running of Labour's campaigns and communications strategy and was to blame for the sacrifice of content to 'glitz' (see, e.g., *Guardian*, 16 May 1992).

What precisely did the SCA do? Its main tasks involved advising and helping formulate advertising and media projection strategies, including creative work, pre-testing campaign themes, concepts and language and conducting qualitative research. But its influence extended well beyond this. Labour regarded the basis of modern electioneering as the regular scrutiny and analysis of public opinion and this set the parameters of policy development, shaped advertising strategy, moulded the choice of campaign themes and messages, and provided the yardstick of feasibility. The SCA was responsible for conducting qualitative research whilst NOP handled quantitative polling. Whereas in earlier elections Bob Worcester of

MORI had also advised on the construction to be placed on his organisation's findings, NOP tended to define its remit more narrowly. All quantitative and qualitative data was processed by Gould and the SCA who also acted as the main channel for conveying – and drawing out the implications of – the data to campaign decision-makers. There was a further enhancement of the role of the Agency in 1991 due largely to fortuitous factors. Whilst Mandelson occupied the post, the making of strategic recommendations was mainly the prerogative of the Director of Communications. His (and Kinnock's) nominee for the job after his resignation (his deputy, the Press Officer Colin Byrne) was rejected by the NEC in favour of the TV journalist John Underwood. Underwood was critical of aspects of the Mandelson approach, never enjoyed the full confidence of the leader and felt that his position within the organisation was being subverted by Mandelson's friend and protege, Byrne. In June 1991, never having been able to secure a full grip over his department, he resigned (as did Byrne six months later). He was succeeded by Hattersley's long-time political aide David Hill. Hill had a thorough understanding of the Party and was adept at managing press relations but had little experience with other aspects of his job – and no time to acquire it. With an election likely at any moment, and on the initiative of the Party's General Secretary, Larry Whitty, the NEC agreed to expand the role of the SCA. In theory, this simply enlarged its responsibility for polling, advertising and PPBs. In practice, it meant that the Agency became the key source of strategic recommendations.[25] To construe this (as some have done) as a take-over by the admen would, however, be misleading. The SCA did not escape political control – although that control was not exercised by the NEC. The SCA throughout worked closely with Kinnock's Office, especially Charles Clarke, the chief political aide of the leader to whom it was accountable and who was eager to exclude the NEC as much as possible from the strategic arena. The SCA formulated strategic proposals but these were only put into effect because they were acceptable to the Party leader and his advisors.

But if it is inaccurate to claim that the professionals, rather than the politicians, ran the campaign, it would be equally wrong to conclude that they simply acted as sources of information and expertise. A key service provided by the SCA was the supply of qualitative political intelligence: the role of focus groups was to penetrate below the surface, to apprehend the meaning of views articulated in quantitative polls and to lay bare voter motivations. Qualitative research was a most valuable campaign instrument and had a substantial influence upon Labour's strategic thinking. But given that its interpretation is inherently more subjective in character than that of quantitative research, it follows that control over the supply of such material and of the right to analyse and interpret it are crucial power resources. This control was vested in top Agency members (in particular, Philip Gould and Patricia Hewitt).[26] It appears that only Agency members enjoyed regular access to the voluminous amount of information collected, hence only they were able to evaluate and draw conclusions from it. The evaluations may well have been correct – but the point is that no one was in the position to challenge them. In consequence, the SCA's interpretation formed the Party's picture of the state of public opinion with Gould and Patricia Hewitt emerging as the chief party strategists. Furthermore, strategic thinking and decision-making slipped into the hands of the Agency – in combination with officials from the Leader's Office – in the absence of institutional structures geared to considering issues from a strategic perspective.

The Leader

A central part of the Tory campaign was to exploit the personal appeal of John Major whilst remorselessly vilifying the Labour leader. The belief that Kinnock was not fitted to be Prime Minister was the most frequently cited reason for not voting Labour (Newton, 1992: 151). But in practice, it is extremely difficult to measure its real significance since, for many respondents who had no intention of supporting Labour or didn't want to be troubled to think out a longer response, this may well have been a rationalisation. Having said this, there is no doubt that, in the leadership stakes, he was well behind Major.[27] The Party, as we have seen, was not unaware of the problem and strove to compensate by raising John Smith's profile, but this tactic failed. Smith (and other articulate Labour front-benchers like Brown and Blair) attracted little media attention given TV's tendency to personalise the campaign. This was especially the case with ITN:

Scammell, Nossiter and Semetko report that the election was framed largely as a contest between three men – John Major, Neil Kinnock and Paddy Ashdown. 'Over 15% of its total coverage (compared to just under 7% of the BBC's) was devoted to the leaders' (Scammel *et al.*, 1992: 12). Personalisation is also 'intrinsic to tabloid journalism' and the tabloids virtually all but eliminated other party notables from their pages (Seymour-Ure, 1993).

Our prime concern, however, is not with the direct effect of Kinnock on the election outcome but with the impact of his leadership on the Party's ability to transmit its campaign messages. Persuasion research has demonstrated that the effectiveness of a communication varies considerably according to estimations of its source. Hovland distinguished between two aspects of source credibility, expertise and trustworthiness. Expertise referred to 'the extent to which a communicator is perceived to be a source of valid assertions' and trustworthiness to 'the degree of confidence in the communicator's intent to communicate the assertions he considers most valid' (Hovland *et al.*, 1953: 21). Haas in addition notes the importance of source attractiveness. He suggests that the audience is likely to be more receptive to his messages to the degree to which a source is seen to possess desirable and relevant qualities (Haas, 1981: 144).

As Labour's main communicator, Kinnock suffered from multiple handicaps. Years of endless vitriolic attacks by the right-wing tabloids had severely damaged his standing in the public's eyes (Miller, 1991: 171–2, 175–6). As a result, few regarded him as attractive – he persistently polled less favourably as a potential Prime Minister than either Major or Ashdown and qualitative research suggested that many regarded him as a lightweight, weak and indecisive, a picture closely corresponding to the portrait drawn of him by the tabloids. This may well have affected the way he was perceived on TV. According to psychological research, people tend to develop simplified perceptual structures of individuals, institutions or events as a way of coping with an information-thick environment: once formed, such structures will render their bearers disproportionately attentive to information which validates rather than contradicts them. (Tajfel and Forgas, 1981: 124). Kinnock was almost certainly seen in such a stereotypical way which rendered him unattractive (in the technical sense used above) and hence undermined his authority as a communicator.

But his problems were compounded by his own style as a communicator. His grasp of issues – particularly economic ones – appeared unimpressive, he often spoke in long and labyrinthian sentences difficult to disentangle and, despite constant urging by his advisors, never seemed fully able to cure himself of verbosity. The *Guardian* rather cruelly commented that on television he 'looks physically inhibited, emotionally constipated and vulnerable to the attentions of a clinical inquisitor . . . [He] radiates a chronic confidence shortage' (*Guardian*, 28 September 1991). He tended to compensate for this by a fondness for jargon and a latinate vocabulary as if to convince his audience of his intellectual mastery of the subject. But to his viewers his language seemed opaque, his manner bombastic and his style bewildering.[28] None of this – following Hovland's analysis – afforded any confidence in his expertise, hence further eroding his persuasiveness as a communicator. Nor – to turn to the second of Hovland's components of source credibility – was he rated as particularly trustworthy. Paradoxically, his very success in transforming the Party's programme operated to his disadvantage. Trust in a party or its leader is likely to influenced by the degree that they display consistency in pronouncements and behaviour over time, hence Kinnock's many reversals of policy were likely to leave an impression of unreliability. This was exploited by the Tory tabloids: a man, they charged, who had changed his mind on so many issues – unilateralism, opposition to the European Community, nationalisation, planning and so forth – was hardly someone in whom the electors could repose their trust. Who could be sure, they queried, that he would not renege once more?

It is impossible to demonstrate with any precision the effects of Kinnock's lack of credibility as a source of communications. But Labour's own qualitative research indicated that he failed to carry conviction as a conveyor of economic messages. He was certainly capable of effective performances, but not consistently so and too often his interviews seemed like damage-limitation exercises. Yet (in ever-more presidentialised campaigning) the lengthy interviews, to which party leaders have privileged access, provide – for a party with little support in the press – virtually the sole opportunity to develop its case before a mass audience otherwise rarely exposed to more than the sound-bites on TV news. In these circumstances, the capacity of a Labour leader to employ scarce broadcasting time to maximum effect is a vital one. From this perspective, the problem with Kinnock was less that he lost votes than that he was unable to gain them.

7

THE DETERMINANTS OF
PARTY TRANSFORMATION

How can we account for Labour's transformation? Though the precise mix of factors was not the same in the fields of policy, organisation and strategy, in this chapter we propose to explore the underlying forces that contributed most substantially to the process. Most theories of party behaviour would interpret Labour's metamorphosis into a more centrist, pragmatic, voter-oriented and disciplined party as a functionally necessary response either to the pressure of evolutionary social trends or as the product of a party's rational vote-maximising behaviour.[1] However these theories tend, mistakenly, to assume that the political significance of environmental trends are self-evident and to assume that the key to the pursuit of an optimal vote-getting course is the ability of office-seeking leaders to overcome internal opposition from a more ideological or purposive-minded rank and file (see, for example, Strom, 1990; Schlesinger, 1984). The power resources it could command and the intensity of internal pressures and constraints it faced were indeed important factors determining the capacity of Labour's leadership to procure change. But, as we shall see, the different components of the Party (whether left or right, leaders or rank and file) whose conduct is often explained by theoretical works in terms of simple motivational drives (Strom, 1990; Schlesinger, 1984) is more accurately understood as that of *reflective* beings who adjust their views, goals and conduct as they think about and react to events. So, too, were options always constrained by environmental forces, but equally it is misleading to treat them as independent causal agents which operate in an objective way; the extent to which the implications of these forces were self-evident and hence predetermined the Party's

152

response, varied to a considerable degree, whilst the precise conclusions its leadership drew were always mediated by its frame of reference. As Ross has observed, 'the nature of environmental challenge is never completely clear to partisan actors, since the evolution of the social world is always uncertain and open-ended, shaped in essential ways by the significance with which actors endow it in their various responses' (Ross, 1992: 43–4). In the following discussion, we distinguish then between three types of determinants of change, external environmental factors (political and economic) the leadership's frame of reference (the new strategic thinking) and internal Party considerations (the power structure, internal party alignments and party culture).

THE POLITICAL ENVIRONMENT

After the SDP schism and the formation of the Liberal–SDP Alliance, Labour faced intensified competitive pressure. The Alliance appeared to have sliced off a substantial portion of Labour's traditional constituency and regaining their allegiance became a prime strategic goal. Mounting evidence from the polls indicated that many former supporters felt estranged from Labour because of its 'lurch to the left' which powerfully reinforced the case of Party strategists that a return to the centre was essential if Labour's broken fortunes were to be repaired. Indeed, whereas initially the 'betrayal' of right-wing defectors had benefited the left, the very narrowness with which the Party escaped relegation to third place and the continued competitive strength of the Alliance were powerful arguments for the casting aside of left-wing policies. Whilst the Alliance challenged Labour from the centre, the Conservatives enacted a set of measures – council house sales at discount prices, the heavy marketing of underpriced privatisation shares and income tax cuts – designed to dislocate its core constituency by appealing to the more prosperous sections of the working class. The strength of the Conservative challenge derived from the degree to which it grasped the dynamics of social change and engaged in systematic social engineering to implement its strategy. The durability and appeal of its programme of sweeping legislative change was legitimated through the dissemination and widespread acceptance of 'Thatcherite' definitions of societal problems and notions of how the world works. As a result, in major fields of policy – industrial relations, taxation, housing, industrial ownership – Labour was confronted by new institutional realities that increasingly constrained its freedom of action in reformulating its policies.

The ideological buoyancy of the new right was fortified by the collapse of the states of the Soviet bloc in the late 1980s, and subsequent revelations demonstrated the degree to which the institutions of state ownership and centralised planning were incapable of matching the economic performance of market economies, a lesson rammed home by the enthusiastic adoption by the new democracies of Eastern Europe of privatisation and free market policies. To the right, this demonstrated the economic bankruptcy of socialism, indeed of any disturbance of the market. To those amongst the left who had persisted in believing that the Soviet system constituted a type of socialism, or that a wholly state-owned and centrally planned economy represented a more rational economic model – beliefs which were by no means confined to admirers of the USSR – the revelation of their total failure was demoralising.[2] It seemed to offer incontrovertible evidence that, in the crucial economic dimension, socialism furnished no convincing alternative to capitalism. More clear-sighted elements on the left had reasoned for decades that the Communist world bore little if any resemblance to any western conception of socialism and that therefore events in Eastern Europe were of little practical relevance to the debate in the West but capitalist triumphalism drowned out such voices and the sense that it was capitalism that marched in step with history contributed within the Labour Party to a loss of confidence in the feasibility of socialist solutions to the country's economic problems.

THE ECONOMIC ENVIRONMENT

Most significant of all in setting boundaries for Labour's programmatic exercises was the continued and accelerating globalisation of the world economy. Shortly after the election, Bryan Gould reprimanded the leadership for failing to come to terms with 'the single most important problem facing the left in the post-war economy: the political implications of the internationalisation of capital' (*Guardian*, 28 May 1992). But this was only partially true in that, in a negative sense, they were fully aware of its importance. Fear of incurring the displeasure of the financial establishment, and, above all, of provoking a speculative crisis the moment a Labour victory appeared on the horizon, pervaded the thinking of its economic policy-makers. One of Crosland's basic propositions, upon which much of the structure of the revisionist case rested, had asserted that since, 'whatever the modes of economic production, economic power will, in fact, belong to the owners of political power' (Crosland, 1964: 10), government had the power to regulate economic activity. Whatever the truth of the matter at the time, it was clear that the proposition was no longer valid. As John Smith warned, we lived in an interdependent and highly unstable world 'where capital movements in Tokyo, New York and London can subvert the economic policies of nation states' (*Tribune*, July 1990). Unstoppable flows of capital and currency poured across the exchanges, dwarfing direct investment and trade in goods and services, tirelessly seeking the highest rate of return. Not only were the money markets 'the true commanding heights of the economy' but they had strong political preferences – were, indeed, 'the guardians of the orthodox view', insistent that governments must 'cut budget deficits, reduce social costs and scale back welfare provision' and wholly convinced of the efficiency of private over public action. Further, given their occupation of 'the very pinnacles of the social and economic pyramid' they were well placed to enforce their prescriptions on government (Will Hutton, *Guardian*, 11 October 1993; 22 November 1993; 4 January 1994). Revisionist social democracy had sought to channel the growth increments of a Keynesian regulated economy into social purposes but by the 1980s this was no longer an acceptable economic strategy to the City (and much of industry) which now regarded a willingness to clamp down on public spending, reduce corporate and income tax and above all assign an absolute priority to combating inflation as a measure of economic rectitude. Globalisation and the immense powers of the money markets, fuelled by the world-wide trend to deregulation and liberalisation now heavily curtailed the practical jurisdiction of the nation-state over economic policy.

The soft leftists within the Party concluded that economic policies, however valid in themselves, would not be politically feasible unless a Labour government had the self-confidence and courage to curb the power of the City and (along with other states) take steps to regulate the financial markets.[3] But the leadership demurred. 'We can curse the irresponsibility, prejudice and power of the currency movers', Kinnock declared. 'All of that is justifiable. It is also idle' (Kinnock, 1986: 168); and indeed a strategy of challenging the power of finance would have been inconsistent with his entrenched belief that Labour could only regain office by adopting studiously moderate and 'responsible' polices.Thus Margaret Beckett, the shadow Chief Secretary, sought to assure the City that under Labour, borrowing would be restrained: 'We have to minimise the level of borrowing, and it has to be judged against what is seen to be prudent, not only in the government's own judgement, but also by markets. We have to take account of what the markets will wear' (*Guardian*, 25 February 1992). As we have seen, the leadership supported ERM membership and the existing sterling parity in part to reassure the City and, over the whole range of economic matters, policy was formed with an understanding of what was tolerable to the financial markets – helping to explain the similarity over macro-economic policy between the two main parties at the 1992 election.

LABOUR'S FRAME OF REFERENCE: THE NEW STRATEGIC THINKING

A crucial key to understanding the form that party transformation took was the extent that decisions were strategy-driven, that is, a function of what we have termed the new strategic thinking. Its value and influence lay in the clarity of its conceptions, its internal coherence, the experience and quality of its exponents and the proven commercial effectiveness of its methods. It became the driving force behind Labour's transformation as it emerged as the yardstick against which all initiatives, strategic, programmatic and organisational, were judged. It comprised five main components:

1 A model of electoral behaviour which, in its original form, saw voting as the outcome of three sets of factors: party image, leadership image and policy preferences. After 1987, much more emphasis was given to perceptions of trust, economic competence and governing ability in shaping public attitudes

to the parties. Hence the necessary condition of electoral revival was seen as overcoming the pervasive lack of trust in Labour, lack of faith in its ability to manage the economy and protect living standards and fear that its economic incompetence would lead to massive tax increases.

2 Positioning referred to attempts to corner as large a share as possible of the electoral market by fashioning policies which more closely matched public preferences than those of competitors. More broadly, it entailed adapting to evolving social realities, as they were construed by strategists. They believed that the shrinkage and decomposition of a once-cohesive working class, the determination of the more affluent groups within Labour's natural constituency (such as 'C1s and C2s') to protect their living standards, the greater availability of mass consumer goods coupled with the spread of wider share and home ownership had encouraged the spread of individualistic aspirations and the desire for material gratification to which Labour must respond if it were to gain their support. Reinforced by polling evidence that suggested dwindling sympathy for collectivist ideas and values, and fearfulness of Labour's profligacy as a 'tax and spend party' they concluded that it must move back to the middle ground and abandon or eschew 'old-fashioned' collectivist policies and values.

3 The heart of campaigning was seen as the struggle for control over the agenda. On the assumption that most contentious policy issues 'belonged' to one or other of the major parties in the sense that the voters had a definite and enduring preference for the respective stances they adopted, electoral choice by floaters would be determined by which issues were uppermost in their minds. Hence the principal communications objective was seen as raising the salience of 'Labour issues'.

4 On the assumption that the electorate's agenda was largely set by the issues aired most frequently on television the key to dominating the agenda was seen as securing as much TV exposure as possible. Hence it was vital to communicate one's campaign themes in an orchestrated and disciplined manner and to concentrate on organising photo-opportunities and other pseudo-events to attract the the broadcasters' interest. Securing maximum television attention was also seen as the most effective way of transmitting the campaign message, for unlike traditional grass-roots campaigning, TV-centred cam-

paigns could reach millions of voters speedily and effectively, and being centrally co-ordinated the leadership could ensure that the right themes were being conveyed.

5 On the assumption that they offered the most effective way of designing and disseminating campaign messages and securing an attentive audience, extensive use should be made of advertising techniques such as image-management, symbolic imagery and appeals to feelings and emotion.

The new strategic thinking was of crucial significance because it established the categories into which the mass of opinion research findings could be fitted, and furnished the structured understanding indispensable for the formulation of strategic decisions. Its effect was to implant a powerful bias towards caution and 'moderation'. 'The essence of making Labour electable', wrote Patricia Hewitt, 'is trust. Trust in Labour's leadership, in the team, in Labour's ability to manage the economy competently. Trust that Labour knows where it is going – and trust in the policies to take it there' (*New Statesman and Society*, 4 August 1988). The absence of trust was seen to derive from the Party's reputation for recklessness, profligacy and extremism. The cure followed logically: to provide balm and convey the message that Labour would be safe, pragmatic and prudent, and eschew controversial policies. This entailed, firstly, discarding unpopular policies like unilateralism and the extension of public ownership and, secondly, accommodation to those aspects of the Thatcher revolution that ran with the popular grain, such as council house sales and the new framework of labour law. Coupled with the desire to elicit the approval of opinion-leaders in the media and within business, this approach also encouraged the adoption of a macro-economic position – support for ERM membership at the existing exchange rate and a cautious fiscal stance – not substantially different from the Government's. Furthermore, it fostered a tough disciplinary stance: considerable pressure was placed on those who queried established policy or strategy, since anything that might expose Labour to charges of 'splits' or 'extremism' would undermine its strategy and unravel the gains so painfully made.

THE POWER STRUCTURE

A party leadership can only procure change to the extent that it commands *power resources* and can overcome *internal resistance*. Constitutionally, rights and powers are distributed amongst a range of institutions in the Labour Party: the NEC, Conference, the Shadow Cabinet, the leader and affiliated unions. Historically, the key to effective leadership has been the ability to institute a system of integrated organisational control which binds together, under the authority of the leader, the main centres of power. This system had existed for decades but broke down in the 1970s, primarily because of a shift to the left within the unions which gave the left control over the NEC. One of Kinnock's prime aims was to reconstitute the system and this was successfully accomplished by the second half of the decade through a mixture of skillful manoeuvring, procedural changes and ability to exploit increasingly fluid alignment patterns.

The emergence of a right/soft-left bloc supporting the leader and its progressive consolidation after 1985 ensured Kinnock overwhelming majorities in the PLP, the Shadow Cabinet and the NEC, making available to him their very extensive combined powers over policy and organisational matters. Mastery over Conference was more difficult to obtain since the bulk of votes belonged to the unions, organisations over which the Party could exert, at most, limited suzerainty. Most commentators have assumed that, as interest- and power-maximisers, the 'union barons' have therefore dominated Party decision-making. However, as Minkin has demonstrated, union leaders are best understood as role occupants whose behaviour is heavily constrained by the responsibilities and expectations attached to these roles and by the unwritten conventions governing the Party–union connection (Minkin, 1991). In consequence, on the bulk of both policy and organisational issues, the unions have been content to leave the initiative to and be guided by the preferences of the Party leadership. On a narrow, though important, range of organisational and policy matters (most notably labour law, pay and parliamentary selection procedures) impinging on what they considered to be vital institutional interests, they (or, more accurately, the more left-wing unions) asserted themselves and significantly narrowed the leadership's freedom of action. Otherwise, union co-operation, along with the emergence of a cohesive governing block, by the mid-1980s, helped to reconstitute the structure of integrated organisational control, the institutional basis of leadership supremacy.

The power of the leadership was further augmented by the remodelling of the policy machinery. The extensive network of study groups and policy sub-committees orbiting around the NEC with their large coteries of advisors and specialists – in which left-inclined pressure group representatives and academics often figured prominently – was swept aside. It was replaced by a much more tightly organised system of joint Shadow Cabinet–NEC committees, in appearance a partnership but in practice run by the front bench and the leader. The creation of sub-committees, the recruitment of outside advisors and the input of ideas and policy options were all subject to a degree of regulation by the leadership which, whilst it should not be exaggerated, was rigorous by the recent standards of the Party. The outcome by the end of the 1980s was a policy-making community and a set of policy practices of a character radically different from in the previous decade. In combination with the broader organisational changes referred to above, the new institutional setting afforded the leader, his aides and senior front bench colleagues an unprecedented amount of power in formulating the Party's approach on matters of policy and strategy.

THE PATTERN OF INTERNAL ALIGNMENTS

A major factor operating to arrest and contain centralising impulses is the existence within a party of autonomous and organised bodies capable of countervailing leadership power, which, within the Labour Party, have traditionally been drawn from the left. In the early 1980s, Labour was a deeply polarised Party and as long as the leadership faced a more or less united left, its capacity to procure major organisational and programmatic change was limited. One of the most critical developments in the internal politics of the Party since the mid-1980s has been the virtual elimination of the left as a sizeable, united and autonomous force. This process took two distinct forms: the eclipse of the hard left, and the fragmentation and integration into the leadership circle of much of the soft left.

Perhaps the major single factor responsible for the decline of the hard left was the succession of electoral defeats. Since the

Party entered the 1983 election on what was widely (if not entirely accurately) seen as a 'Bennite' manifesto, its catastrophic loss discredited hard left policies and political strategies. But they were further undermined by the failure of the miners' strike and by the 1987 defeat as many within the Party lost confidence in the ability of Labour to win unless it watered down its policies, and the hard left response of demanding more radical policies and a more combative and class-based strategy evoked little enthusiasm. They had also contributed to their own political demise by their ill-thought out rate-capping strategy and by a series of tactical mistakes, for example the decision in 1988 to field Tony Benn and Eric Heffer as candidates for the leadership and deputy leadership against Kinnock and Hattersley. Designed to rally left-wing opinion, they completely miscalculated and both left-wingers went down to a stunning defeat. The effect of this and similar errors was to accelerate a process of decline underway for a number of years. In the PLP the hard left suffered constant attrition as members alienated by its unyielding political stance quit to swell the ranks of the rival soft left. Thus, for a number of influential left-wingers who had sought to straddle the divide between soft and hard left (Jo Richardson, Margaret Beckett, Clare Short and Joan Ruddock) the decision to launch what they saw as the divisive and pointless Benn/Heffer challenge was the final straw and they attached themselves firmly to the former.[4] At the same time, support for the hard left in the constituencies was steadily falling. According to an NEC analysis, in 1990 votes for hard left candidates for the constituency section of the NEC slipped in all regions outside the South (*Guardian*, 4 October 1990) and from 1984 to 1990 Benn's vote was down by 40 per cent. (P. Kellner in the *Independent*, 5 October 1990). Few hard left candidates triumphed at parliamentary selection contests so the prospect for future representation was grim. By the end of the decade the hard left had lost the capacity to mobilise effective rank and file protest against the relentless drift of the Party to the right. Furthermore, they were almost completely isolated as the soft left swung decisively behind the leadership.

We have already traced the division of the left between hard and soft left currents (see p. 39ff). After 1987, the process of fragmentation intensified as the soft left progressively lost whatever cohesion it had possessed. As early as 1985 one of its adherents, Chris Smith MP, had complained that the soft left was 'unorganised, it lacks direction, it hasn't any coherent definition and it has precious little influence on Neil' (*Guardian*, 11 November 1985). After the 1987 election, disagreement became more intense over the core strategic question of whether to co-operate on at least some matters with the hard left or tie themselves more closely to the leadership. The issue crystallised within the Parliamentary party in a landmark debate in the Tribune Group in July 1987 over the formation of a joint slate with the Campaign Group for the Shadow Cabinet elections. Constructing such a slate had always been a fraught process. In 1984 and 1985 a joint slate had been agreed but not in 1986, helping the right to maintain control of the Shadow Cabinet. But after the 1987 election a flood of new recruits swelled the Tribune Group into the largest in the PLP. Officers from the two left-wing groups managed with difficulty to agree a common slate on terms distinctly favourable to the Tribune Group but after a heated debate the Group rejected the agreement (by 37 votes to 27)[5] not – as had happened in the past – because the conditions were not right but on principle. According to Jack Straw the idea of a joint slate was based on a 'pretence' since left unity 'palpably does not exist' and 'fundamental divisions' now separated the hard and soft left (*Tribune*, 3 July 1987). In fact there were now two tendencies within the Tribune Group, those who continued to regard the hard left as potential allies, at least for limited objectives, and those – which included rising young stars Gordon Brown and Tony Blair as well as Straw – who wanted a firmer *rapprochement* with the right with whom, as soon became evident, they shared much in common.[6]

Ironically, by this time Tribune Group members had at last managed to secure a majority on the Shadow Cabinet, but in practice this had little significance. It was now divided between those who were essentially pragmatists difficult to differentiate from the old right, and the soft left proper.[7] Blunkett lamented that 'to many Party members who yearn for a cohesive and positive left approach, existing groupings inside and outside the parliamentary party appear to have lost that role' (*Guardian*, 17 October 1988) whilst from outside Parliament (though shortly to join it as MP for Neath in 1990) Hain complained there was 'no longer an identifiably coherent Tribune Left' (*Tribune*, 21 October 1988).[8] In response soft left Tribunites (including NEC members and front-benchers) formed a new group, the so-called 'Supper Club'. However, this merely acted as a loose association where like-minded people could discuss matters of common interest and plans for a new soft left organisation (advocated by Hain and others) never got off the ground.

By the late 1980s, many prominent soft leftists had come to occupy senior positions in the Party hierarchy: for example as chair of the Home Policy committee of the NEC Sawyer played a major role in the organisation of the Policy Review and as consensus-builder, and Gould, Blunkett, Jo Richardson, Meacher and several other soft leftists were front-benchers and Policy Review conveners. Even Margaret Beckett, who had in 1981 made a stinging attack on Kinnock for 'betraying the left' over the Benn bid for the deputy leadership, was appointed to the front bench, eventually as an influential shadow Chief Secretary. (All the above, except Gould, had been Bennites earlier in the decade.) Members of the soft left joined the front bench in the hope of influencing Party policy as well as to further their careers but, for some at least, it was *their* views that were more often altered. There were several mechanisms at work here. New responsibilities and new relationships encouraged a different way of looking at politics; the convention of collective responsibility, rigorously enforced by Kinnock, inhibited open criticism; and adjustments in behaviour brought about by new role requirements helped stimulate attitude change, because of the psychological tendency to justify one's conduct (Pfeffer, 1981: 168–9). Perhaps most important of all, many former Bennites changed their minds, because of the conclusions they had drawn after their experience of the strife of the early 1980s, in response to electoral defeats or because they no longer believed that policies they had earlier espoused were workable, politically viable or electorally acceptable. Thus whilst initially, in the mid-1980s, the soft left occupied a midway position, this was only a staging post towards alliance with the leadership. By damaging – probably beyond repair – the unity of the left, the effect of realignment was the isolation of the hard left who, by the end of the 1980s, were left as the only organised yet largely impotent focus of resistance to Kinnock's modernisation project. Given the pronounced advantages that the leadership normally enjoys – in terms of control over power resources such as information, communication, organisation, penalties and rewards – only the existence of organised groups capable of concerting resistance and propagating alternative perspectives can hold it in check and enforce the need to compromise. In the Labour Party, the traditional source of this restraint had been the left, so its decomposition and the marginalisation of its remaining oppositional elements considerably enhanced the leadership's innovating capability.

THE INFLUENCE OF PARTY CULTURE

Rational choice theories that analyse political parties as aggregates of individuals pursuing their own goals fail to appreciate that the behaviour of their members is also shaped by organisational culture.[9] Members do not act exclusively as individuals, but as actors within an organisation with its own independently existing ethos, norms, customs and traditions. The degree to which they imbibe this culture and the effectiveness of internal socialisation mechanisms can have a substantial effect on the attitudes and behaviour of the rank and file. Whilst Labour never generated that strong sense of deep personal involvement, of being a part of a solidaristic and close-knit community that Duverger suggests once typified socialist parties (Duverger, 1964: 129) nevertheless long-standing members often exhibited an affective identification with the Party and an instinctive sense of loyalty towards the leader, which Drucker had identified as a central Labour norm (Drucker, 1979, 12). In the early 1980s, a breakdown in internal socialisation mechanisms and the crumbling of leadership legitimacy produced a rank and file permeated with a deep mistrust and antagonism towards all authority-holders in the Party. The shock of the 1983 election defeat (repeated four years later) helped restore these mechanisms and instigate profound changes in membership outlook. There developed a much finer sensitivity to the effects of their actions on Labour's image and a much enhanced appreciation of the need for Party unity which reflected not only the pragmatic understanding that policies cannot be implemented out of office but also the re-awakening of feelings of loyalty and attachment to the Party in its own right. Further, by the end of the decade members came to appreciate that the prestige and standing of a leader influenced the disposition of voters to back a party and increasingly concurred with the view – articulated by Gould –

that 'the betrayal theory' of leadership had inflicted serious damage on the Party by engendering 'a constant climate of suspicion and grievance . . . which makes it difficult for the Labour Party to maintain the unity and discipline rightly expected of a party seeking office' (*Guardian*, 14 June 1988). This was coupled with a growing awareness of the danger that too sharply or overtly articulated disagreement would be exploited by the press eager to discredit the Party. Orientations to leadership were also modified by institutional change. The establishment of the electoral college, by widening the franchise to the Party as a whole, contributed to replenishing the legitimacy of leadership. Both in 1983 and again in 1988 Kinnock was able to claim that, having granted him a mandate by overwhelming margins, the membership owed him their loyalty – an argument that if never universally accepted, carried conviction in an organisation which regarded majority rule as the basis of political obligation. Ironically, at the moment when reservations about his leadership were at their most intense,[10] challenged by Benn, he won a crushing victory with almost 90 per cent of the vote – allowing him to claim that his leadership had been decisively endorsed. As Anthony Howard commented, the electoral college meant that 'far from being a leasehold, the Party leadership had become a virtual freehold' (*Observer*, 1 January 1989).

Kinnock was well-equipped to capitalise on this new mood. Through his upbringing and experience as a radical young MP he acquired a thorough familiarity with the conventions and folkways of the Party. 'He was', as Peter Jenkins has observed, 'a Party insider through and through, a man who knew a thousand Christian names, at home in every twist and turn of the sub-culture of the Labour Movement' (Jenkins, 1987: 221). As a tenacious and experienced Party manager he knew how to make use of the widespread desire for unity to elicit a positive response to his demands for loyalty and self-discipline – and it was a short step from this to portray public criticism as a threat less to himself personally than to the Party. By the turn of the decade, outspoken critics who at one time might have accumulated political capital by assailing the right-ward drift of the Party were more likely to find themselves condemned (and, like Livingstone who lost his seat on the NEC in 1989, penalised) by exasperated members for being (in Robin Cook's words) 'always on the television slagging the Party off' (*Independent*, 3 October 1989).

This leads us to the most potent factor explaining the altered mood in the Party – the urge for electoral victory. The deep yearning to rid Britain of the much reviled Thatcherite Government fed a growing disposition to compromise and swallow unpalatable leadership decisions if this facilitated victory at the polls. An illustration of this was the surprisingly muted response to the reversal of Labour's defence policy. In the spring of 1988, when Kinnock first appeared to waver over his support for unilateralism, Blunkett had warned that 'if an unnecessary and devastating split in the Party is to be avoided, the leader needs to make clear that his words were not an abandonment of his long-standing commitment, on which so many of his allies have placed their trust' (*Guardian*, 11 June 1988). Kinnock retreated, but only temporarily. At the NEC meeting of May 1989 he passionately and unequivocally repudiated unilateralism, but no 'devastating' split took place as the soft left offered only token resistance and the anticipated wave of protests amongst the rank and file never materialised – despite the fact that Kinnock, by the time of the election had moved very close indeed to the Government's position of pledging to maintain nuclear weapons as long as any other country held them – that is to say it would not even negotiate them away in multilateral bargaining. The total renunciation of what was for many on the soft left virtually an article of faith and which would have precipitated an outburst of outrage within the Party only a couple of years previously was digested – albeit unhappily – with remarkably little public protest.[11] The reversal of policy, and the soft left's acquiescence in it, had nothing to do with the merits of the issue but was due to what one shrewd and experienced commentator called the 'profound, genuine and largely spontaneous change of mood in the grassroots', engendered by the driving conviction 'that nothing, not even the most cherished items of dogma, must be allowed to stand in the way of beating Mrs Thatcher' (Ian Aitken, *Guardian*, 1 October 1990).

8

ASSESSING LABOUR'S CAMPAIGN AND COMMUNICATIONS STRATEGY

THE COMMUNICATIONS CONTEXT

Our analysis in earlier chapters has chronicled the tremendous improvement in Labour's campaigns and communications strategy which in terms of professionalism, meticulous planning and disciplined execution attained an unprecedented and consistently high level of proficiency. The fact that Labour never came close to winning is not in itself evidence that its campaign strategy failed as many other factors determine the outcome of an election. This chapter will open by considering a major impediment to its capacity to diffuse its case, over which it has little control, the nature of the communications context in which it must perforce operate.

By the 1980s the nature of party competition and electoral mobilisation had been fundamentally altered by 'the modern publicity process' which impels rival parties to seek to shape public perceptions of major political events and issues by obtaining maximum favourable exposure for their case in the mass media (Blumler, 1990: 103). Labour's problem is that the media does not afford a level playing field but one with in-built advantages for the Conservative Party for two reasons, which we shall explore in turn: information-management by the Government and the role of the tabloids.

Government communications

The Government has the great advantage of possessing a large publicity machine staffed by about twelve hundred civil servants employed in the preparation and dissemination of official information. In the past, governments have respected the distinction between public information and partisan propaganda, but since 1979 this has become increasingly blurred (Golding, 1990: 95). Government expenditure on publicity and press relations activities has risen massively from £20 million in 1975 to £200 million in 1988, making government the third largest advertiser in the country. Whilst a fair slice of this consists of communicating information of genuine interest to the public (e.g. the AIDS public health campaign) a very large proportion has been used for campaigns which, at best, straddle the boundary between public enlightenment and party interest. Lavish amounts have been devoted to promoting the Government's various privatisation measures. Thus around £20 million was spent on privatising gas, about £42 million on promoting water privatisation whilst the sum spent on electricity was estimated to be over £100 million (Golding, 1992: 507). Not only was privatisation as a policy probably of direct electoral benefit to the Conservatives, but TV adverts helped create a climate of opinion helpful to the Tory cause by associating privatisation with greater efficiency and a glowing high-tech future.

An interesting example of the mobilisation of the government publicity service for partisan campaign purposes was afforded by the 'Action for Jobs' campaign which was ostensibly designed to promote various measures to help the unemployed. According to a Panorama report, the timing and placement of the adverts on television suggested that they were aimed at a relatively affluent audience, a fact confirmed by leaked government documents which indicated they were targeted on 'upmarket groups,' not the unemployed (Tumber, 1993: 40; *Guardian*, 7 September 1989). Furthermore, the 'action' slogan was utilised as a theme at the Conservative Party conference and a copy of its soaring arrow logo appeared soon after in official Conservative publicity material (*Sunday Times*, 30 April 1989). The campaign took place whilst the Tories were seeking to cultivate a 'caring government' image and Tumber concluded that 'it was in effect a public relations exercise to promote the Government rather than a public information one to help the unemployed' (Tumber, 1993: 40). Other instances confirm that this was not an isolated incident. According to the Institution of Professional Civil Servants, which organises government information officers, officials were being asked to prepare explanations of government policy which mirror Conservative campaign slogans and research was being selectively presented to fit Conservative campaign themes and arguments (*Observer*, 23 April 1989).

The media

To communicate to the public, a party requires channels. As a senior SCA member commented: 'Little is direct, most issues are conveyed via the media and the Parties must, therefore, deal through the media to reach their audience.' The most important of these are television and the press. Of these two, the former – more precisely BBC and ITN news with their mass audiences comprising a large majority of the electorate – was the prime channel for the communication of Labour's message. However, two problems limited TV's value for campaigning. Firstly, broadcaster authorities were heavily constrained by the require- ments of balance; this was especially the case for news bulletins which could register points of view but (unlike the press) not promote them. As a result, competing party views were always carefully balanced against each other, in contrast to the vigorous and unabashed partisanship of the tabloids. Secondly, the very nature of news bulletins, consisting mainly of short items with politicians' contributions limited to sound-bites, rendered them an inadequate vehicle for the exposition of an argument.

There are also some grounds to query television's objectivity. Government pressure on television, in particular the BBC (more vulnerable because of the threat of reducing or removing the license fee), intended to induce greater circumspection in reporting government activities, has been well documented (see e.g. Cockerell, 1988). According to recent research into tele- vision coverage of the politically highly sensitive issue of health in 1991 and 1992, the efforts may not have been wasted. After a series of Conservative attacks on the BBC's handling of the issue 'the BBC tended to report developments in the NHS with more caution than ITN and occasionally news commentaries would favour or endorse Government perspectives and down play those of the opposition' (Miller, 1993: 25). Lack of balance also emanated from internal processes. In addition to their specialist correspondents, the news broadcasts rely on outside experts and practitioners to provide informed commentary, especially on economic and financial matters. Their function is to elucidate the significance of complex information, to provide context for the news and to offer an objective, non-partisan judgement about the overall state of the economy and upon the plausibility and credibility of the policies on offer, and in this way they contribute to the formation of mass opinion (Harrop, 1990: 282). The outside practitioners whose views are most commonly elicited are drawn mainly from industrial firms, trade associations, employers' organisations and the financial institutions (rarely, nowadays, from the unions). Although they may adhere to a range of views, they all tend to identify the interests of their organisations with the type of policies more likely to be pursued by the Conservatives than Labour. Further, the choice of experts reflects editorial judgements by the broadcasting hierarchies about what type of people merit the status of 'experts' and, indeed, what views are sufficiently within the mainstream to warrant exposure to the public. Within the last decade or so, the main news channels have been increasingly reliant on economists from the City to enact the role of independent commentators – but as a community City economists and financial executives tend to be more right-wing than their academic counterparts and, according to a MORI poll (cited by Peter Golding in the *Guardian*, 4 April 1992) an overwhelming 90 per cent majority were Conservative in their political sympathies.

The partisanship of the tabloid press was much more overt and unrestrained. They acted as active propagandists – all (except the Labour-supporting *Mirror*) on behalf of the Conservatives. Until recently, most commentators have been sceptical of claims that this mattered much, doubting the capacity of the media to shape opinion to any significant degree. This 'minimal effects' approach holds that, on most issues, voters have clear beliefs or partisan preferences which then act to filter inconsistent information. According to one exponent, 'there is a good deal of selective exposure, and in 'decoding' media messages most voters appear to seek reinforcement for their political positions' (Denver, 1989: 102). The reluctance to attend to other views derives from the desire to avoid cognitive dissonance, 'a psychological state of unease or tension which occurs when an individual encounters facts or arguments that are at variance with his or her beliefs or attitudes' (Denver, 1989: 98).

This theory is, however, based on faulty reasoning. Insofar as voters have firm political allegiances or coherent belief systems, and insofar as such voters are able to grasp the political significance and line of a story, then the minimal effects hypothesis may well apply. But this defines a section of the electorate which, having fixed political beliefs or loyalties, is unavailable for partisan conversion: hence the question of media effects is not relevant. In addressing the question of media influence, we are interested in the floaters, who form at least half the electorate and are the targets of the political campaigners' efforts (Miller, 1991: 4). But since floaters are by definition those without firm political preferences or belief systems, then, logically, cognitive dissonance, in the sense envisaged, cannot apply. Another aspect of the thesis is equally flawed. It claims that the effects of the press are largely confined to setting the agenda: to influence what we think about, but not what we think. But this distinction between 'thinking' and 'thinking about' is, as Entman has noted, a misleading one: 'The way to control attitudes is to provide a partial selection of information for a person to think about, or process' (Entman, 1989: 349). Further, the notion that a particular report from a media source – say about the state of the economy – cannot influence views about the economy implies that the average voter is able to judge whether the report is 'biased' or 'factual'. But the concept of 'factual' makes very little sense when the reader has no independent means of ascertaining 'the facts' and where, indeed, the concept of fact is hardly a relevant one. How does one develop a 'factual' view of the effect of the internal market on the NHS, or the causes of falling educational standards? Given that economists disagree sharply amongst themselves, how can the voter reach a judgement about the real state of the economy, the effects of government policy or the appropriateness of Labour's alternatives? As Entman comments, 'the notion of an audience that actively resists all potentially conflicting information rests upon an assumption of a deeply involved and knowledgeable citizenry, a vision that does not apply to most people' (Entman, 1989: 350).

The theory of minimal effects has recently been challenged by Miller. He has distinguished between two forms of response to the media: they may be used either as a source of information or of guidance on how to vote. Whilst the majority of voters prefer television as a source of issue-information, they draw almost equally upon TV and the press as a source of guidance. This is particularly the case for tabloid readers (Miller, 1991: 118–19, 125). A rather neglected element in Downs' analysis helps explain the importance of this guidance function. He argues that, for the undecided voter, spending a considerable time acquiring sufficient information to make an informed choice is not rational, given the limited effect of a single vote. Hence the voter chooses 'selection principles' which will help him make a decision consistent with his conception of the social state he most desires (Downs, 1957: 212–14). The next step – to economise on time and effort – is to discover a media source sharing these selection principles. This then acts to supply processed information which can be used to make a rational voting decision.

But what if the voter cannot easily find a media source that shares his or her selection principles? Downs suggests here that:

> since the mass media of communication in many democracies are owned or dominated more by higher-income interests than low-income ones, low-income citizens are more likely to receive data selected by principles conflicting with their own than are upper income groups . . . [this] contributes to the general advantage of high-income groups produced by the necessity of bearing costs to obtain political information.
>
> (Downs, 1957: 235)

Voters in higher income groups, then, are able to procure a given amount of information more 'cheaply' than low income ones, but it would not be rational for the latter to seek to attain the same degree of information. He concludes that the effect is to undermine the principle of political equality (Downs, 1957: 236). If Downs' unrealistic assumption that voters' choice of newspapers is motivated by the search for an information source is dropped, then his conclusion acquires added strength, given that voters are yet more likely to be exposed to information organised by selection criteria not their own. It is worth noting here that two newspapers, the *Sun* and the *Star*, have a disproportionate number of readers who are low-income, with limited education, with little interest in politics and with no fixed political allegiances – a mix of qualities which renders them particularly apt subjects for political persuasion (Miller, 1991: 191–2; Harrop, 1987: 47–8). Miller's findings do indeed demonstrate that *Sun* and *Star* readers are especially prone to adjust their views and voting behaviour in line with the right-wing ideology of these papers. Thus he found that they were more likely to approve of the performance of the Government, especially over the management of the economy, a stance closely correlated with Conservative voting (Miller, 1991: 182–4; Sanders, 1992: 201). Overall, when controlled for their party identification and ideological self-placement they exhibited a more positive attitude to the Government's record on major issues. In addition, amongst readers of the *Sun* and the *Star* there was a disproportionate swing to the Tories between April–May 1986 (when Labour led in the polls) and the general election a year later. Far from mid-term criticism of the Tories by the right-wing press causing the Government any lasting embarrassment, it served a useful purpose by enhancing the credibility of the right-wing press (Miller, 1991: 193–5, 207–8 – unfortunately, Miller's research was not repeated for the 1992 election).

Whatever the precise relationship between newspaper reading and the vote, there can be little doubt that the tabloid press substantially impaired Labour's communications efforts, in a variety of ways. Fear of tabloid reaction helped contribute to the defensive temper of the Party's strategy, reinforcing the inclination towards caution and the 'play-safe' approach. All the tabloids (including the *Mirror*) operated as auxiliaries for the major parties, indeed as election times neared, co-operated in the development of campaign strategies – articulating their party's major themes, relentlessly exposing the enemy's weaknesses. The difference was the unevenness in tabloid support, hence accessibility to the electorate, between Labour and the Conservatives. Thus one reason why Tory campaigns – for instance the near-term campaign over tax – proved far more effective in capturing the public's attention was the role played by their tabloid allies in amplifying, elaborating (often with much greater verve and ingenuity) and incessantly repeating their central themes and motifs. Finally, for a Party which, for a range of reasons, was afflicted by a loss of confidence, perpetual tabloid pillorying and ridicule of Labour politicians caused a sapping of morale.

Any political party in shaping its strategy faces a mass of assumptions, beliefs and values which, from the point of view of the strategist comprises part of the reality he or she faces. But from a longer-term perspective than a single election, the formation of public opinion is a dynamic process in which the accumulated encounter with past media messages is of considerably greater import than current political reporting and the mental categories which voters use to process political communications may themselves have been moulded or modified by media influence in earlier years. As Golding *et al.* have recently observed, what really counts is not tabloid *election* coverage but 'the longer term forging of beliefs and values in a culture that may well have become inexorably conservative' (Golding *et al.*, 1992: 8).

LABOUR'S STRATEGY EVALUATED

Unchanging perceptions

As Bowler *et al.* note, little is known about how campaigning affects voters, largely because of the immense methodological problems involved (Bowler *et al.*, 1992: 205). So there are no precise yardsticks by which Labour's campaigning and communications strategy can easily be evaluated. The closest we can come is to examine the extent to which it realised the prime goals it set itself – to regain the electorate's trust, reassure the voters of its ability to manage the economy and run the country and generally refurbish its image.

In earlier chapters, we surveyed voter perceptions of Labour. If we compare these with the findings of post-election qualitative research conducted in 1992 by the SCA, we discover that remarkably little has changed. It was still seen as backward-looking, out-of-touch, economically incompetent, unreliable, vulnerable to an extremist take-over and, above all, not meriting trust. It was associated with the unions, old-style industrial workers, 'minorities', the poor and the losers in life rather than with 'ordinary' people. It was seen as antipathetic to the upwardly mobile, the diligent and the able and there was little faith in its ability to govern, to protect individual well-being or promote popular aspirations.[1] Indeed, there is an uncanny resemblance between these findings and those uncovered by Philip Gould in his report for the Party seven years previously. Further, research conducted by NOP also indicated that the level of public knowledge of Labour's stance on key issues was noticeably lower than of the Tories'.[2] In other words, none of the Party's key campaigning objectives were realised: virtually all the stereotypes and caricatures that had plagued Labour in the mid-1980s continued to do so. In this sense its campaigning and communications strategy was not a success. This bleak picture was confirmed in a further report carried out for the Party in December 1992, after six months of Conservative vicissitudes including 'Black Wednesday'. Despite the fact that the opinion polls suggested a handsome Labour lead, underlying attitudes had hardly altered. The Party was still seen as outdated, untrustworthy and prejudiced in favour of minorities rather than ordinary people (*Guardian*, 5 January 1993).

On the surface, Labour's failure is puzzling. By and large it pursued a 'rational' strategy: making systematic use of polling to supply relevant data, it sought to reposition itself in line with the preferences of the median voter and pursue a moderate and responsible course designed to regain trust. The bulk of Labour's strategists thereby concluded that since the most appropriate strategy was followed, the problem must lie with the 'product' – that is the Party itself. Negative perceptions of the Party had proved obdurate because they, to a large extent, reflected reality: testimony not to the failure of their strategy but to the incompleteness of modernisation. Whilst impressive progress had been achieved in modernising policy, Kinnock had lacked the time and support to transform the Party itself – a fatal weakness since the character and behaviour of its activists, its procedures, its ethos, language and rituals, and its close association with the unions, all alienated the electorate.[3] Further, 'there were too many who went along with the Kinnock project of change not because they believed in the need for change or in the kind of change he was offering, but because they thought it might win.' If the Party was not convinced, why should the voters be (Hewitt and Gould, 1993: 47)?

This interpretation has been endorsed by most media commentators but we shall suggest in this chapter that it is misplaced and that the failure of Labour's campaigns and communications strategy was, in part, due to flaws in its own design. We shall explore its basic assumptions and precepts and conclude by sketching the contours of an alternative.

The interpretation of public opinion

We noted early that a major source of the power of Party strategists was their control over the gathering and interpretation of opinion research findings. They proved to be shrewd and perceptive in their portrayal of public opinion and their qualitative research was often more accurate (with hindsight) than quantitative data. However, their *interpretation* of the research findings – the basis for their strategic recommendations – was less convincing. This was particularly the case of their explanation of the tenacity with which voters adhered to a bleak picture of the Party which endured, the strategists contended, *despite* a well-designed and executed campaign strategy because, ultimately, there was a large measure of truth in it. The Party had only reluctantly and superficially embraced modernisation, it *was* backward-looking and out of tune with the aspirations of ordinary people.

In so doing, they tended to assume that the reasons respondents gave for disliking Labour constituted the *full* explanation of why they did so – rather as if psychologists accepted, without further analysis, as a satisfactory explanation of the behaviour of their subjects the reasons offered by the subjects themselves. The strategists also tended to assume that the perceptions respondents had of the Party constituted an accurate representation of what it was actually like. For example, if respondents stated they felt alienated from Labour, because it was 'the party of minorities' not only was this taken to account fully for their alienation (rather than a description of how they felt) it was also inferred that Labour was, indeed, a party for the minorities: to continue our analogy – rather as if a social psychologist interested in the relationship between, say, the family and his subjects assumed without further ado that the conception of the family as an institution held by the subjects was a fully adequate one. Beyond this, no attempt appears to have been made by strategists to explore *why* Labour was portrayed as a party of minorities and other poorly regarded groups – and why, indeed, this so aggravated people. This might have been understandable if, in terms either of policy or strategy, the Party had geared its appeal to 'minorities', such as blacks, gays and lesbians and so forth, but, as we have seen, this was not the case.[4]

The strategists' understanding of the process of opinion-formation was flawed because it was derived almost entirely from current polling data and it was assumed that only the impact of relatively recent events (such as the Winter of Discontent and the Party's civil war of the early 1980s) was of relevance. This reflected the assumption that images and attitudes stemmed from individual perceptions of current or recent politics – rather than seeing that they were also *social* products emanating from an historically and socially embedded political culture. To illustrate the point, we shall explore the problem of why the Conservatives held a consistent lead on the questions of governing capacity and trustworthiness. Whilst Party strategists never looked beyond beyond contemporary events, research conducted in the radically different (and much more pro-Labour) circumstances of the early and mid-1960s uncovered a not radically dissimilar pattern of perceptions. Thus McKenzie and Silver in their investigation of working class electoral attitudes found that 'many Labour voters readily endorse the Labour Party as the agent of their class interests but widely concede that the Conservatives are generally more competent and qualified in other respects, including the defence of the national interests' (McKenzie and Silver, 1968: 247). Similarly, in the same period, Nordlinger discovered that:

> even among those workers who subscribe to an achievement or class orientation, and who are consequently prone to be critical of various aspects of the social stratification system, there is a hardy respect and admiration for high born, well bred and exclusively educated men as political leaders.
>
> (Nordlinger, 1967: 81)

Both studies agreed that the origins of these perceptions lay in the political culture. According to Nordlinger, 'it is basically the Tory conception of the relationship between Government and electorate which is widely diffused throughout the population' (Nordlinger, 1967:17). The majority of Labour as well as Tory working-class voters subscribed to a form of secularised deference which assumed that those who occupied high positions in the social and occupational hierarchies had developed or demonstrated leadership abilities which rendered them better qualified to run the country than their Labour opponents. As McKenzie and Silver noted, the acquisition of a powerful sense of national identity fostered deference, given 'the extent to which national symbols are drawn from the history and institutions of the privileged elite' (McKenzie and Silver, 1968: 250). The studies agreed that the most important single factor differentiating the political behaviour of Labour from that of Tory supporting members of the working class was not values or policies but subjective class identity and their perception of Labour as the party most likely to promote their class interests. Thus McKenzie and Silver reported how 'Labour-voting workers see themselves as having to choose between class interests on the one hand, and a party that is *fundamentally more competent* and national, on the other' (McKenzie and Silver, 1968: 248; emphasis added). It followed that if class identification weakened, then widely diffused conceptions and values imbibed from the dominant political culture would have greater behavioural consequences. Thus McKenzie and Silver observed that, though its strength may be diminishing, the importance of deference might well persist 'as younger workers encounter a less class-bound society and therefore [become] less insulated from many traditional norms of English life – deference among them – to which they have previously been unexposed or hostile' (McKenzie and Silver, 1968: 251).

Current opinion is not, however, formed only by beliefs acquired from the past. Whilst Labour's strategists tended to assume that images and attitudes derived from an *individual* encounter with the outside world, research into opinion-formation across a range of disciplines has demonstrated that the process is a *social* one influenced especially by social identity, that is a person's 'knowledge that he belongs to a certain social group together with some emotional and value significance of his membership' (Tajfel and Forgas, 1981: 124). It is also a vital element in cognition since, as cognitive psychologists have argued, in the act of absorbing information people engage in 'social categorisation' that is the ordering of the environment through the grouping of persons and events. This process of attributing 'collective traits and intentions to various social groups' functions as 'a form of understanding' and an 'aid to the cognitive structuring of his environment' (Tajfel and Forgas, 1981: 124). Thus social categorisation contributes to the manner in which incoming information is processed, by telling 'the social perceiver what data to look for and how to interpret the data that is found' and hence to the understanding of social and political relations (Taylor and Crocker, 1981: 94; Miller and Wlezien, 1993: 7–8).

Since groups often derive a sense of themselves 'from comparison with and differentiation from the other' the felt intensity of group allegiance is powerfully influenced by the existence of an out-group and these out-groups represent symbols that trigger hostile responses and hence contribute to structuring attitudes (Conover, 1988: 56). Price suggests that the designation of 'out-group' status from amongst a variety of 'other groups' is often a product of negative stereotyping or stigmatising by the media. Their coverage of conflicts shapes people's understanding of the most politically salient social cleavage patterns: 'by depicting *which* groups are at odds over a particular issue, media reports can signal which group identities are relevant to the issue'; and by describing (and often stereotyping) the characteristics of groups and the stance taken by them over issues, they affect how they are evaluated (Price, 1988: 671–3). In the 1970s, many of the issues which received most extensive publicity in the mass circulation papers concerned groups with which Labour was associated, most notably social security 'scroungers', immigrants receiving 'preferential' and 'privileged' treatment and 'rapacious trade union militants'. Not only were they portrayed in a caricatured fashion, they were imputed with motives, interests and behavioural patterns which portrayed them as at loggerheads with 'ordinary people' and the interests of the community as a whole (Golding and Middleton, 1982; Braham, 1982; Seaton, 1991). A crucial point is the gradual, cumulative nature of the process: 'each successive encounter with an issue . . . contributes to ongoing opinion formation. Social identification effects may thus accumulate as message recipients come to understand a given issue in terms of particular social group differences' (Price, 1988: 671–3).

By applying this reasoning we arrive at a radically different explanation of why voters felt alienated from Labour since it seems reasonable to conclude that the continuous and cumulative nature of press coverage – combined as we shall see with Conservative campaigning – contributed significantly to opinion formation and, therefore, to the group and party images voters acquired. Given that a political party is likely to incur resentment if it is seen to favour undeserving and stigmatised groups (Conover, 1988: 54), the association of Labour with a sympathetic

179

stance towards social security recipients, ethnic minorities, gays and so forth was bound to arouse antagonism since any partiality would be seen as excessive and unjustified. In other words, the reason why the perception of Labour as too close to these groups angered and estranged so many of its natural supporters was less a response to its stance, strategy or very character (as strategists claimed) and much more the projection upon the Party of the animosity felt towards these groups.[5]

Approaches to persuasion

Labour's strategy also displayed an inadequate grasp of the way voters received incoming political information. It was rooted in the 'screening hypothesis' which argues that a message is either digested or repelled by the audience according to the degree of affinity it has with existing dispositions. Most theories in cognitive psychology, nowadays, regard the process of audience response as more complex and ambiguous than this:

> Confronted with a blizzard of facts, figures, and images on which impressions are formed and judgements made, the individual must somehow selectively attend to some stimuli and disregard others, group together and categorise events that share common attributes, encode and store in memory some representation of the event, and then retrieve and utilise this information to interpret and structure new stimuli.
>
> (Hill and Lodge, 1986: 60)

Rather than being filtered in a more or less mechanistic manner, incoming information is processed by the recipients 'cognitive structures'. Cognitive structures or 'schemas' can be defined as maps which 'provide the means by which persons organise objects and events in their environment' (Petty *et al.*, 1981: 47). They determine 'what type of information is relevant, and therefore what is noticed, stored and available for later recall' (Lau and Sears, 1986: 352). They act as cognitive templates ordering and rendering intelligible the mass of information which people nowadays encounter. In this way, they enable most people who have only a modest amount of interest in political issues, who lack the contextual understanding or knowledge –

and the incentive to acquire them – to reach an informed or rational judgement, to meet what appears to be a psychological need to impose a pattern on a confusing and complex world, hence enabling them to make decisions with minimal effort. In this sense, cognitive maps are exercises in 'psychic economy' which can be activated when a behavioural response is required (Hill and Lodge, 1986: 71).

This analysis raises serious doubts, given the weight placed upon them, about the effectiveness of two major components of Labour's campaigning and communications strategy – the advertising mode of message delivery and agenda-setting. The advertising mode corresponded to Petty and Cacioppo's 'peripheral route to persuasion'. By 'peripheral route to persuasion' the authors refer to a situation where a voter is persuaded by the style and mode of presentation of a message, that is by 'drawing a simple inference based on various cues in the persuasion context'. These cues may include pleasant music, vivid visual impressions or positive source characteristics such as trustworthiness (Petty and Cacioppo, 1986: 13, 158). In following this route Labour's communicators utilised such techniques as concentrating on the appearance and style of message-exponents and employing sophisticated audio-visual effects to generate (what we have called) symbolic images, crafted to cast the Party and its leaders in an attractive light. Thus, the formal ambience of Smith's 'alternative budget' was designed to project the image of a responsible party well-equipped to enact the role of government and similarly 'Labour was particularly lavish in its deployment of black limousines to promote its image of government-in-waiting' (Butler and Kavanagh, 1992: 167).

This approach can be effective, but, we shall contend, it was inappropriate for Labour. It is, Petty and Cacioppo argue, most likely to succeed on matters of relatively slight concern to its audience, where it can activate or exploit existing beliefs and preferences and where it does not disturb strongly-held sentiments: conditions present to a greater extent with the Conservatives than with Labour. They further suggest that even where attitude changes are accomplished via the peripheral route, they tend to be less 'persistent, resistant, and predictive of behaviour' than changes induced via the active consideration of an argument.' This they refer to as the 'central route' where a higher degree of 'elaboration' takes place, that is where a 'person scrutinises the issue-relevant arguments contained in the persuasive communication' (Petty and Cacioppo, 1986: 217, 7). According to social psychological research, the central route is more closely correlated with a sustained change of attitude and – crucially – with actual modification of behaviour (Perloff and Brock, 1980: 70). By focusing mainly on the transmission of appealing images and sound-bite phrases rather than by elaborating and (as we shall contend below) framing key arguments, Labour adopted an approach of considerably less persuasive force.

A second component of the strategic paradigm, agenda-setting (that is, the view that effective campaigning is about ensuring that the issues that protrude most in the electorate's mind are those that favour one's party) was equally defective as a method of political persuasion. Its rationale as a long-term persuasive strategy[6] was rooted in the theory of cognitive dissonance. As we have noted, this emphasises the limited capacity of communicators to alter attitudes by arguing that the desire for cognitive equilibrium renders people highly allergic to the psychological discomfort produced by exposure to conflicting ideas, inhibiting them from attending to messages incongruent with existing beliefs. Hence, agenda-setting advised against raising issues which 'belonged' to the other side on the grounds that it was better to 'close down' discussion on these issues (such as the role of trade unions or defence) rather than 'feeding' them by engaging in debate. The way Party strategists envisaged achieving maximum salience for campaign themes also rested on a narrow 'stimulus–response' notion of audience reception in which the persistent and orchestrated repetition of a pre-tested slogan or phrase was seen as the best way to evoke a positive response. Thus at one strategy meeting, discussing ways of getting across the key 1992 campaign theme, that it was 'Time for Change', Philip Gould urged everyone 'to use the phrase relentlessly. Every sentence everybody says has to begin "It's time . . ."'. He was convinced, according to the playwright David Hare who attended the meeting, 'that only by saying "it's time, it's time, it's time, it's time . . ." over and over again will they get the momentum that will get them over forty [per cent of the vote]' (Hare, 1993: 201).[7]

We shall contend that the premises upon which the agenda-setting was based were defective. McGuire has contrasted the dissonance model with theories which derive from the cognitive approach that we have outlined above. 'These theories suggest that persuasion involves not so much changing one's attitude or behaviour towards a situation as changing one's perception of the situation to which one is responding' (McGuire, 1989: 56). This approach to persuasion holds that by modifying people's cognitive maps, a communicator *can* secure significant alterations in beliefs. It has been labelled 'framing', which we can define as a communicating strategy whereby communicators 'assign meaning to and interpret relevant events and conditions in ways that are intended to mobilise potential adherents' (Snow and Benford, 1988: 198, 208). Thus, whereas the agenda-setting approach directs persuasive efforts towards influencing what is on the voters' mind, a framing approach emphasises the importance of influencing the cognitive categories used to organise incoming messages. Social psychological and political science research in the US suggests that the main properties of cognitive maps are conceptions of causal, moral and treatment responsibility: that is to say, they consist of notions of what causes a particular problem, who bears moral responsibility for it, how (or whether) it should be remedied and what agent is capable of so doing (Iyengar, 1989). In theory, there may be myriad types of such maps, but both British and American research indicates that notions of causation and responsibility tend to take one of two main forms, the societal or the individualistic (see, e.g., Furnham, 1982a, Furnham 1982b). For the impact of the ideology of economic individualism in shaping attributions of responsibility in the US see, e.g., Feldman, 1982; Abramowitz *et al.*, 1988) Framing, we shall argue, constitutes a more effective persuasive strategy than agenda-setting. To develop this argument a little further, we shall apply it to what Labour's strategists saw as the Achilles' heel of the Party: the electorate's conviction that the Conservatives were more capable of running the economy than Labour.

The question of economic competence

In 1987, the Conservatives earned credit for the (apparently) booming economy yet, five years later, escaped blame when it faltered. The Conservative Government's reputation for superior economic competence was one of the most consistent of quantitative polling findings (see e.g. NOP polls in the *Independent*, 12 February 1990, 19 July 1991, 21 February 1992; and Newton, 1992: 142) and survived intact despite the two worst recessions since the 1930s and a growth, industrial investment, employment and balance of payments performance worse than any of its predecessors since the War. A range of factors are obviously relevant in accounting for this phenomenon, including recollections and folk memories of the last Labour Government,[8] the genuine improvements in personal living standards enjoyed by large numbers of voters, Kinnock's lack of credibility as a purveyor of economic messages, the impact of the media and (as we have seen) a form of deference rooted in Britain's elitist political culture which regards the party of businessmen and the rich as better qualified to run the economy.[9]

Nevertheless, given that the recession followed over a decade of Conservative rule, the relative confidence in Tory handling of the economy remains puzzling. As Newton reflects at the conclusion of a paper on economic voting: 'Given the endorsement of Labour by the *Financial Times*, albeit by a cautious and fine margin, the general public's faith in the economic competence of the Conservatives needs a bit of explaining and understanding' (Newton, 1992). We shall suggest that a major reason for this faith was that the Conservative Party communicated its case more effectively than did Labour. To understand how and why, one must grasp the process by which voters absorb economic information. Most voters lack an informed understanding of how the economy operates or of the linkages between the macro-economy and the political system. (For some striking evidence of voter unawareness of basic economic terms, see Radice and Pollard, 1993.) Given the complexity of economic information, voters will seek to 'reduce information and decision costs and simplify information processing' in conditions of uncertainty by relying heavily on the cognitive mechanism of responsibility attribution. (Peffley *et al.*, 1987: 104). Whether a government is held responsible for economic problems depends on whether they are seen as 'caused by personal or systemic forces' which is, in turn, largely a function of adhesion to an economic individualist or a collectivist ideology. (Peffley, 1984: 285, 286). If a government is not held responsible, then information about economic performance is irrelevant to assessments of competence. However, Peffley adds:

citizen judgements do not occur in a vacuum, but in a political context that is shaped as much by the actions of strategic elites as by objective material conditions. Most voters are highly dependent upon elites for distilling the complex machinations of the macro-economy to more accessible interpretations.

(Peffley, 1984: 288, 289)

In other words, parties do have significant leeway in shaping voters' definitions of economic situations. If we compare the approach pursued by the two major parties, we find marked differences. Rather than simply focusing on their 'strong' issues the Conservatives under Mrs Thatcher set out consciously to reconstruct the political agenda by mobilising popular acceptance for its definitions of economic problems. Quantitative opinion surveys, unfortunately, have generally been limited to elucidating responses to Thatcherite values – and here the consensus has been that it has made few inroads. But this is largely to miss the point for its enduring ideological significance has lain in its ability to recast not the moral sensibility (how things should be) of the community but its 'practical sense' (how things are). Thus the Conservatives' economic discourse always concentrated on identifying those responsible for economic ills – the incompetence of the previous Labour administration, 'profligate' public spending, trade union power, bureaucratic waste and mismanagement, global factors and the dependency culture of the welfare state, and there is evidence that this approach succeeded. Thus Marshall *et al.* found that amongst their respondents over 40 per cent cited as causes of Britain's economic problems explanations consistent with Tory diagnoses; only 13 per cent directly blamed the Government (Marshall *et al.*, 1989: 159). Qualitative research amongst target groups commissioned for Labour in 1985 from MORI indicated that voters were worried by high unemployment, but the world recession, poor management and bureaucratic over-staffing, not the Government, were seen as the main culprits.[10] A strategy paper based on earlier qualitative research concluded that 'Labour has lost the economic argument. People do not believe our policies will work. The Keynesian argument appears wholly unconvincing.' The Tories had succeeded in distilling into a widely accepted 'commonsense' language many of the key precepts of their economic creed: for example, that unproductive public spending must be cut to release resources for more profitable private industries; that market forces, and not the Government, could best be relied upon to rebuild industry and that they practised 'good house-keeping' rather than (as with Labour) borrowing beyond the nation's means.[11] Qualitative research conducted two years later confirmed these findings. Target voter groups appeared to be deeply impregnated with Thatcherite economic and social conceptions: collectivism was associated with inefficiency and regimentation, and poverty was seen as often self-inflicted (Hughes and Wintour, 1990: 137–8). According to quantitative research from Gallup, in the early months of 1992, around 50 per cent consistently held the world recession responsible for the recession in Britain (Sanders, 1992: 200; this, however, was a very restricted choice question). GMA Monitor concluded from its qualitative research into Southern waverers shortly after the 1992 election that 'the Conservatives have generally escaped blame for the current recession. Instead they are thought to be natural managers of the economy who have done a good job over the last decade or so.'[12]

The way in which the Conservatives neutralised unemployment as a political issue offers evidence of the effectiveness of framing. Until the 1970s unemployment was seen not only as something unpleasant for those who experienced it but – electorally more significant – as a measure of a government's economic competence. Thus Butler and Stokes argued that, as a result of wartime experience, 'the mass of the people, as well as the political and economic elite, came to accept a more Keynesian view and to expect government to take effective action against unemployment' (Butler and Stokes, 1974: 391). Mrs Thatcher and her new right advisors understood that if such a belief persisted the argument over economic competence would be conducted on a terrain more favourable to Labour. The issue therefore had to be stripped of its broader political significance by altering its meaning: and this the Tories did by blaming the unemployed for their own plight because of their slothfulness ('get on your bike' in Tebbit's immortal phrase) or their welfare-dependency, by suggesting that the real problem was 'over-manning' and that technological change demanded 'leaner, fitter' industries, or that it was excess pay exacted by trade unions or, alternatively, world market forces that caused joblessness. Because the questions of causal (and moral) responsibility were answered with such clarity, because the explanations often tapped existing sentiments in the popular culture (e.g. hostility to the unions and to 'welfare scroungers') and not least because the Tories had the means to communicate and amplify their message, their object of 'depoliticising' unemployment was achieved. Thus, particularly in the early years of Thatcherism, 'shedding labour' came to be perceived as a necessary purgative to revive the work ethic and the competitive spirit and to end overmanning. In Hugo Young's words, 'by a brilliant feat of propaganda, unemployment ceased to be the proof of economic failure and became the key to economic success' (*Guardian*, 9 September 1986). Subsequently, the Tories were able to convince many voters that it was the result either of personal failings or of global and technological factors out of the control of government (Rentoul, 1989: 109–10, citing Gallup polls and qualitative research). Not everyone accepted this diagnosis, but enough were convinced to help neutralise the issue.

As we have seen, one of Labour's prime objectives in the run-up to the 1992 election was to eliminate the Tory lead on the issue of economic competence. To achieve this, Labour employed a mixture of methods. It relied heavily on presenting an attractive economic team (Brown, Beckett and, in particular, Smith) that could convey an air of authority and studied moderation; it utilised symbolic images – such as the 'alternative budget' – to convey the air of governmental authority. The policy package – carefully pre-tested to ensure public approval – was designed to communicate the theme that, unlike the dogma-ridden Tories, Labour was a pragmatic party pursuing a goal, economic modernisation, to which no one could seriously object. Yet, the Party did not come near to achieving its objective. Its own opinion surveys showed that whilst people agreed with the individual policies themselves (such as a higher priority for training and R&D), the modernisation message as a whole failed to strike them as a convincing response to the problems of the economy – as one senior Party strategist commented, 'it lacked resonance' – and, therefore, to diminish their doubts about Labour's capacity to resolve them.[13]

Party modernisers have argued that this was not because the approach was wrong but because it was not pursued in a sufficiently single-minded and unambiguous manner. Thus Radice contended that Labour had been too ambivalent about the role of the market and private enterprise. Its 'failure to accept the market economy fully has been a major handicap', by enabling the Tories to charge Labour with wishing to install a command economy. To win the confidence of the voters, the Party's task must be to convince them that it can manage capitalism better than the Tories – which entailed unequivocally admitting the success of the market economy (Radice, 1992: 18–19). The effect of accepting this advice – that is, taking the pre-1992 strategy a step further – would, in fact, be quite self-defeating. Firstly, it would help legitimise the notion that the market is the most effective form of economic and social organisation – hence encouraging voters to opt for the party whose support for the market is strongest. Secondly, it would involve asking the electorate to evaluate the merits of the two parties on the most crucial policy area of all not in terms of rival policy prescriptions but of their respective competence to manage the market economy: given that this would entail persuading the voters to disregard the greater confidence that the practitioners of the market economy – industry and finance – clearly reposed in the Conservatives, indeed also to overlook the Tory claim that, as a party of businessmen, they naturally understood it better, this seems a contest Labour is unlikely to win. Finally, the logic of such a response would be to continue to attribute Britain's economic ills primarily to 'Tory mismanagement and incompetence': an explanation which clearly lacked plausibility – perhaps because voters regarded 'blaming the other party' as too obviously self-serving or because it struck many voters as too superficial for what were long-running and deep-seated economic afflictions. Lau *et al.* point out that politicians can 'manipulate the issue positions of voters by manipulating the interpretations to which voters are exposed' (Lau *et al.*, 1991: 670). Where voters are faced with only one interpretation about a policy question and where it is formulated in such a way as to appear credible, they will tend to accept it. Further, 'that interpretation can be persuasive with many voters regardless of their general political beliefs' given that 'cognitively limited' voters won't be sufficiently motivated to devise or search out alternative interpretations for themselves (Lau *et al.*, 1991: 668). Labour's strategic precepts prevented it from recognising that by foregoing any sustained effort to challenge the philosophy and interpretative understanding that underpinned the Government's polices, it vacated a crucial terrain of battle.

REPOSITIONING AND THE PLAY-SAFE STRATEGY

Failure to frame was not simply a matter of communications discourse. Framing was a more natural response for the Thatcherite Tory Party because its economic strategy was located in a coherent theory of Britain's economic failings. As we have seen, Bryan Gould sought to root the Party's economic and industrial strategy in a diagnosis which attributed responsibility for economic failure to the City. This approach was unacceptable to the leadership since it conflicted with the paramount strategic objective of projecting an image of prudence and responsibility. Since one means to achieve these ends was to impress opinion-formers in the broadsheets and amongst TV commentators, amongst whom (as we have noted) City economists were disproportionately represented, attacks on the financial institutions appeared very unwise. In consequence, as Will Hutton noted in a prescient article written in May 1990, defensiveness 'abounds throughout. There is caution on taxation; caution on spending pledges; caution about how much intervention promises to be successful' (*Guardian*, 23 May 1990). When Britain joined the ERM with a clearly over-valued currency, Labour's criticism was (for fear of appearing 'irresponsible') muted and, as the election neared, it stressed that it would stand by the existing exchange rate. This strategy always had its critics within the Party such as Gould and Blunkett, who urged 'a spark of radicalism, a degree of imagination and risk, in offering people a challenge' (*Tribune*, 1 February 1991). Party strategists were dismissive since opinion research indicated that the main bars to voting Labour were lack of confidence in its capacity to govern the country, and fear of hefty tax increases. Demonstrating – in Kinnock's words – 'that we were serious and capable . . . respectable, acceptable and trustworthy'[14] coupled with lacerating Tory misrule seemed the most appropriate way of reassuring the voters and, above all, encouraging them to vote Labour.

This strategy encouraged a tendency to treat the economy as a valence issue, (that is, one where the parties have broadly the same ends but differed over means and priorities, rather than a position one, where there is conflict over goals and values (Butler and Stokes, 1974: 292)) but this may well have been self-defeating since, as Stokes has observed, a valence approach invites voters to choose not on the merits of alternative policies but on the relative capacity of the parties to handle issues – precisely where Labour was most vulnerable (Stokes, 1992: 148–49, 159). It also, Stokes adds, lends itself to negative campaigning where the Tories have persistently proved themselves more proficient.

One can take the argument a step further. Floating voters act, as we have seen, as information-processing economisers and search for some simple means to discriminate between the parties: hence the importance of party ideologies. As van Praag has argued, 'those voters who are only fitfully interested in politics associate a party's identity primarily with the issues a party is prepared to contest with other parties' (van Praag, forthcoming). The clarity and sharpness of the Conservative Party's ideology enabled it to convey a clear understanding of what it stood for, but Kinnock's driving concern to 'get the party back to respectability' (quoted in Hare, 1993: 234) prevented the Labour Party from generating a distinct, well-defined identity. By pursuing a centrist, play-safe course the Party not only deprived potential supporters of motivations to vote for it – as occurred with the Dutch Labour Party, which suffered disastrous electoral losses (van Praag, forthcoming) – but left a vacuum which the Conservatives and the tabloids were able to fill by foisting upon it a host of damaging attributes.

The transmission of the campaign message

A major premise of the new strategic thinking was that television provided the crucial means by which the Party could communicate its message to the wider public. Many of the techniques Labour's strategists deployed with such skill – the manufacture of images, the use of visually attractive symbols, the arrangement of photo-events – were all designed for TV consumption. This emphasis reflected Labour's move towards the 'capital-intensive party', that is, 'one which relies on linkage to potential voters by methods which do not involve personal contact or the extensive use of human labour' (Ware, 1992: 73). However, whilst TV-based communication is indispensable it does have significant drawbacks, such as the political pressure to which it is subjected,[15] its pursuit of its own distinctive agenda and the sound-bite culture of mass-audience news bulletins which limit their utility as transmitters of political messages.[16] Whilst Labour did not ignore local grass-roots campaigning, in line with political science orthodoxy that has for years disparaged its significance, it was regarded as a subsidiary activity useful to shore up support but of limited value as a campaigning aide. Recent research suggests this was mistaken. Thus Seyd and Whiteley conclude 'that an active party membership is absolutely vital to the Labour Party's electoral performance' (Seyd and Whiteley, 1992a: 199). Indeed they calculate that if the average CLP membership had been double its actual size, the Labour vote in 1992 would have been raised sufficiently to have produced a minority Labour government (Seyd and Whiteley, 1992b: 592). Research conducted by Denver and Hands also indicates 'a strong relationship between the intensity of a party's local campaign and the share of the vote that it obtained in the 1992 election' (Denver and Hands, 1993: 11). The precise mechanisms by which a large and active local party membership improves electoral performance is unclear, but activists carry out a range of important campaigning tasks such as door-to-door canvassing and bringing out the vote on polling day. However it may be that their most important function is to act as networks disseminating the Party's message. As Seyd and Whiteley comment, 'they provide a voice in the community, often becoming key opinion-formers in the neighbourhood' (Seyd and Whiteley, 1992a : 220). Similarly, a recent study of the campaign strategies of the wealthy and well-organised German Christian Democratic and Social Democratic parties notes how much emphasis they:

> still place on quite traditional grassroots canvassing and at permanent efforts aimed at creating a positive image of the party in the neighbourhood and community. . . . Even in the age of mass media, face-to face campaigning is still considered to be an important element of a successful campaign. Clearly the image that parties attempt to create through media strategies and promotion of their elites needs validation on the local level.
>
> (Boll and Poguntke, 1992: 140)

SOCIAL IDENTITY AND ELECTORAL STRATEGY

Strategists saw that there was little mileage to be made in seeking to revive old-style class politics since traditional, solidaristic attachments and easily engendered loyalties were clearly decaying whilst a demographically shrinking working class could no longer supply sufficient votes. They recognised that some groups within the electorate were more readily available for mobilisation than others but these groups were seen primarily as aggregates of individuals defined by the possession of shared demographic characteristics but without any necessary sense of group identity or shared collective interests. No sustained attempt was made to direct specific messages to target groups, largely because such groups (and they varied over time) were not seen as very distinctive in terms of outlook or interests and, generally speaking, Labour designed its policies and strategy to attract people from all quarters of society on the assumption that the key voter motivations and concerns were common to the electorate as a whole.

This encompassing approach was as flawed as old-style class politics since whereas the former exaggerates the significance of class identity, the latter dismisses the relevance of all social identities. This displays a failure to grasp that social identity is, in fact, a constitutive principle of social life, one that affords people a sense of personal identity and self-esteem and an awareness of their own place in the pattern of social life (Conover, 1988: 58). We have argued that social identity is an inherent feature of social life structuring the way in which political phenomena are apprehended and policy preferences emerge, hence:

> no political party can hope to play an important political role for any length of time unless the guise in which it succeeds in presenting itself evokes some real resonance in the sense of their own social identity actually held by large numbers of human beings.
>
> (Dunn, 1984: 27)

Social identities, however, are multiple in character and do not necessarily become politically activated. A key question is which out of several social identities does so, for once activated, a 'social identity operates as an interpretive framework. . . . Thoughts and feelings about issues may be produced and organised in quite different ways, depending on the particular group perspective one assumes in approaching the issue' (Price, 1988: 673; see also Milburn, 1991). This the Conservatives recognised since, unlike Labour, their strategy apprehended the importance of the politics of social identity and negative stereotyping. As Leadbeater observed, Thatcherism was 'superb at parcelling people up as outsiders, malcontents or moral undeservers – "on your bike", "moaning minnies", "scroungers."' (Leadbeater, 1989: 15). Thus, the real significance of the Tory and tabloid 'loony left' assault was its invitation to voters to define themselves as white and respectable rather than as working-class, to identify with the Conservatives as the party of whites and the upwardly mobile – and to reject Labour as the party of minorities and the failures. This strategy was pivoted on driving a wedge though Labour's working-class constituency, which effectively involved exploiting, politicising and sharpening existing cleavage patterns and rival social identities, dividing the more affluent, socially mobile and owner-occupiers from the poor, welfare recipients, one-parent families and so forth (Pahl and Wallace, 1988: 139–40). The Government also pursued social engineering to give added force to their strategy seeking not only 'to align [the Tory party] with rising social groups, but to create them, by offering people new cultural identities to live within: as home-owners, shareholders, credit-card holders' (Leadbeater, 1989: 17). In Krieger's words, ' "We" are the solid citizens who feel swamped, can afford to buy the better range of council flats, buy British Telecom stock, and are outraged by the violence of the miners and by welfare cheats. "They" are blacks, the unemployed, the renters, the clients of the welfare state, the strikers.' (Krieger, 1991: 54; some evidence that the strategy had an effect is supplied by Pahl and Wallace who discovered (in their working-class sample) 'a degree of collective identity based on occupation' which expressed itself in support for the Conservatives (Pahl and Wallace, 1988: 137)).

Recent elections in Belgium, Sweden, France and in the German laender indicate that extreme right-wing parties have, using racist appeals, attracted substantial backing from working-class voters – often at the expense of parties of the left – by inducing them to identify themselves primarily as whites or Germans, French and Belgians and to view non-whites as the main threat to their status and well-being. This may also be contributing to the drift of working-class and other voters from Labour. There is already evidence that racist sentiment is common[17] whilst according to Heath *et al.*, the elections of 1983 and 1987 for the first time showed that race (or immigration) as an issue had 'a significant net association with vote' (Heath *et al.*, 1991: 39).[18] All this suggests that a party which foregoes the struggle to foster group identities creates a situation where, by default, other electorally more harmful group identities can be exploited. If this analysis is correct, it follows that, by abjuring a social-identity strategy in favour of an encompassing one, Labour was leaving the initiative to others to depict it in negative group terms, as the party of the socially marginal and – even more damagingly – of 'blacks, gays and extremists'.

What, then, is the alternative for Labour? Dunn suggests that constructing a politics of social identity is a three-stage process entailing tapping or reinforcing a sense of social identity, or seeking a political subject; forging a connection between the social group that possesses social identity and the party as the custodian of its needs and interests, or establishing a political identity; and persuading the members of the social group of one's capacity to determine and defend these needs and interests (Dunn, 1984: 27). What then, of the political subject? The most thorough recent investigation into class found that class remains 'still the most common source of social identity and retains its salience as such' (Marshall *et al.*, 1989: 143). Class, however, is a complex phenomenon which assumes constantly mutating forms. A generation ago, Goldthorpe *et al.* distinguished between 'solidaristic' and 'instrumental' forms of class identity and concluded that the latter was increasingly displacing the former. (Goldthorpe *et al.*, 1968). Since then this trend has almost certainly accelerated. As Evans has observed, 'contemporary class-based consciousness is instrumental reflecting self-interest, rather than based on some sort of affective solidarism, class loyalty, or principled concern with equality'. Hence the working class is unlikely to respond to altruistic or egalitarian urging to support policies that appear to help the disadvantaged at their expense – but the basis does exist for appeals to a sense of collective self-interest (Evans, 1992: 253). Both quantitative and qualitative research indicates that many who complained that Labour had ceased to be a serious vehicle for the promotion of their interests and aspirations continued to identify themselves as 'ordinary working people' (Marshall *et al.*, 1989: 254–5; Devine, 1992).[19] This was actually confirmed by a point made in the Party's own post-election (qualitative) research which reported considerable 'uncertainty about what interests the Labour Party represents – a vote for Labour was no longer seen as a "self-interested working-class vote" '.[20]

But Labour needs to designate a social coalition sufficiently wide to deliver a requisite number of voters and the working class alone does not constitute a large enough political subject. This need not form an insurmountable obstacle since a narrow focus on the the manual working class rests on the false premise that the working-class/middle-class division is the only occupationally based demarcation line of political relevance. Indeed, Westergaard argues that this line is now of fairly limited relevance. A better understanding of the core social cleavage, in terms of the allocation of income, employment conditions, status and autonomy at work, is furnished by distinguishing 'between two broad groups of people whose different 'life-cycle' expectations and experience mark them off from one another'. On the one hand are those – the majority – 'whose lives are confined within the resources and horizons of routine jobs'. They have little discretion at work, little variety, limited promotion prospects and are relatively vulnerable to redundancy and hardship in old age. On the other hand are those with *careers*. They enjoy regular increments of pay, the opportunity for advancement, a degree of discretion and variety at work, decent pensions and less risk of redundancy (Westergaard, 1984: 31–2; emphasis in the original). On the basis of this analysis, job-holders in both manual and routine clerical occupations would compose Labour's 'political subject'.

Its size can be further expanded by adding public sector white collar workers employed in careers as well as jobs. Whilst most commentators (correctly) highlight the problems facing Labour as a result of a receding working-class electorate they too easily assume that they are compounded by white collar growth. In fact, comparative experience indicates that this demographic trend is not necessarily adverse and can offer the potential for electoral advance. As one authority on Norwegian politics has observed, public sector employees 'constitute an increasingly homogeneous ideological grouping which is consistently more 'leftist', more pro-statist, more radically democratic, more environmentalist, and more feminist than employees in the private sector' (Lafferty, 1990: 84). Similarly, in Sweden and Denmark where the left as a whole regularly obtains the support of over 45 per cent of the electorate, they record high rates of support from public sector white collar employees (Esping-Andersen, 1985). In France 70 per cent of public sector employees in education and welfare backed Mitterrand in the decisive second round of the presidential elections of 1988, with majorities or near majorities of other white collar groups voting likewise (Goldey and Johnson, 1988). Research in Britain too indicates that in terms of values, interests and voting patterns the public sector middle class is significantly to the left of its counterpart in the private sector (Savage, 1991; Goldthorpe *et al.*, 1987: 350; Edgell and Duke, 1986; Heath *et al.*, 1991: 95–6).

Secondly, some strategy is required to mobilise and bind this social coalition to Labour – the question of political identity. Tory strategy was rooted not only in modern communications methods but in a grasp of social dynamics, an approach that Labour needs to emulate. This involves not simply monitoring opinion research but engaging in systematic social analysis in order to gain insights into the process of collective interest formation and social attachments in a changing society (Lead-beater, 1989: 17). We can only sketch the lineaments of such a strategy here. Its core must be a 'new populism' that unites the mass of ordinary people – the social coalition we have outlined above – against the 'establishment' or 'the vested interests'. This requires a *political* strategy, that is, one that combines and integrates both programmatic and campaigning elements, expressly designed to solder a new social alliance by appealing to shared material interests – just as the Conservatives sought to build a powerful new social bloc in 1979 by fracturing Labour's working-class constituency and enticing the skilled, more affluent workers through material incentives (lower taxation, council house sales) reinforced and legitimated by value-based rhetoric (attacks on 'spongers', propounding the virtues of thrift, individual striving, etc.). As the Conservatives understood, a new populist alliance can be cemented with a sense of shared identity and interest only to the extent that feeling is mobilised against a credible 'out-group' that is seen to threaten group values and interests (Wilder and Shapiro, 1984: 342). This, in turn, entails a persuasive strategy that concentrates on 'framing' issues, that is formulating and communicating policies that clearly attributes to the 'out-group' responsibility for societal ills and demonstrates how they have acquired an unfair and undeserved share of scarce resources.

The most appropriate candidate for 'out-group' status is that complex of interests that span the hierarchies of wealth, power and prestige and that has benefited greatly from the redistribution of resources since 1979. The new populism would aim to replace the 'two-thirds–one-third' cleavage by one that set the mass of 'ordinary people' against powerful and immensely wealthy elites, above all the financial institutions (the City). As Hutton has commented, 'For the Labour Party, some old fashioned populism about the workings of foreign exchange speculators and life assurance salesmen alike could pay rich dividends.' It both credibly locates the prime cause of Britain's economic decline whilst being 'part of the serious business of building a commonality of interest between the regions, manufacturers, the public sector, and C2s' (*Guardian*, 29 September 1992). The most effective way Labour can limit the damaging fall-out of its connection in the public mind with negatively-rated 'out-groups' such as ethnic minorities and social 'scroungers' (aside from publicly repudiating them – the approach arguably adopted by the 'new Democrats' in the US) is by generating and rendering politically more obtrusive a stronger sense of grievance and resentment against the privileged elites, so that its links with 'minorities' lose something of their salience. An effective social group strategy, in other words, involves highlighting conflicts of interests and challenging the establishment: a high risk strategy but perhaps – given that the play-safe one failed – one with a greater chance of success.

Thirdly, rendering credible Labour's role as champion of 'the people' requires both a relevant and feasible policy package and a mobilising message which can encapsulate what the Party stands for and sharpens its profile. On central economic issues, Labour has no option (in terms both of policy and strategy) but to revive a Keynesian approach (perhaps with a European dimension) geared to achieving full employment and growth and to aggressively defend the principles of industrial intervention, purposeful social action and the developmental state as the spurs to economic dynamism. It has to challenge the prevailing assumptions that the untrammelled market, a regressive low tax regime and the unconstrained profit motive are the key to economic vibrancy, and place the debate on a terrain where it can make some realistic claim to have some economic expertise and competence.

The most appropriate mobilising idea would be community, that is the 'sense of common purpose . . . the willingness of citizens to work together, to share together, to provide for the needs of all' (Blunkett and Crick, 1988: 22). Community, in other words, focuses on the way people relate to each other and hence upon the creation of social and economic arrangements that institutionalise and strengthen ties of mutual and reciprocal obligation, solidarity and fellow feeling. By presenting its legitimating creed as the pursuit of individual liberty, post revisionism found that the supply of collective goods other than those that clearly conduced to expanding opportunities for individuals could only be defended in terms of altruism. In contrast, the notion of community can be employed to convince people that 'the interests of others matter to them, and . . . that their concern will be reciprocated when their own interests are at stake' (Miller, 1991: 354).

In a society where the continuous jostling for individual advancement and the relentless pursuit of personal gain is straining the social fabric, and where social cohesion and ethical codes are being corroded by the ever greater power of the market and the acquisitive society, it seems plausible to argue that a reaffirmation of the ethic of community could provide a rallying cry 'of unmatched potency' (Wright, 1993). But this would entail Labour abandoning its 'play-safe' strategy, its fear of the 'tax and spend' label and conveying an understanding that the immediate individual benefits procured by tax cuts are purchased at the expense of their long-term interests as they find – as they or their parents sicken and age – their resources eaten up by the rapidly mounting costs of private health and nursing homes (*Independent*, 3 July 1993; *Guardian*, 5 August 1993) with vanishing or inferior public services no longer providing a palatable option. It would involve a concerted campaign to propagate the principles underpinning the welfare state, including fair shares, mutual obligation and the public service ethic. The more that people understand that what is of greatest value derives from the quality of communal bonds, the more they appreciate that security and well-being can best be protected by a resilient social fabric, then the more they will recognise that the collective organisation of resources and the supply of collective goods and services is a matter not of altruism but of enlightened self-interest.

9

CONCLUSION

THE TRIPLE CRISIS

Labour in 1979 confronted a triple crisis: ideological decomposition, a breakdown of governance and electoral disintegration. Although in each case the roots lay in the period before 1979, they only reached crisis proportions in the following four years. **The ideological crisis** arose from the disintegration of Labour's ruling discourse, revisionist social democracy. A combination of Keynesian economics, social welfare and corporatist decision-making, it was posited on the belief that socialist goals could be realised within the framework of a largely privately owned regulated market economy. This fell apart under the strains of government between 1974 and 1979 which gave impetus to the adoption of a far more radical programme during the transient period of left-wing ascendancy. The 1983 manifesto, *New Hope for Britain*, promised a massive programme of public sector-led reflation to regain full employment and expand the public services, the reinstatement of exchange controls, the introduction of selective controls on imports, a comprehensive system of planning and withdrawal from the European Community. Although the 1983 programme was not the massive departure from traditional thinking that it has been portrayed to be, it nevertheless displayed a degree of radicalism which was wholly unpalatable to both elite and mass opinion. The left exhibited curiously little interest in the profound changes that were reconstructing the political economy both at home and abroad and undermining the feasibility of purely national-based alternative strategies whilst displaying undue confidence in the capacity of their programme to galvanise public opinion. The sheer scale of the 1983 defeat both discredited the left and its most distinctive policy planks whilst seriously exacerbating Labour's ideological crisis.

Crisis of governance: Labour rests upon a pluralistic constitutional foundation which apportions power to a range of institutions – the leader, the Shadow Cabinet, the NEC, Conference and the larger unions. Historically, the key to effective leadership command has been the existence of a structure of integrated organisational control rooted in a pattern of concurrent majorities in which the right controlled all key institutions, thereby maintaining the supremacy of the parliamentary leadership. This system had existed for decades but broke down in the 1970s as the left gained a majority on the NEC. This was used to hasten the passage of constitutional reforms intended to establish a form of activist democracy whereby MPs were individually and collectively accountable to the rank and file and where policy choices reflected the preferences of grass-roots activists, not the parliamentary leadership. However, even in their heyday the left's influence was balanced by a predominantly right-wing parliamentary party and by a solid block of centre–right unions. Their drive to transform Labour's programme and organisation was countered by the right's fierce resistance, leading to prolonged internal strife and a polarisation which destroyed the cohesion of the Party and debilitated the authority of its leader.

The electoral crisis: in 1979 Labour had suffered a major defeat – the third election in which it had won less than 40 per cent of the vote. To the left, prime responsibility for the Party's plight lay with the record of the 1974–9 Labour Government with its use of pay restraint to squeeze working-class living standards, its cuts in social welfare and its acquiescence in mass unemployment. The key to electoral revival, they reasoned, was the mobilisation of the Party's natural constituency via a programme based on the restoration of full employment and improved public services. To be credible, the programme required a leadership seriously committed to implementing it – which would be obtained only by constitutional changes ending the effective autonomy of the parliamentary party. However the combination of these changes and programmatic radicalisation precipitated the defection of a group of right-wing MPs, the formation of the SDP and the Alliance which, in conjunction with the dramatic retrieval of the Government's fortunes after the Falklands War demolished any hopes of victory at the polls. A poorly composed and mismanaged election campaign snatched disaster out of the teeth of defeat with Labour narrowly escaping the humiliation of being pushed, in terms of vote share, into third place.

ORGANISATIONAL TRANSFORMATION

The Party which the new leader, Neil Kinnock, inherited was demoralised, deeply polarised and virtually ungovernable. He was determined to restore the authority of the leadership and to transform Labour into a cohesive, disciplined and tightly managed political organisation, a task which, in due course, he accomplished. The means used were the subordination of the extra-parliamentary party to the collective parliamentary leadership, firmer control over local party organisations and the transfer of decision-making rights from activist-run CLP General Committees to the more moderate ordinary membership. However, in the first two years of his leadership, Kinnock made little progress in modernising either organisation or policy. His foiled first bid to reform parliamentary selection procedures, his inability to steer the Party's response over the rate-capping controversy and the miners' strike demonstrated his inability to organise the Party's response to externally generated pressures. But the collapse of both the rate-capping campaign and the miners' strike inflicted highly damaging blows on the morale of the left, discredited class-based and extra-parliamentary strategies and hastened the emergence of rival hard and soft left camps. The effect was to facilitate Kinnock's drive to modernise party organisation via the twin strategies of centralisation and direct membership enfranchisement.

Centralisation

Centralisation referred to the accumulation of power by the parliamentary leadership at the expense both of the NEC and constituency party organisations and this process, which began hesitantly in 1983 progressively gathered speed. The NEC-controlled network of policy committees and study groups was replaced by a system of joint NEC–Shadow Cabinet policy committees – or Policy Review Groups after 1987. Further, policy-making resources, in terms of researchers, funds and access to specialist advice, were re-allocated in favour of the leader and the front bench (at the expense of Party Head Office) and the number and influence of front-benchers on the Executive steadily rose. At the apex of the revamped policy process stood a much stronger Leader's Office whose staff played key roles in overseeing policy-making, mustering support for the leader and isolating critics.

In the field of campaigning, communications and electoral strategy, new planning and decision-making arrangements placed overall control in the hands of the leader and the inner circle of strategists. The initial step, taken in 1983, was to vest major responsibilities in the hands of a newly-established Campaign Strategy Committee, chaired by Kinnock and composed of union and parliamentary leaders as well as NEC members. But this soon became a 'dignified' part of Labour's constitution as the responsibility for fashioning and implementing strategy passed to unofficial bodies and informal networks in which the key positions were occupied by top officials from the Campaigns and Communications Directorate (notably Mandelson) senior Shadow Communication Agency members (e.g. Philip Gould) and aides from the Leader's Office (especially Patricia Hewitt and Charles Clarke) with the strategy-making community as a whole answerable to Kinnock.

Finally, a range of measures were taken to subject constituency parties to considerably tighter central control, especially in the realm of parliamentary selection. Largely in response to the the embarrassment caused by the Greenwich by-election when, in the run-up to the 1987 election, a hard left candidate was selected against the advice of the leadership and a safe seat lost to the SDP, the NEC acquired the right to choose by-election candidates. This was employed on a number of occasions to veto the choice of electorally 'risky' candidates, replacing them with the NEC's chosen nominees. In addition, a new disciplinary system was instituted in order to facilitate a crackdown on the Trotskyist Militant Tendency.

Direct membership enfranchisement

Kinnock regarded constituency activists as the main power-base of the hard left and this he sought to dismantle by devolving rights and responsibilities traditionally a prerogative of constituency General Committees to the individual membership as a whole (popularly known as OMOV, one member, one vote). Thus in 1987 the right to select (and deselect) parliamentary candidates was given to an electoral college, in which a minimum of 60 per cent of the vote was cast by individual members and the rest by union organisations. In the following years, OMOV was extended to voting for the constituency sections of the leadership electoral college and the NEC, and for the constituency conference delegate. The rule changes appear to have achieved their objective – most strikingly in the composition of the NEC. By 1993, the last member of the hard left, Tony Benn, had been ejected, four of the seven constituency representatives were from the right and all but Kinnock (by then the former leader) were front-benchers. In conjunction with a major shift in the internal political equilibrium of the Party, the overall impact of organisational reform was far-reaching and the prospect of Labour's extra-parliamentary machinery with its extensive range of policy and managerial powers falling again into the hands of the left was greatly reduced for the foreseeable future. By the late 1980's, a structure of integrated organisational control had been rebuilt. The system of joint policy-making in practice relegated the NEC to the status of junior partner of the Shadow Cabinet. The building up of the Leader's Office provided Kinnock with the means to project his authority more effectively and union leaders resumed their traditional roles as allies of the leadership and stabilising agents. The decomposition and demoralisation of the left, the erosion of the powers of intermediary organisations capable of sustaining dissent produced by the extension of the principle of direct enfranchisement and the leader's tough managerial regime all contributed to the centralisation of power in the hands of the leader and senior members of the Shadow Cabinet.

However the process of organisational reform was neither smooth nor untroubled. Kinnock's desire for a parliamentary selection system in which voting rights were confined to individual members was thwarted by the majority of trade unions who insisted on retaining a say. Instead, key unions like the normally loyalist General and Municipal Workers became more hostile to OMOV as they began to suspect that the reform was designed to reduce the role of the unions in the Party. The upshot was a compromise, the local election college introduced in 1987, but this was riddled with so many faults that, after only having been used once, it was abolished in 1990. A new arrangement was only agreed after the election, at the 1993 Conference when, after intense pressure from the new Smith leadership and amidst acute controversy, a form of OMOV was installed which, nevertheless, gave voting rights to union levy-payer supporters on payment of an additional £3.

As a result of two further major organisational reforms the future shape of Labour's power structure will be more fluid and more difficult to predict. The Constituency share of the Conference vote has been increased to 30 per cent with the possibility, if membership grows significantly, of rising to half – a change which had immediate consequences as, for the first time ever, with the unions evenly split, constituency delegates at the 1993 Conference found themselves being lobbied by the leadership.[1] In addition, the policy-making system has been thoroughly remodelled with the setting up of a Policy Forum and Policy Commissions, with representatives from all sections of the Party. A considerable degree of ambiguity surrounds the questions of how these new bodies will function, their powers and the precise nature of their relationship with Conference, the NEC and the Shadow Cabinet. It is unclear as yet whether it might (as at least some of the modernisers hope) further dilute the influence of Conference with its still numerous trade union contingents or conversely – if the system works well and accrues support – it loosens the grip over policy-formation that the front-bench has succeeded in obtaining.

PROGRAMMATIC TRANSFORMATION

In the aftermath of the 1983 debacle, the new leadership was determined to return the Party to the political mainstream. Though the years 1983 to 1987 witnessed a series of significant policy modifications, the leadership hesitated to challenge fundamentals. In part, this was due to the restraints imposed by the need to maintain the co-operation of the soft left and the more left-wing unions: thus efforts to adjust policy on industrial relations in line with public sentiment made only tepid progress, the abandonment of nationalisation in favour of 'social ownership' was ambiguous and could be construed to entail a substantial extension of the public sector, whilst the lynchpin of the understanding with the soft left was the retention of the highly controversial non-nuclear defence policy. Nevertheless, one should not overlook the substantial programmatic adaptation that did occur: opposition to council house sales and membership of the European Community was reversed, the Alternative Economic Strategy was scrapped, proposals for planning, state intervention and public participation in the investment process were watered down, spending commitments pruned, pledges to restore full employment made much more tentative and industrial democracy vanished from the agenda. Yet all this appeared to make little public impression. The problem here was that, in order to avoid antagonising opinion within the Party, policy shifts were often surreptitiously introduced – which greatly dulled the impact on a sceptical public, since messages which are not congruent with existing perceptions need to be openly and insistently proclaimed to have any effect.

The Policy Review represented a much more systematic effort to resolve the ideological crisis of revisionist social democracy and it did so by accommodating to many of the changes wrought by the Conservative Government. Though Labour's highly publicised conversion to the market economy was interpreted by many commentators as a major ideological breakthrough, the significance of this was much exaggerated. The Party had frequently in its rhetorical pronouncements denounced 'the anarchy and wastefulness of the free market', but in practice the continuation of a market economy was taken for granted by Labour governments. What *was* significant was that the leadership felt obliged to publicly declare its faith in the market. There were a variety of reasons for this, including the triumph of the market economy in the wake of the collapse of communism, the frailty of opposition from the left (who had previously inhibited such outspokenness) and the need to adjust to prevailing economic conceptions in order to acquire economic credibility.[2]

In fact, the two most important substantive policy shifts were over other matters – the retreat from industrial intervention and from Keynesianism. A major bone of contention within Labour's ranks has always been not the survival but the governance of the market, that is the role played by the state in the market. Within the first phase of the Review soft left advocates of the 'developmental' and right-wing exponents of the 'enabling' state differed over the contribution that an active state could make to economic growth. On the premise that the market suffered from serious failings, the former favoured sectoral intervention and powerful interventionist institutions, such as a much-strengthened and proactive Department of Industry. They contended that the power of the City lay at the roots of Britain's manufacturing weakness, and pressed for a significant public role in the investment process. The latter (which included the inner leadership) was sceptical of these interventionist ideas; they doubted whether state initiatives would galvanise economic activity, and rejected the notion that government could 'pick winners.' Defining market failure more narrowly in terms of its inability to supply collective goods like adequate training and Research and Development, they urged a more modest dose of what we called functional intervention, which was designed to contribute to market efficiency by providing, in co-operation with industrial firms, better training, higher quality skills and more R&D. In the second phase of the Review, from the summer of 1989 onwards, the consolidation of leadership power ensured that the views of the enablers prevailed. The old debates over the state versus market, and public versus private ownership were declared outdated and the key themes in Labour's new industrial policy were deemed to be 'modernisation', defined in terms of raising educational and skill standards, investing more heavily in R&D and exploiting more fully advances in technology; and partnership between government and industry, encapsulated in the slogan 'business where appropriate: government where necessary'.[3]

However, the most notable innovation of the Policy Review was the retreat from Keynesianism. Keynesianism was the kernel of revisionist social democracy in that it offered the means by which government could recycle the economic surplus into welfare spending whilst at the same time pursuing growth and full employment as the chief goals of economic policy. Post-revisionists (as we termed them) doubted the viability of demand-management due to its internal deficiencies, insuperable practical problems (such as operating an effective policy of wage restraint) and to altered international and domestic circumstances. Under the influence of Keynesian thinking, revisionist Labour believed that government had the capacity to tackle sluggish growth and encourage higher investment by a combination of boosting demand and fiscal incentives. This was now seen to run too serious a risk of an inflationary upsurge, a rapid widening of the payments deficit and a loss of confidence in the money markets. Instead, private investment was regarded as the key to economic revival. Labour's new analysis (associated especially closely with the Shadow Industry Secretary, Gordon Brown) highlighted problems on the supply-side, notably inadequate training and investment in R&D, and argued that government's chief tasks should be to address supply-side problems whilst promoting business confidence by establishing a stable and predictable monetary framework. Gould's antipathy to the City was – after his replacement by Brown in 1989 – jettisoned in favour of a campaign to secure its approval for Labour's policies and the enhanced reputation for economic responsibility it was believed this would afford. The Party's keen acceptance of ERM membership (at a high exchange rate) completed its conversion to financial orthodoxy. The import of this was much greater than Labour's alleged Pauline conversion to the market. It entailed effective surrender of control over exchange and interest rate policy and – to all intents and purposes – the discarding of full employment as the overriding economic priority (as Gould and other members of the soft left complained in private[4]). As the *Guardian* commented, it made Labour's macro-economic strategy 'virtually indistinguishable from Mr Major's. The ERM will mean low inflation but it also guarantees unemployment of 2.5 million or above for the foreseeable future' (*Guardian*, 26 August 1991).

Post-revisionism adjusted to the changes wrought since 1979: it accepted both the bulk of the new framework of labour law that so tightly constrained the unions and the massive privatisation wave with all its consequences for the government's diminished revenue base and for a further widening in already huge inequalities in the distribution of wealth. It detected no conflict between the pursuit of corporate interests and the public good and, indeed, assumed a broad commonality of purpose with state intervention aimed at 'championing – rather than apologising for – a role for government working with industry as well as acting as custodian for the welfare state' (Gordon Brown, "A New Popular Socialism", *Guardian*, 30 September 1991). The assertion of a basic harmony between capital and labour implied an endorsement of the established structures of power, wealth and authority: with such material advancement as labour might enjoy confined to the benefits accruing from the proceeds of economic growth.

In their reflections on the election defeat, modernisers called for a yet sharper rupture with the past. Labour's 'new economic thinking,' as defined by Gordon Brown, the Shadow Chancellor, and a leading post-revisionist, repudiated 'the old battles between market and state, public sector and private, capital and labour, and the old dividing line on tax and spending' instead putting 'individual potential at the core of Labour's policy' (*Guardian*, 27 February 1993). Other modernisers, unconstrained by high political office, and free to proclaim their case more starkly, complained that the Party had hedged its support for the market and private enterprise with too many qualifications, continuing to exhibit too great a propensity for interventionist schemes, and concluded that Labour must unequivocally affirm its support for the market economy (Radice, 1992: 18–19; Willman, 1992; Lipsey, 1992). 'Only by exorcising its historic claim of replacing capitalism can the party think, and sell, serious thoughts about how to bring capitalist prosperity to all' (Peter Kellner in the *Independent*, quoted Radice, 1992: 19).

TRANSFORMATION OF CAMPAIGNING AND COMMUNICATIONS STRATEGY

The 1983 election saw a ham-fisted Labour Party totally overwhelmed by the highly professional, well-oiled Tory campaign machine – yet the verdict by most observers in both the following elections was that, whatever their outcome, Labour had won the campaigns. Nowhere did transformation proceed as thoroughly and apparently successfully than in the Party's approach to campaigning and communication. In the winter of 1985–6, with the appointment of Mandelson as Director of Communication, the establishment of the Shadow Communications Agency and the expansion of the Leader's Office a powerful strategy-making community had emerged. Equipped by a coherent body of strategic thought (what we have called the new strategic thinking) this influential group of strategists set about re-organising and streamlining campaigning and communication.

Centralised control of communications

The overhaul of Labour's campaigning and communications entailed restructuring the process by which strategy was evolved. An institutional triangle was formed between Head Office, the Campaigns and Communications Directorate, the Shadow Agency and the Leader's Office in which the former two bodies provided the expertise, the ideas and the means to put them into effect whilst the latter furnished the essential political backing – by-passing the NEC which was formally entrusted with the management of election campaigns. As one key strategist later reflected, the real novelty of the new approach lay less in the use of particular techniques (many of which had been applied before) than in the integrated, systematic approach they pioneered – viewing communications 'as a totality'.[5] Viewing communications as a totality came to mean viewing all Labour's operations as a totality in which the requirements of communications and strategy should govern all else.

Modern advertising techniques

The bulk of recruits to the SCA were from the advertising world and this was reflected in the systematic use of advertising techniques in designing and delivering the campaign message. Party strategists exhibited a new organised awareness of the importance of both linguistic and audio-visual forms of communication. Attempts were made to improve the intelligibility of Labour's case by pre-testing language and phraseology; and to facilitate message assimilation by the orchestrated repetition of key messages as encapsulated in easily digested formulations. Considerable use was made of the 'symbolic image' which was designed to burnish the image of the Party and its leader by associating them with qualities – such as modern, dynamic, capable – symbolised by other phenomena. A visit by Kinnock after the launch of the 1992 Manifesto to a computer software firm was aimed to symbolise a forward-looking, modernising party (*Guardian*, 19 March 1992). And one PEB opened 'with the camera swooping from snowy mountains over picturesque villages . . . [to] the throbbing chords of Labour's campaign theme' to symbolise life under Labour. (Butler and Kavanagh, 1992: 176–7)

Communications objectives

Labour's strategic objectives did not vary much between 1986 and 1992 largely because its diagnosis of the problem remained broadly the same: the Party was perceived as backward-looking, out-of-touch and unrepresentative and its reputation continued to suffer from memories of the Winter of Discontent; voters lacked trust in it, feared it would succumb to an extremist take-over and could not match the ability of the Tories in managing the economy, improving living standards and providing effective leadership. On the basis of this diagnosis, strategists concluded that Labour's key communications aims should be to reposition itself in the middle-ground of politics, convince sceptics of its ability to handle the economy and above all, earn the voters' trust.

Changes in policy, presentation and organisation were all used to alter mass perceptions of the Party. Controversial and unpopular policies were shed and, under the aegis of the Policy Review, the Party's move towards the centre was accelerated. Improved presentational techniques were deployed to present a more voter-friendly profile whilst the left was gradually brought to heel and a tough managerial regime installed to allay the voters' fears of extremism. More discreetly, both policy and organisational reforms were designed to demonstrate that the leadership was fully capable of mastering union power. Labour coupled these moves with a two-step effort to influence the electorate by formulating 'responsible' and 'practical' policies designed to impress opinion-formers within industry, the City and the media. In short, the top priority was to convince the electorate that it was 'fit and able to govern' (Mandelson, *World in Action*, ITV, 11 May 1989).

The nature of the appeal

In an influential analysis Marquand has claimed that 'Labour's class appeal has always been fundamental to it' since at its heart 'lay the assumption that the class dimension must, by definition, have primacy over all other dimensions' and therefore working-class interests must be accorded 'a special legitimacy'. This determined the shape of its electoral strategy since ' it was bound by its very nature to stress class identities and appeal to class loyalties' (Marquand, 1991: 22–5). A close inspection of many of the Party's strategy documents from 1983 to 1992 (and interviews with virtually all leading strategists) shows no trace whatsoever of this mode of reasoning: the vocabulary, imagery and cognitive patterns of class analysis, far from being accorded 'primacy' were quite alien to Labour's strategic community. Indeed a class mobilisation strategy of the type espoused by the hard left was never even seriously considered. To the contrary, strategists strove to distance the Party from the trade unions and to deploy an ostensibly classless (that is, middle class) style and demeanour whilst, during actual election campaigns, ensuring that union leaders were kept at arms length and never figured in media-designed events, however considerable the material contributions made by their organisations.

Attempts were made to locate segments of the electorate most likely to be attracted by Labour's message. At varying times, these included 'Green voters', women (seen to hold Labour-type values to a greater extent than men) and C1 and C2 market research groupings. The choice was, however, ad hoc in character, derived from opinion polling and not from class or indeed any other form of theoretical reasoning. In fact, strategists grew increasingly sceptical of the value of classifying the electorate on a demographic basis preferring to identify targets in terms of the nature and intensity of their partisan attachments. Furthermore, and crucially, the assumption was made that floating voters (i.e. roughly half the electorate) were actuated by similar concerns, so there was little point in developing policies designed to appeal to any particular group.[6]

The campaign message

The absence of any specifically class appeal is demonstrated by the nature of Labour's message. Attitudes were seen as loose combinations rather than tightly constrained belief systems: on some issues voters favoured Labour stances (e.g., health) and on others Conservative ones (e.g., defence) the remainder representing contested territory. Since the way weakly or non-aligned electors finally voted would be heavily influenced by the concerns that were uppermost in their minds it followed that a prime campaigning goal must be to control the agenda of political debate. On issues where it was seen to be vulnerable, like defence and industrial relations the Party's tactics were twofold: firstly to discard those polices which most jarred with public opinion, like unilateralism and the repeal of the bulk of Tory trade union legislation and, secondly, to try and keep them off the agenda by avoiding discussion of them. It sought to allay public anxieties by the 'moderation' and 'practical good sense' of its policies, by impressing opinion-leaders and by projecting an image of respectability, trustworthiness and governing stature. It contrasted the ideological zealotry of Mrs Thatcher with its own pragmatic approach, chary of doctrine and wild social experiments, a theme that did not alter after the entry into No. 10 of John Major in November 1990.

This strategy lent the Party's campaigning a defensive tone as illustrated by its reaction to the Tories tax assault in early 1992. It forewent any attempt to highlight the extent to which income, wealth, and power was concentrated in the hands of a small privileged caste and to query the principles upon which so uneven a distribution was based, to expound the social case for increased public spending, or to attack the Tories for redistributing taxation in favour of the rich but instead concentrated on persuading the electorate that the Party could be trusted to act 'prudently' over tax and spending.

Voter receptivity and Labour's campaigning and communications strategy

A widely accepted argument is that Labour lost the 1992 election despite having run 'an excellent campaign' (Moran, 1993: 137). Technically and tactically, its campaign was indeed well-organised and efficiently executed and since there are many other factors that influence the outcome of elections, successive defeats are not in themselves evidence of defects. While it is extremely difficult to assess the impact of campaign strategies, there is nevertheless some reason to query the above judgement. Opinion polls indicated that, consistently, voters were more likely to believe the Conservatives than Labour, as illustrated by the success of the (as it transpired) highly disingenuous Tory 'tax bombshell' campaign; the Party's efforts to improve its image made virtually no progress, and even where voters sympathised with its policies, they distrusted and shied away from it. In short, despite all the improvements in organisation and technique, Labour's communications campaigns persistently made less impression on their audience than did their main opponents'. How can we account for this?

Source credibility

One problem was the leader. Party competition is now highly personalised: party leaders act as the focal points of the campaign, have unrivalled access to television, their speeches are far more extensively reported and their views much more often sought than other politicians. Hence, they become their parties' main communicators. One of the most common findings of research into persuasion is that audience receptiveness to a message varies significantly with the characteristics of the communicator – in particular, his or her perceived trustworthiness, expertise (that is, the degree to which he is seen to be the source of valid claims) and attractiveness (the possession of relevant and desirable qualities). Kinnock suffered in comparison with other party leaders in that he was poorly rated in each of these characteristics. This was in part due to his record, where his major reversals of policy raised questions about his reliability; in part due to his television performances, which were uneven and often lacked clarity; and in part due to hostile press stereotyping, which meant that many people viewed him through a prism that accentuated his negative attributes. The outcome was that the Party messages lacked persuasive power because of the persistent lack of source credibility.

Professionalisation

In the wake of the 1992 defeat the Shadow Agency was blamed by internal Party critics for what was alleged to be a major failing of the campaign – too much glitz and too little substance. This exaggerates the power of the Agency though it did perform important functions. It was responsible for conducting qualitative research, evaluating findings from both qualitative and quantitative polls, providing advertising copy, and advising on advertising and media strategies. Its role expanded particularly after Mandelson's departure from Head Office in 1990 as it operated both as the main conduit for political intelligence and the major source of strategic recommendations. However, claims that the SCA effectively ran the campaign were inaccurate: the power it came to possess was derived in part from its monopoly of professional expertise, in part from its strategic emplacement within the decision-making structure but not least because it enjoyed the full confidence of the leadership to which it was always accountable. Labour's strategic community, we have emphasised, was composed of the apex of the Party's hierarchy – notably the Leader himself and his senior aides and confidantes – as well as SCA members. There was a close meeting of minds between professional communicators and politicians who both adhered to the basic precepts of what we have called the new strategic thinking and were jointly responsible for shaping campaigning and communications strategy.

Panebianco suggests that the impact of the mass media and the emergence of more complex and technical campaign techniques is leading to the displacement of bureaucratic roles by professional ones (Panebianco, 1988: 266; for the application of this thesis to the Labour Party, see Webb, 1992). The growth in Labour's Campaigns and Communications Directorate's influence at the expense of the Policy and Organisation departments, and the heavy reliance of the Party on the professional skills of the SCA members seems to substantiate the thesis. Nevertheless, it is inadequate because it ignores the question of the *type* of professional expertise drawn upon. Although initially the SCA drew upon a wide range of professional skills, it soon came to rely primarily upon specialists from advertising and, to a lesser degree, polling agencies. Holders of other types of expertise – for example broadcasters, print journalists and academic specialists in communications studies, sociology and political science – were, for the most part, ignored.

This was reflected in the Party's approach to opinion-formation. After the election, senior strategists attributed the tenacity with which the electorate continued to adhere to a negative image of Labour to faults in the Party itself: it was, at best, half-hearted in its response to modernisation, clung to archaic practices and rituals, spoke a language and acted in ways

unattractive to the voters and contained undemocratic and alienating structural features, above all, a very powerful union
voice. It remained too narrowly the party of the poor, the
traditional working class and other marginal elements rather
than appealing to the electorate as a whole. This analysis – which
assumed that the the mental picture voters held of the Party was
in large part a reflection of reality – was bound by a limited time
span, lacking any sense of an encompassing political culture or
social context. It assumed that people's views of political objects
could be extracted from their broader web of thoughts and
feelings about the social universe, and were primarily reactions
to political stimuli. In fact, opinion formation is a gradual,
incremental process in which the reception of political information is mediated by people's interpretive frames or cognitive
maps which are, themselves *social* products shaped by the cultural milieu and kneaded by social affiliations. Thus the widespread perception that the Conservatives were better qualified
to rule the country has deep historical roots and probably reflects a secularised form of deference emanating from the highly
traditional British political culture.[7] Furthermore, the estrange-
ment from Labour felt by many voters due to its perceived
association with the poor, ethnic minorities and so forth, interpreted by strategists and modernisers to testify to its unduly
narrow appeal, in fact can more accurately be seen to derive
from the transference to the Party of the enmity and resentment
felt towards these groups.[8]

The strategy of persuasion

Labour's communications efforts also faltered because its two
key precepts, the use of modern advertising methods and
agenda-setting, were flawed. Strategists relied heavily on more
effective packaging and promotion – personal image-building,
photo-opportunities and symbolic images – as cues to communicate Labour's message. Borrowing from Petty and Cacioppo
(1986) we have termed this 'the peripheral route to persuasion'.
This was pursued at the expense of Petty and Cacioppo's 'central
route to persuasion', that is attempting to convince an audience
by elaborating an argument. Whilst the two are not mutually
exclusive, the Party gave greater weight to the former and
(according to Petty and Cacioppo) less effective route.

216

Furthermore, while agenda-setting is the only realistic option during the actual election campaign, as a long-term persuasive device it is defective. It assumed that people respond to political messages by mechanistically absorbing matching communications whilst screening out discordant ones. It rested on a narrow stimulus–response view of the relationship between message reception and conduct where the repeated airing of a strong 'positive' issue (for instance, health) was seen more or less automatically to procure desired behavioural change. It reflected campaign strategists' view that political communication was primarily a matter of devising the best 'product mix' – that is, a policy package with maximum public appeal – and then applying the most sophisticated selling techniques. However, in making a political choice, voters are not (as Labour's strategists assumed) simply registering exogenously determined preferences but reaching a decision about what these preferences were. As Lindblom has argued, voters form 'volitions' shaped by the interaction between their cognitive maps and information circulating within the political system. The key task for parties, then, is not to respond to given preferences but to participate in the forming of these volitions (Lindblom, 1977: 135–7). Political communication (unlike commercial advertising) then can more plausibly be seen as a process whereby the perception of and meaning conferred upon a message – and therefore the response to it – may vary considerably according to the explanatory frameworks or cognitive maps to which recipients subscribe. It follows that to persuade their target audience communicators need to try and alter existing cognitive maps by framing their messages, that is mobilising support by modifying voters' definition of societal problems, their understanding of how problems arise, who is responsible and how they can be resolved. This was the approach the Conservatives followed, providing for instance a free market model of how the economy works, attributing responsibility for economic ills to a range of culprits such as the unions, feather-bedding and global forces. Whereas this diagnosis was widely shared by the public, few were impressed by Labour's counter-argument which, rather than constructing an alternative economic narrative, laid the blame primarily on the Tory government.

Problems of transmission

Labour concentrated overwhelmingly on television as the main means to transmit its case but although invaluable as a conduit for the Party's photo-events and image-management efforts, it did have disadvantages. Mass audience TV news bulletins were wedded to the sound-bite culture, which permitted only condensed and often sloganised particles of party messages to be broadcast; often, for political reasons, this produced bland reporting whilst their coverage of economic information – the central arena of party competition – was frequently framed by outside experts drawn disproportionately from the City, a stronghold of free market and orthodox economic ideology.

Conventional wisdom has tended to deprecate the role of the press claiming that at most, the press influences what people think about, not what they think. This is misleading, for a range of reasons. Firstly, the segment of the electorate that party communicators seek to reach – floating voters – by definition lack strong partisan beliefs and can hardly respond mentally in the way predicted by the 'minimal effects' hypothesis. Secondly, the distinction between 'thinking' and 'thinking about' is a false one, since how people think is bound to be affected by selection of material available to them. Thirdly, the hypothesis rests on the assumption that readers are able to identify coverage which is biased, or which represents a standpoint distinct from their own by some implicit yardstick of truth or objectivity. This rests on the fallacious premise that the realm of facts – for example, the real state of the economy, or the actual impact of the internal market on the NHS – exists independently from interpretation and can be ascertained by the average voter who can thereby discount slanted reporting. Research into persuasive communication has demonstrated that messages will have a greater impact the more frequently and forcefully they are repeated. Tory campaigners could rely on the bulk of tabloids to mould and reinforce over time right-wing attitudes and understandings and then amplify their current election communications. As a result, the mass readership press formed a major impediment to Labour's ability to communicate its message.

Labour's only mass outlet is the *Mirror*. There is now evidence that, under its present management, it is reducing its news coverage and distancing itself from Labour (Roy Greenslade,

Guardian, 10 May 1993). This raises a serious question mark over the Party's ability to transmit its values and policies to a public with a generally low tolerance for politics. The position within the broadcasting media is similarly deteriorating for Labour. With the rapid spread of video use and unregulated satellite channels (owned largely by hostile businessmen) almost inevitably the numbers watching BBC and ITN news and current affairs programmes (especially the generally less politically minded floaters) will fall significantly – with the role of the press as the main news source thereby expanding. In addition, in response to the auctioning system for renewing franchises introduced by the Government as well as to intensified competition from Sky TV, there are already clear signs that ITV channels are devoting more high-audience air time to commercial products at the expense of current affairs programmes and news bulletins (Sir Paul Fox [former managing director of BBC Television and Yorkshire Television], 'TV News on a Hiding to Nothing', *Observer*, 15 August 1993). The outcome is likely to be a trend towards a depoliticised information environment, particularly for working class and routine clerical voters whose allegiance Labour must recapture.

The effect of these trends will be to intensify 'the spiral of silence'. The theory of 'the spiral of silence', developed by Noelle-Neumann, takes as its point of departure the premise that people prefer to align themselves with majority opinion to avoid the danger of isolation. One's confidence in one's views and judgement is likely to be impaired by the sense one is voicing minority views but enhanced by the belief one is running with the grain of popular opinion. Hence there is always a pressure towards conformity and the marginalisation of deviant opinion. The media play a crucial role in this process. 'They provide the environmental pressure to which people respond with alacrity, or with acquiescence, or with silence' (Noelle-Neumann, 1974). Much depends, Noelle-Neumann argues, on the variability of its output: the more homogeneous the media, the more potent its influence. Given an already conservative political culture, given, for tabloid-reading voters, an ever more homogeneous press, and given broadcasting institutions (bound by statutory impartiality and exposed to increasingly fierce commercial pressures) less capable of balancing the press, then the effect of the spiral of silence in delegitimating even marginally 'deviant' left-wing views is likely to grow. In these circumstances, the problems Labour will face in communicating its message will become even more difficult to surmount.

Yet there is one resource that the Party has neglected. The new strategic thinking disparaged grass-roots campaigning as an outmoded and ineffectual form of communication, but recent research suggests that there is in fact a marked correlation between the size and activism of local party membership and electoral success (Seyd and Whiteley, 1992a; Seyd and Whiteley, 1992b; Denver and Hands, 1993). Whilst the precise nature of the causal link is unclear, it appears to be a combination of traditional local campaign techniques and the presence and voice within a community provided by a large and involved membership. This resource, however, has been steadily depleted, partly because – despite periodic recruitment campaigns – membership has stagnated but also as a direct consequence of Kinnock's modernisation strategy. On the grounds that activists were predominantly left-wing[9] the leader as we have seen, sought to strip them of power by tightening central control over CLPs and by relieving them of key tasks. The effect of depriving activists of a range of rights, including control over the selection process and the election of NEC constituency representatives, has been to reduce the incentives for activist participation. Since a core group of activists forms the driving force for recruiting, organising and motivating a wider involved membership, constricting their role seems likely to contribute to what Seyd and Whiteley have described as 'de-energization', that is a waning in both the scale and intensity of participation in the Party (Seyd and Whiteley, 1992a: 202; Seyd and Whiteley 1993).

THE DILEMMAS OF MODERNISATION

The pursuit of modernisation

The organisation and power structure of the Party has traditionally been characterised by ambiguities, anomalies and unresolved tensions and the left's constitutional campaign of the late 1970s and early 1980s can be interpreted as a bid to resolve them by installing what Wright has called 'the party democracy model' (Wright, 1971) in which the leadership would be clearly accountable to the membership, with key decisions made by the rank and file or by bodies elected by them, and with membership involvement in policy-making institutionalised by formal procedures for extra-parliamentary party control. The left was only partially successful and almost immediately, on his accession to the leadership, Kinnock set about unravelling their gains and 'modernising' the Party. Modernisation can be seen as an effort to enhance Labour's ability to compete in the electoral market by transforming into what Wright has described as the 'rational efficient model' (Wright, 1971). This envisaged bolstering leadership power to enable it to formulate a coherent election platform intended to maximise its voting support without the distraction of ideologically minded party activists blocking the return to the electorally crucial middle ground. The Kinnock modernising drive moved the Party significantly closer to the rational efficient model. The most salient innovations included:

- the determination of all key decisions by the inner Parliamentary leadership;
- the subordination of the institutions of the extra-parliamentary party to the Shadow Cabinet;
- policy-making driven primarily by strategic positioning requirements, with vote-getting established as the Party's core function;
- the narrowing of the tasks of lower-level Party bodies to routine administration and vote-gathering, with limited input into policy-making.

However, in one crucial respect, the modernisation drive had faltered. Though agreement had been reached to cut their share of the Conference vote from 90 per cent to 70 per cent, the unions continued to play a major role in Labour's internal life. This was demonstrated by their success in thwarting – in 1984 and again in 1987 – the leadership's desire to institute a new procedure for candidate selection based on the individual member ballot. After the election, and backed by senior modernisers like Tony Blair and Gordon Brown, the new leader John Smith sought to transact this unfinished item of business but immediately encountered stiff resistance from the unions led by the TGWU and the GMB and the issue became a flashpoint in the clash between modernisers and the 'traditionalists'. Ostensibly, the debate was about party democracy and, given the manipulation to which earlier systems of candidate selection had leant themselves, and the problems of enfranchising union political levy-players (the preferred solution of the anti-OMOV camp) the modernisers' case was a powerful one. But a disagreement over what to the great mass of the population was a minor and obscure matter was presented by the media – encouraged by briefings from modernisers – as part of Labour's struggle (in the language used by television news broadcasts as well as the press) to shake free of 'domination by union bosses' This angered the anti-OMOV unions and greatly raised the temperature within the Party.

Whatever the merits of (a relatively minor) matter there seems little doubt that for the modernisers it raised two much larger issues: the distribution of power within and the representational role of the Party. The modernisers' goal of a centralised party with power legitimated by a system of 'direct membership democracy' could not be fully consolidated as long as the unions maintained their considerable stake in internal party processes. Opportunities for leadership control via agenda management, non decision-making and so forth were bound to be less as long as the unions were able to operate as powerful, organised sources of dissent within the Party. As Minkin has observed, 'on constitutional change the trade union majority at the Party Conference formed the ultimate boundary – the ultimate defence that 'the Party' (as opposed to simply its Leadership) should make policy' (Minkin, 1991: 630).

More fundamental still, the unions were held responsible by the modernisers for Labour's old-fashioned and off-putting image. Indeed (by some rather strained reasoning) OMOV in parliamentary selection was presented by otherwise sympathetic commentators as the test case for the seriousness of the leadership's commitment to the modernisation of the Party and of Britain's institutions as a whole. (See, e.g., Will Hutton in the *Guardian*, 4 January 1993; Martin Kettle in the *Guardian*, 8 May 1993; and Andrew Rawnsley in the *Observer*, 5 September 1993). Indeed, it seems likely that the modernisers' real long-term aim was to loosen the organic ties between Labour and the unions in order to reformulate its representational role. A similar debate occurred in the German SPD with whom the unions have close but not formal ties. 'The trade unions were the revisionists' [or modernisers] main target, since they symbolised traditional party orthodoxy including its association with its core working class constituency and its attachment to the principle of social solidarity' (Padgett, 1993: 30). The modernisers – in both countries – wanted a clearer and more emphatic identity for their parties as catch-all organisations seeking to articulate and aggregate a wide range of interests and views. Whilst to the so-called 'traditionalists' (in Britain) unions were part of a wider labour movement committed to the values of social justice, equality and solidarity and the only strong countervailing force to capital, to the modernisers they were Labour's own 'vested interest' which had to be challenged if its transformation into a broad-based party fighting on behalf of ordinary people was to gain credence (see, e.g., Radice, 1992).

Formally the modernisers triumphed in the debate over OMOV, though in conditions which emptied it of a good deal of its meaning. To woo sufficient support (amongst constituency parties as well as the unions) Smith felt impelled to affirm his commitment to the union link and disavow any intention of altering the essentials of the relationship. Even then, the vote was only (very narrowly) won because it had become an issue of confidence in the new leader – and after an impassioned speech in favour of the reform by John Prescott, a defender of the union bond and an outspoken critic of the modernisers. So whilst the modernisers had achieved one aim, it was left unclear what, if anything, the victory signified.

Problems of a Modernised Party

The – predictable – effects of organisational modernisation have been a loss of membership vitality and mounting evidence of organisational atrophy. If present trends continue, the Party may well become 'nothing more than a credit-card organisation' (Seyd and Whiteley, 1993) hence squandering a major cam-paigning and communications resource. Further, essential tests of the democratic credentials of any political party are the tolerance it extends to dissenting minorities and the opportunity it affords for rank and file participation in decision-making. But the organisational transformation achieved under Kinnock has resulted in the reinforcement of oligarchical tendencies in-herent in all voluntary organisations. A range of factors – a more cohesive and institutionally integrated leadership stratum, a fragmented left, procedural changes tightening the leadership's grip over policy-making, the weakening of constituency organisations, a tougher disciplinary code, a pervasive fear that any public articulation of dissent will be exploited by a hostile press – has tilted power decisively in favour of the Party elite.

The transformation of Labour has also produced acute problems of identity: what does it stand for, what are its governing ideals and what distinguishes it from its rivals? In post-revisionism it formulated a new synthesis which adjusted revisionism to an age characterised by the ever-greater penetration of market relations, the fragmenting of traditional class alignments, the growth of possessive individualism and a concerted assault on all collective institutions. The predicament for Labour is how to respond to cultural patterns which fit uneasily with traditional collectivist ideals – whether to adapt or to resist.

The post-revisionist answer was to adapt by redefining Labour's purpose as the enlargement of individual freedom, but this had little public resonance. Under Smith, there was a shift back to emphasising the values of community and mutual responsibility but, given the pragmatic approach to matters of policy and strategy the new leader favoured, these never figured as part of an organised ideological challenge to the Conservatives and the Party continued to be troubled by doubts about its identity and purpose.

POSTSCRIPT

Unexpectedly, with his sudden death in the spring of 1994, the Smith leadership proved all too brief. It is too early to reach any judgement about the nature and effects of his short period as leader though one can make some preliminary observations. His style of leadership was notably more collegial, conciliatory and consensual than his predecessor, displaying a greater willingness to give leeway to Shadow Cabinet colleagues and to seek solutions which accommodated the various viewpoints within the Party. His quality as leader impressed the public and the long period under which Labour lagged behind the Tories in the leadership stakes ended. Whatever the impact of leadership on voter choice, leaders play a vital role in the communications process and it was a role that Smith performed considerably more effectively than the man he replaced. An analysis of voting behaviour outside the province of this study – though the

Government's shedding of election pledges by imposing heavier taxation and disenchantment with Major's leadership seem to be central factors – but by the close of Smith's leadership, Labour's prospects for returning to power seemed considerably better than for many years.

At the time of writing (June 1994) Tony Blair appears likely to emerge as next leader. Bryan Gould, who probably would have been Blair's most formidable opponent, had adventitiously removed himself from the running. Progressively marginalised since 1989, his decisive defeat by Smith in the 1992 leadership election led to a further demotion and, increasingly out of sympathy with the drift of policy, he resigned from the Shadow Cabinet in September 1993 in order to voice more openly his opposition to the leadership's economic strategy. To the dismay of his supporters early the following year he announced his decision to retire from politics and take up an academic post in his native New Zealand.

As a leading 'moderniser' Blair will probably wish to resume the course Neil Kinnock pursued in both strategy and policy with greater single-mindedness than his immediate predecessor. Indeed, most media comment assumed that in the continued 'modernisation' of policy (a term which appeared to mean moving further to the right) lies the key to electoral victory. However, a yet more emphatic *rapprochement* with the established order, and a reliance primarily on the growth dividend is not going to release the resources needed to repair the damaged fabric of the NHS or state education, or tackle the many social problems which have proliferated in recent years. A more radical approach, entailing the adoption of redistributory policies challenging the existing spread of income and wealth, is a condition of achieving any of the goals with which the Party has been historically associated. The risk may well be to provoke the hostility which 'modernisation' has sought to allay but, as Victor Keegan observed, the alternative is that Labour 'will simply lose its soul' (*Guardian* 31 May 1994).

NOTES

PREFACE

1 It is also often argued that Labour has become a European-style social democratic party. (Smith, 1992: 223) Not only is there no such phenomenon as a 'European model' of social democracy, there are very substantial differences indeed between, for example, the German brand, which has in the main stood for a mildly humanised social capitalism, (see, e.g., Padgett, 1993) and the far more egalitarian Swedish brand which has striven to to create a social order rooted in the principle of social solidarity (See, e.g., Milner, 1989; Tilton, 1990; Sainsbury, 1993).

2 We use the term 'modernisation' in a neutral way to denote the type of changes Kinnock sought and achieved, as this became the term that was most commonly employed in party discourse.

3 After a statistical analysis of eleven countries, Kitschelt concludes 'that there is precious little relationship between the relative magnitude of the working class across countries or changes of the working class within countries over time, on the one hand, and the respective electoral performance of socialist parties, on the other.' Only in two countries, Britain and Austria, was there a fairly close correspondence between the decline of the working class and of the left. (Kitschelt, 1992: 313).

1 LABOUR'S MULTIPLE CRISES, 1979–83

1 Healey's view was that the realities of the world economy left Britain with no option: 'So long as we live in an open and mixed economy', he told the cabinet in November 1976, 'we shall depend on the market judgement to determine our future.' Accepting the Loan and its conditions 'is like the Seal of Good Housekeeping: it is regarded by the markets as a guarantee of responsible economic management' (Benn, 1989: 659; Healey, 1989: 435).

2 Labour Party NEC *Labour's Programme 1973*, London, Labour Party, 1973, pp. 13, 30.

3 Labour Party NEC *New Hope for Britain*, London, Labour Party, 1983, pp. 7–8.
4 Ibid., p. 10. Here Shore prevailed in toning down the tighter regime favoured by the left to a simple pledge to re-introduce the pre-1979 controls (Minkin, 1991: 424).
5 Tony Benn *Unpublished Diaries*. Entry for 16 February 1982.
6 *New Hope for Britain*, p. 9.
7 TUC–Labour Party Liaison Committee *Partners in Rebuilding Britain* London, Labour Party, 1983 p. 13.
8 In the words of a Party economic researcher: 'The concern with detailed intervention in industry reflects a shift away from a preoccupation with the spheres of distribution and exchange which is associated with Keynesianism, and which dominated Labour Party thinking in most of the post war period, towards a recognition of the need to pay much greater attention to the nature and control of the process of production' (Sharples, 1982: 80).
9 TUC–Labour Party Liaison Committee *Economic Planning and Industrial Democracy*, London, Labour Party, 1982, p. 4.
10 Ibid., p. 12.
11 Interview. During one meeting of the Industrial Democracy and Planning sub-committee of the Liaison Committee, left-wing NEC member Norman Atkinson commented 'I don't see any rejection of the market mechanism' to which the (then) left-wing Research Secretary had riposted 'Well the Party hasn't opposed the market mechanism for a decade or more.' Benn *Unpublished Diaries*, 21 September 1981. Benn commented that, in response to Atkinson's remark, 'people really looked as if someone had said at a coronation, "Thou shall love thy neighbour as thyself." It was just like shouting in the British museum'.
12 *New Hope for Britain*, p. 9.
13 *Economic Planning and Industrial Democracy*, p. 25; *Partners in Rebuilding Britain*, p. 10. The Party and the unions were agreed in emphasising that the trade union monopoly of representation be retained – which rendered public acceptance of the proposals questionable.
14 Labour Party NEC *Labour's Programme 1982*, London, Labour Party, 1982, p. 9.
15 The manifesto stated it would 'return to public ownership the public assets and rights hived off by the Tories with compensation of no more than that received when the assets were denationalised' *New Hope for Britain*, p. 12.
16 LPCR 1979, p. 186.
17 Ibid., p. 189.

2   TRANSITION: ORGANISATIONAL AND POLICY CHANGE 1983–7

1 LPCR 1983, p. 29.
2 LPCR 1984, p. 66.

3 LPCR 1984, pp. 128, 130.

4 LPCR 1984 pp. 102, 55.

5 Interview with David Dimbleby, BBC 2, 5 December 1992.

6 Later, he was to regret his 'gross mistake' in not calling, publicly and strongly, for a ballot. Interview with Roy Hattersley, Channel 4, 22 May 1993.

7 LPCR 1985, p. 128.

8 The second disciplinary drive against Militant was to be far more effective than the first, but success was achieved only after a long, protracted process in which Kinnock had to use all his powers of persuasion and his steely resolve before he could rally a sufficiently large block of support on the NEC. (For a detailed account see Shaw, 1988: 259–90.)

9 Interview in *Kinnock: The Inside Story* ITV, 26 July 1993.

10 NEC minutes, 12 December 1984.

11 This, by making it possible for Kinnock to speak from the platform on behalf of the NEC, enabled him to deliver his critique of Scargill. Benn recorded bitterly in his diary 'any residual links I had with [Meacher] are finished and done with' (Benn, 1992: 423). Meacher later recalled, 'the vote was exceptionally difficult: I felt torn apart.' Interview on *Kinnock: The Inside Story*, ITV, 26 July 1993.

12 Conference endorsed the NEC policy statement, *Defence and Security for Britain*, which recommended decommissioning Polaris, scrapping Trident, and the unconditional removal of all US nuclear bases from British soil and waters including the Cruise missile, F111 and nuclear submarine bases. Labour Party NEC *Defence and Security for Britain*, London, Labour Party 1984.

13 Right-wing front-benchers like Healey and Hattersley were prepared to swallow their doubts about the decommissioning of Polaris and saw little virtue in Cruise and Trident but harboured serious reservations about the commitment to remove all US bases, which Healey regarded as, in practice, incompatible with membership of NATO (Healey, 1985).

14 As Peter Kellner commented: 'There is nothing like a right of centre Labour Party leader to keep the disparate elements that compose the left together' (*New Statesman*, 1 November 1985).

15 An ingenious 'capital repatriation scheme' designed to attract sterling holdings and to allow for reductions in interest rates was devised by the Party's City and economic advisors in 1985 as a way of protecting an incoming Labour Government from an anticipated flight from sterling (Kinnock, 1986: 68–9).

16 Labour Party NEC *Investing in Britain*, London, Labour Party, 1985, p. 16; Labour Party NEC *New Industrial Strength for Britain*, London, Labour Party, 1987, pp. 6–7.

17 The attitude of the giant TGWU was a particular problem. Its General Secretary, Ron Todd, complained that, 'what Hattersley wants is for us to give him a blank cheque . . . the public knows we could not deliver' (*Guardian*, 30 July 1985).

18 TUC–Labour Party Liaison Committee *A New Partnership. A New Britain*, London, Labour Party, 1985.

19 Labour Party Manifesto *Britain Will Win*, London, Labour Party, 1987.

20 *A New Partnership, A New Britain*, p. 27.

21 *New Industrial Strength for Britain*, pp. 13, 14; *Britain Will Win*, p. 4.

22 TUC–Labour Party Liaison Committee *People at Work: New Rights, New Responsibilities*, London, Labour Party, 1986.

23 *Investing in Britain*, pp. 17, 20–21. BIB-supplied finance would require the development of a 'business plan' agreed between government, management and workforce and would be funded by requiring financial institutions with large overseas holdings to invest a proportion of their portfolios in NIB loan stock on pain of losing fiscal privileges. Ibid., p. 24.

24 *New Industrial Strength for Britain*, p. 14.

25 Labour Party NEC *Social Ownership*, London, Labour Party, 1986.

26 Labour Party NEC *A Future That Works*, London, Labour Party, 1984, p. 15.

27 Interview with Party official.

28 *Social Ownership*, pp. 1–2. The document identified the following priorities for social ownership:

   1 All utilities.These included the recently privatised British Telecom plus the soon-to-be-privatised British Gas.The return of BT to the public sector – a potentially highly expensive operation – would be funded by swapping interest-bearing bonds for shares. Existing BT shareholders would – if they decided to hold on to their stake – in effect be fully compensated by the award of these bonds.

   2 Labour would acquire or maintain a 'strategic stake' in 'vital national industries' (such as oil, aerospace, steel, information technology) 'centres of innovation' and industries supplying the public sector (two were specified: pharmaceuticals and construction).The major responsibility for managing public equities would be vested in a new state holding company, British Enterprise.

   3 In the financial sector Labour would establish a British Investment Bank to provide finance for industry, and a British Savings Bank.

29 Ibid., p. 6.

30 Ibid., p. 2.

31 Interview with Party official. In three key areas, the details of Labour's industrial policy were left vague: the precise criteria which would govern the BE's choice of priorities for intervention; the extent to which it was willing and able to use pressure to achieve its goals; and the amount of funds it would have at its disposal.

32 *People at Work: New Rights, New Responsibilities*, p. 48; *New Industrial Strength for Britain*, p. 7.

33 Interview, *Kinnock: The Inside Story*, ITV, 25 July 1993.

3 LABOUR'S CAMPAIGN AND COMMUNICATIONS STRATEGY 1983–7

1 See, e.g., Labour Party NEC Report 1982, 13–14.
2 Ibid., p. 36
3 NEC Report 1984, p. 10.
4 Interview with Party official.
5 Interview with Party official.
6 P. Mandelson 'Communications Planning: Future Organisation' CSC February 1986.
7 P. Mandelson 'Communications Planning: Future Organisation' February 1986; Butler and Kavanagh, 1988: 63.
8 Interview with Party strategist.
9 Interview with Party strategist.
10 Interview with Party strategist.
11 Interview with Party strategist.
12 Interview with Party strategist.
13 With the advent of the campaign, the Leader's Committee became the formal campaign committee.This had a dual responsibility: 'first, to ensure that the leader and his colleagues had coherent proposals for the campaign's political strategy, based on comprehensive quantitative and qualitative research; and secondly, to establish an organisation which could manage the campaign professionally and efficiently' (Hewitt and Mandelson, 1989: 51). The CMT was in fact in a constitutionally anomalous position: in theory it should have reported to the NEC, but did not partly because the latter was not regarded as sufficiently leakproof and partly because the leadership wanted to exclude it as much as possible from campaigning strategy.
14 The CMT's extra-constitutional status, however, deprived it of political legitimacy and meant that it had to operate in a somewhat clandestine way (in the days before Kinnock could rely on the unswerving loyalty of the NEC). As a result, there was a lack of co-ordination between day-to-day campaigning and preparations for the election campaign with only one or two key figures possessing an overall strategic grasp. Interviews with Party officials.
15 R. Worcester 'Campaign Polling Presentation' May–June 1987. In the run-up to the election a small group of polling analysts was set up consisting of, in addition to Party officials, the journalist Peter Kellner, Andrew Mackintosh (of IFF Research Ltd.) and senior Shadow Agency member Chris Powell. Memo 'Polling Requirements' from P. Hewitt to Leader's Committee, December 1986.
16 'Polling Requirements' Memo to Leader's Committee, December 1986.
17 Interview with Party strategist. For this reason, at least one senior member of the Shadow Agency would regularly attend focus groups to get a sense of how people were thinking. Interview with Party strategist.
18 'Labour's Jobs and Industry Campaign' CSC 1 November 1984.

19 MORI Confidential Presentation to Labour Party Jobs and Industry Committee, 19 September 1985.
20 Mandelson,1988. Mandelson P., 'The Proposed Campaign on Social Policy' CSC 59/25/11/85.
21 Interview with Party strategist.
22 P. Hewitt memo to CMT 21 January 1986. Emphasis in the original.
23 SCA 'Defence Strategy' October 1986.
24 P. Mandelson 'General Election Strategy' 27 October 1986.
25 Thus during the election, the morning press conferences, the speeches of leading campaigners and the schedule of Kinnock's visits were all designed to illustrate a common theme.
26 T. Mainwaring 'First Thoughts on a "Jobs and Industry Campaign"' RD 2932, February 1984.
27 NEC Report 1985, p. 104.
28 CSC 38/19/11/84 October 1984, CSC 31/14/1/85 December 1984.
29 LPCR 1985, p. 124.
30 Ibid.
31 'Media Presentation and Campaign Activities' RD 3162 October 1984.
32 'The Second Phase of the Campaign' RD 3556.
33 Interview with Party strategist.
34 The proposal, moved by Cook, was agreed only by 12 votes to 8. CSC Minutes, 16 July 1985.
35 SCA The Labour Party Social Policy Campaign 'Second Stage of Research and Recommendations', 27 February 1986; Report of Qualitative Research presentation to Social Policy Campaign Group, February 1986; *Guardian*, 31 January 1986.
36 Proposed Campaign on Social Policy CSC 59/25/11/85; Kinnock, *Guardian*, 12 September 1986; LPCR 1985 pp. 122–3.
37 R. Barr, C. Fisher and D. Mattinson 'Development of a Campaign Theme' CSC 62/25/11/85 November 1985. Kinnock was much taken by the concept of 'symbolic policies' designed, he claimed, 'to illustrate our commitment to general values'. The rationale for this was that – as opinion research had shown – 'in the abstract, people found it difficult to see how our values related to their daily lives. Linked to particular policies, those values came alive' (Hughes and Wintour, 1990: 57–8).
38 MORI Presentation to Labour Party Jobs and Industry Campaign Committee, 19 September 1985; P. Mandelson 'Campaign Strategy' 1987 CSC 2/24/11/86.
39 SCA Transcript 'Second Stage of Research and Recommendations' 27 February 1986. Interestingly, the concept of the 'enabling state' was found to arouse anxiety about excessive state power.
40 Interviews with Party strategists; *Guardian*, 9 January 1987. It was also totally overshadowed by the Tory/tabloid 'loony left' offensive.
41 R. Cook 'Towards 1987'.CSC 16/7/85 July 1985.
42 M. Gapes, 1988: p. 101.'Proposed Campaign on International/Defence Issues.' Internal International Department paper. Undated.

43 'Public Opinion and Defence' PD 190 February 1986. (See also K. Young, 1988: 79; and Baylis and Balsom, 1986: 190).

44 SCA 'Defence Strategy' October 1986.

45 Ibid.

46 Labour Party. *British Defence Policy: the Choice*, December 1986 (campaign leaflet). Labour Party *The Power to Defend our Country*, 1987, Party Political Broadcast 3 December 1986 (transcript). The main campaign document, *The Power To Defend our Country*, was drafted under the auspices of Mandelson in close consultation with Healey, Kinnock and Davies (interview with Party official) and though ostensibly a campaigning statement, it contained significant modifications in tone, emphasis and content which were largely a response to the recommendations of the SCA. The most notable policy adjustment was the pledge that all savings from the cancellation of Trident, which *Defence and Security in Britain* had envisaged would be used for civilian use, would now all go to expanding conventional military spending (*The Power to Defend our Country*, p. 7). The point was underlined by the 1987 Manifesto which intimated that under Labour no cuts in defence spending could be anticipated. As Hugo Young observed 'an ironic result of the definitive rejection of a nuclear policy has been the elevation of defence spending into a key socialist priority' (*Guardian*, 11 December 1986).

47 MORI confidential memo to NEC January 1987.

48 Although the non-nuclear policy was later dropped by Labour, it transpired that the basic point made by the defence campaign – that Britain could not sustain both an adequate conventional force and its nuclear weaponry – was proved correct. Ironically, by the time this became evident beyond any doubt, Labour was committed to the retention of Trident. (*Guardian*, 19 October 1993).

49 SCA 'Labour Party – Policy and Advertising Research Summary Report March 1987. Even officials in Conservative Central Office experienced 'almost a sense of shock that Labour had been made to appear so vulnerable so quickly' (Tyler, 1987: 73).

50 'The Proposed Campaign on Social Policy' CSC 59/25/11/85, November 1985. Hewitt and Mandelson, 1989: 51.

51 Interview with Party strategist. At one point, consideration was given to switching the focus to Labour's Achilles' heel of economic competence but it was decided to stick (as one influential figure put it) with 'the remorselessly strategic decision to play to our strengths' Interview Party strategist.

52 Gould, Herd and Powell, 1989: 73.

53 Hewitt memo to Kinnock, 17 November 1986. P Mandelson 'General Election Strategy' 27 October 1986.

54 Mandelson 'General Election Strategy' 27 October 1986.

55 The proportion of non-Labour voters giving as their reason 'Labour's defence policy is dangerous' rose from 21 per cent at the start of the campaign to 52 per cent at its close (Dunleavy, 1988: 115).

4 A PALER SHADE OF PINK: THE POLICY REVIEW

1 NEC Report 1987, p. 3.
2 Labour Party NEC *Labour and Britain in the 1990s*, London, Labour Party 1988.
3 *Labour and Britain in the 1990s*, p. 24.
4 Interview with Party strategist.
5 The results of one piece of qualitative research,which appeared to leave a deep impression, were (as one senior strategist recalled) 'devastating'. The sample members were asked to draw pictures of and comment upon the characteristics of the two main parties.The Tories were associated with success, smiling families, high tech – all painted in bright colours.With Labour we are plunged into a grim and Dickensian world of decay and failure: cloth caps, smoke-stack industries, poverty and failure – all portrayed in plain black and white. Interview with Party strategist.
6 *Labour and Britain in the 1990s*, p. 12 (from MORI poll).
7 For details of the process of policy-formulation, see Chapter 5, pp. 111–12.
8 The Review was very ambitious in its scope, covering all aspects of policy. Seven Policy Review Groups (PRGs) were set up with very broad remits: A Productive and Competitive Economy, People at Work, Economic Equality, Consumers and the Community, Physical and Social Environment and Britain in the World.
9 *Meet the Challenge, Make the Change*, p. 10.
10 Ibid., p. 15.
11 Labour Party NEC *Meet the Challenge, Make the Change*, London, Labour Party, 1989, p. 15 This ambiguity reflected disagreements amongst policy-makers. Public sector unions were keen to maintain some commitment to renationalise the major utilities where many of their members worked, a view shared by Gould, the main drafter of the report and other influential figures on the soft left, like Blunkett. On the other hand, Kinnock was chary about any binding commitments to reverse privatisation (Hughes and Wintour, 1990: 132–3).
12 Labour Party election manifesto *It's Time to get Britain Working Together Again*, London, Labour Party, 1992 pp. 13, 21.
13 The thinking of its advocates is spelt out more fully in an earlier draft of *Meet the Challenge, Make the Change* entitled *Supply-side Socialism*, in Gould's own published work and in the work of the Industrial Strategy Group.
14 *Meet the Challenge, Make the Change*, p. 12; Cowling, 1989: 16.
15 *Meet the Challenge, Make the Change*, p. 13; *Supply-side Socialism*, pp. 13, 14.
16 *Supply-Side Socialism*, p. 14.
17 Labour Party NEC *Opportunity Britain*, London, Labour Party, 1991, p. 5.
18 Labour Party NEC *Looking to the Future*, London, Labour Party, 1990, p. 66.

19 However, a survey of top City fund managers suggested that Labour's so-called 'prawn cocktail' offensive to reassure the City had only limited impact as 55 per cent indicated that they intended to transfer money overseas if Labour won the election (*Sunday Correspondent*, 29 April 1990).

20 *Looking to the Future*, p. 15; *It's Time to get Britain Working Together Again*.

21 See, e.g., interview with Chris Smith, *Chartist* 132 Winter 1991; and Peter Jay interview with Gordon Brown, *On the Record* BBC 1, 3 March 1991.

22 *Meet the Challenge, Make the Change*, p. 13.

23 *Looking to the Future*, p. 7. (See also article by John Smith in *Tribune*, 7 September 1990.)

24 *Opportunity Britain*, p. 12.

25 Unsigned paper to IPPR Conference (attended by Labour leaders and strategists). January 1989.

26 *Meet the Challenge, Make the Change*, p. 14; *Looking to the Future*, pp. 7–8. Smith, transcript of speech, 16 April 1990.

27 *It's Time to get Britain Working Together Again*, p. 12.

28 Interview with Party official.

29 The path to agreement was smoothed by the availability of a range of consultative mechanisms which ensured that no step was taken without being thoroughly explored and thrashed out behind the scenes such as the regular meetings between senior front-benchers and the 'Contact Group' of top trade union leaders (Minkin, 1991: 469–70).

30 *It's Time to get Britain Working Together Again*, p. 13. Minkin comments: 'In securing these changes [over industrial relations law] Labour's leadership transcended ninety years of history and overcame what seemed an impassable barrier in the form of ninety percent of the Party Conference votes. There could be fewer stronger tests of power over Labour Party policymaking' (Minkin, 1991: 624).

31 Labour Party NEC *Democratic Socialist Aims and Values*, London, Labour Party, 1988, p. 3.

32 Ibid., p. 7.

33 After the election he revised his view and expressed anxiety that Labour had moved too far to the right. (See, for example, Hattersley in *New Statesman and Society*, 4 June 1993.)

5 ORGANISATIONAL MODERNISATION

1 G. Bish 'Future Policy Development' RD 2806 July 1983.

2 Interview with Party official.

3 Thus Policy Review Groups were chaired by two joint convenors and membership was drawn equally from the NEC and the Shadow Cabinet, supplemented by a few senior trade unionists.

4 One instance of this was Kinnock's vacillating and clumsy conduct over the defence issue in the summer of 1988 which precipitated the

sudden resignation of the Shadow Defence Secretary, Denzil Davis, over the Leader's failure to consult him (Hughes and Wintour, 1990: 89).

5 L. Whitty and G. Bish *Policy-Making during 1990: Role of Policy Review Groups* PD 2274 September 1989; N. Kinnock *Note for PRG Conveners Meeting*, 30 November 1989.

6 Kinnock's chief of staff, Charles Clarke, in particular showed himself to be, in the words of one insider, 'subtle, effective, and very skilled at lobbying'. Interview with Party official.

7 Interview with Party official.

8 Interviews with Party officials and MPs.

9 CLP Rules Clause XV (11) NEC paper 'Parliamentary By-Election Candidates DO 117/1/1989 25 January 1989.

10 J. Gould *Selection of Parliamentary By-Election Candidates* GS 12/1/90, undated; NEC minutes 28 February 1990.

11 Org. Sub. Minutes 17 September 1990.

12 *New Statesman and Society*, 25 October 1991; *Guardian*, 18 October 1991, 19 October 1991.

13 See *Birkenhead Constituency and Allied Matters* DO/85/6/90 June 1990. The unusually large number of eight NEC members voted for a motion to endorse Davies. NEC minutes 27 June 1990.

14 Given that the unions were left to decide the precise way in which their vote would be cast, one effect – in more centrally organised unions like the electricians and the GMB – was to shift voting rights from union branch delegates to the GC to central or regional union officials. A number of powerful Scottish union officers agreed that union votes would not be used to oust any sitting MPs. This saved George Galloway, MP for Glasgow Hillhead and (initially) Ron Brown, MP for Edinburgh Leith who individual Party members had voted to remove. A further unfortunate consequence was adverse media publicity where the union vote appeared to be thwarting the wishes of individually balloted members. The change also gave union levy-payers the right to participate in parliamentary selections in their own right for the first time.

15 At the 1993 Conference a version of OMOV was adopted by a very narrow majority after intense lobbying.

16 NEC Report 1989, p. 28; Org. Sub. 19 February 1990. Livingstone commented, 'I would have survived if One member, One Vote had not been introduced into the constituency section'. (*Independent*, 4 October 1989).

17 Another factor was geographic. Altrincham and Sale CLP consistently voted for Kaufman – MP for the nearby Gorton constituency – during the 1980s, even in its most left-wing period. Personal observation as teller.

18 Seyd and Whitely have shown that activists tend to be somewhat further to the left than ordinary members, though the membership is as a whole inclined to the (soft) left. (Seyd and Whiteley, 1992a: 43–7).

19 *Making Policy for the 1990s: Future of Labour Party Conference and*

Policy-Making GS: 21 June 1990. In addition votes in future would be announced in percentages rather than in – easily mocked – numerical values in the millions.

20 Ibid.

21 See *National Policy Forum* GS: 2/10/92, October 1992.

22 The hard left was strongly opposed to the new system but for a more positive early assessment by a soft left member of the Policy Forum see Atkins, 1993.

6 LABOUR'S CAMPAIGN AND COMMUNICATIONS STRATEGY 1987–92

1 General Secretary's Report to Labour Party NEC (henceforth *GS Report*) *The General Election 1992*, pp. 19–20; General Secretary memo *General Election Management* 10 January 1992.

2 Memo from Larry Whitty, General Secretary of the Labour Party, 6 May 1988.

3 SCA *Developing the Policy Review* 1988.

4 N. Kinnock *Campaigning Framework for 1989 : Working to Improve the Quality of Life* 1988.

5 LPCR 1988, p. 33.

6 P. Mandelson *Projecting Labour's Policies for the Environment: A Fresh Campaign Strategy* CSC 14/88/89 1989.

7 P. Mandelson *Campaign Plans* CSC 14/87/88 September 1988.

8 *Campaigning Framework for 1989: Working to Improve the Quality of Life.*

9 P. Mandelson *Campaign Plans* CSC 5/89/90 March 1990.

10 P. Mandelson *Projecting Labour's Policies for the Environment: A Fresh Campaign Strategy* CSC 14/88/89 July 1989.

11 CSC 3/88/89 November 1988.

12 Thus in a speech to a Fabian conference in July 1989, Patricia Hewitt stressed the importance of Labour becoming a 'red–green' party, synthesising socialist values and environmental concerns. Author's notes.

13 According to a senior SCA member, 'your best chance is before the real campaign starts. Now the TV coverage has to be even-handed, ad campaigns will tend to cancel each other out. A quarter of voters may still be making up their minds but the key was to get your view of the issues uppermost in their minds long ago' (*Marketing Week*, 27 March 1992).

14 Internal Labour Party report, *War Book*.

15 *GS Report* p. 53; Internal Party memo, *The Final Week* p. 3.

16 Ibid. Emphasis in original.

17 *GS Report*, p. 46; *The Final Week*, p. 1.

18 *GS Report*, p. 46.

19 *GS Report*, p. 47.

20 Ibid., p. 55.

21 Ibid., p. 48; *The Final Week*, p. 5.

22 A black prisoner, Horton had been released on furlough by

Massachusetts Governor and Democratic presidential candidate Dukakis and then proceeded to commit rape and murder. Research using focus groups indicated to the Republican campaign that an ad. exploiting the incident would bring floaters flocking behind Bush.

23 Billig and Golding (1992) suggested that race was 'the hidden factor' in the polling upset of the 1992 election.

24 However, it may well be inevitable that for Labour – like parties of the left elsewhere – race is a vote-loser.

25 *GS Report*, p. 21.

26 The research was actually mainly carried out by planners employed or formerly employed by BMP.

27 In answer to the question 'Who would make the best PM?' Major's lead in March and April 1992 ranged between 10 per cent and 20 per cent, Gallup Political Index, (Newton, 1992: 15). As Labour's own post-election report tactfully put it: 'the long-running attack on the leader of the Party did have a considerable effect upon the general unease about Labour and its fitness to govern' *GS Report*, p. 53.

28 As one hostile observer commented, 'His interviews are like processed cheese coming out of a mincing machine – nothing meaty, just one mass of meaningless rhetoric that defuses and anaesthetises the listener' (Benn, 1992: 352; Diary entry, 20 May 1984).

7 THE DETERMINANTS OF PARTY TRANSFORMATION

1 The key texts are still Kircheimer, 1966 and Downs, 1957.

2 See, for example, Dunn, 1993: 521.

3 One measure mooted was an international tax on foreign exchange dealings to contain speculative currency movements (Kelly, 1993; Gibson and Tsakalotos, 1993).

4 The steady flow of defectors from the Campaign Group also found that their claims were not ignored when it came to filling vacancies on the front bench.

5 In addition Kinnock had encouraged MPs to join the Tribune Group specifically to block the formation of a joint slate (interview, *Tribune* 3 July 1987).

6 The extra-parliamentary soft left, too, was divided, though the alignments were somewhat different. Shortly after the rejection of the common slate, seven members of the executives of the LCC and the hard left umbrella group, Labour Left Liaison issued a call for greater collaboration on the the left to combat the right more effectively. But the initiative was overwhelmingly repudiated by the LCC executive (including by members like Robin Cook who had backed the joint slate).

7 Hain complained that the Tribune Group had been converted into 'a forum through which the leadership can pull people into line. Whenever there is a key decision, the payroll vote appears en bloc and stifles the Group's independence and radicalism' (*Tribune*, 21 October 1988). By 1990, of the hundred-odd members of the

Tribune Group, no less than forty-five served on the front bench of which fourteen were Shadow Cabinet members (*Tribune*, 10 January 1991).

8 After the 1992 election, Hain was elected secretary of the Tribune Group and managed to breathe some life into it. The following year, he was voted out of the post (in an unusually well attended meeting of the Tribune Group) largely because he was seen as too critical of the leadership.

9 This passage relies heavily on interviews.

10 At one point, a leading political columnist reported that amongst fellow Labour MPs it was 'hard to find any whose private words are not laced with venom or contempt' (Hugo Young in the *Guardian*, 7 February 1989).

11 One reason of course was that the Cold War had come to a close, yet this could equally be construed as eliminating the strategic rationale for a British deterrent, which Kinnock now promised to preserve almost in perpetuity.

8   ASSESSING LABOUR'S CAMPAIGN AND COMMUNICATIONS STRATEGY

1 SCA *Election and Post Election Polling June 1992*, GMA [Gould Mattinson Associates] Monitor for Fabian Society September 1992.

2 Interview with pollster.

3 Interview with Party strategist.

4 Party strategists could counter that people derived their impressions from the behaviour of a few Labour local authorities, or the speeches of left-wing politicians, but that merely begs the question why perceptions should be formed from the conduct of marginal elements within Labour's ranks rather than from that of the Party itself.

5 Recent research has found that judgements applied to the groups most commonly associated by the public with a political party come in time to be extended to the party itself (Miller and Wlezien, 1993: 7–8).

6 Agenda-setting is obviously the only realistic approach a party can use in the actual campaign period where the prospects of altering beliefs, or conversion, are minimal. However, in Labour's case, as we have seen, agenda-setting was the preferred mode in the total communication effort.

7 David Hare was given access to all Labour's strategy meetings during the 1992 election (Hare, 1993).

8 In fact, the overall judgement of a team of economists was that its economic record was reasonable, given the difficult circumstances (Artis and Cobham, 1991).

9 This was a finding of Labour Party research. Interview. A year into the fourth Conservative term, after 'Black Wednesday' and other economic upsets, qualitative research into politically non-attached C1 and C2 voters found that 'on the key area of economic com-

petence, the Tories win hands down . . . if for no other reason than that *"its their reputation'"* (Radice and Pollard, 1993: 8, emphasis added).

10 MORI Presentation to Labour Party Jobs and Industry Campaign Committee, 19 September 1985.

11 *Labour's Jobs and Industry Campaign, 1985* CSC 1/11/84.

12 GMA Monitor/Fabian Society, 1992: 19.

13 Interview with Party strategist.

14 'Kinnock: the Inside Story' Episode 4, ITV 8 August 1993.

15 Immediately prior to the 1992 election, the BBC decided to defer showing a Panorama programme analysing the Conservatives' economic record, under pressure, it was claimed, from the Government (Butler and Kavanagh, 1992: 156).

16 As Tim Gardam, editor of BBC 2's *Newsnight* programme, observed 'interviews aren't real conversations, questions are framed by the journalist just to get the right clip to fit into a package' (Hare, 1993: 209).

17 For instance, whereas 31 per cent of respondents in a survey conducted in 1991 were willing to acknowledge they were racially prejudiced, the same survey disclosed that 91 per cent of respondents believed that there was a lot or a little prejudice against blacks and Asians (Young, 1992: 183, 181; see also Devine, 238–9: 1992).

18 Rentoul concluded (on the basis of qualitative research carried out just after the 1987 election) that the issues of race (and gays) 'may have more power to influence people's voting decisions, by tapping great reservoirs of irrational feeling, than any supposed shift in values which are more conventionally thought of as political' (Rentoul, 1989: 49).

19 It is worth noting here that, according to a leading authority, the Swedish Social Democratic Party remains a class-based party with its sympathisers viewing it as favouring working-class interests (Sainsbury, 1990: 46–9).

20 SCA *Election and Post-election Polling* June 1992.

9   CONCLUSION

1 The issue was the controversy over parliamentary selection.

2 From around 1983, an even more emphatic process of rhetorical, along with policy, change took place amongst the ruling French Socialists (Ross, Hoffman and Malzacher, 1987).

3 *Looking to the Future*, p. 6.

4 Gould publicised his profound unease over Labour's economic strategy after his resignation from the Shadow Cabinet in September 1992. (See, for example, B. Gould, 'A Radical Recipe for Labour', *New Statesman and Society*, 19 February 1993).

5 Interview with Party strategist.

6 The pledges on pensions and child benefits represent a partial exception in that, in addition to internal party concerns, they were intended to appeal in particular to women.

7 Thus we noted that research conducted in the 1960s by Mackenzie and Silver, and Nordlinger indicated that, even in these more class-bound years, the majority of working-class people believed that the Conservatives were better qualified to govern the country than Labour.

8 For evidence from qualitative research conducted in 1993 amongst C1 and C2 floaters who reluctantly plumped for the Conservatives in 1992, of continuing, though a little attenuated, hostility to 'scroungers' 'malingerers' and the 'work shy', see Radice and Pollard, 1993: 9.

9 Whilst opinion polls do indicate that Labour's activists were widely perceived as 'extreme' this was largely due to negative stereotyping by the press and was not supported by the major piece of research conducted into the matter (Seyd and Whiteley 1992a: 211–18; for press coverage, see Hollingworth, 1986).

REFERENCES

Abramowitz, A. L., Lanoue, D. J., Ramesh, S. 1988 'Economic Conditions, Causal Attributions and Political Evaluations in the 1984 Presidential Election' *Journal of Politics* 50 (4)

Andrews, G. 1991 *Citizenship* London, Lawrence and Wishart

Artis, M. and Cobham, D. (eds) 1991 *Labour's Economic Policies 1974–79* Manchester, Manchester University Press

Atkins, C. 1993 'Constructing an Alternative' *Chartist* July–Aug.

Baylis, J. and Balsom, D. 1986 'Public Opinion and the Parties' Defence Policies' *Political Quarterly* 57

Beer, S. H. 1969 *Modern British Politics* London, Faber and Faber

Bell, D. and Shaw, E. D. (eds) forthcoming *Conflict and Cohesion in Contemporary Social Democracy* London, Pinter Publishers

Benn, T. 1980 *The Case for Party Democracy* Nottingham, IWC

Benn, T. 1989 *Against the Tide. Diaries 1973–6* London, Hutchinson

Benn, T. 1990 *Conflict of Interest: Diaries 1977–80* London, Hutchinson

Benn, T. 1992 *The End of an Era. Diaries 1980–1990* London, Hutchinson

Berry, S. 1992 'Labour's Strategy and the Media: the Failure of Labour's 1992 Election Campaign' *Parliamentary Affairs* 45 (4)

Billig, M. and Golding, P. 1992 'The Hidden Factor: Race, The News Media, and the 1992 Election' *Representation* 31 (114)

Blair, T. 1991 'Forging a new Agenda' *Marxism Today* Oct.

Blair, T. 1993 'Why Modernisation Matters' *Renewal* 1 (4) Oct.

Blumler, J. 1990 'Elections, the Media and the Modern Publicity Process' in Ferguson (ed.)

Blunkett, D. and Crick, B. 1988 *The Labour Party's Aims and Values: An Unofficial Statement* Nottingham, Spokesman

Boll, B. and Poguntke, T. 1992 'Germany: The 1990 All-German Campaign' in Bowler and Farrell

Bowler S., Broughton, D., Donovan, T. and Snipp, J. 1992 'The Informed Electorate? Voter Responsiveness to Campaigns in Britain and Germany' in Bowler and Farrell

Bowler, S. and Farrell, D. (eds) 1992 *Electoral Strategy and Political Marketing* London, Macmillan

241

Braham, P. 1982 'How the Media Report Race' in Gurevitch, M., Bennett, T., Curran, C. and Woollacott, J. *Culture, Society and the Media* London, Methuen and Co.

Bruce, B. 1992 *Images of Power* London, Kogan Page

Burt, G. (ed.) 1988 *Alternative Defence Policy* London, Croom Helm

Butler, D. and Kavanagh, D. 1984 *The British General Election of 1983* London, Macmillan

Butler, D. and Kavanagh, D. 1988 *The British General Election of 1987* London, Macmillan

Butler, D. and Kavanagh, D, 1992 *The British General Election of 1992* London, Macmillan

Butler, D. and King, A. 1965 *The British General Election of 1964* London, Macmillan

Butler, D. and Stokes, D. 1974 *Political Change in Britain* London, Macmillan

Cockerell, M. 1988 *Live from No. 10* London, Faber and Faber

Conover, P. J. 1984 'The Influence of Group Identifications on Political Perception and Evaluation' *Journal of Politics* 46

Conover, P. J. 1988 'The Role of Social Groups in Political Thinking' *British Journal Of Political Science* 18 (1)

Cowling, K. 'The Strategic Approach' in Industrial Strategy Group 1989

Crewe, I. 1982 'The Labour Party and the Electorate' in Kavanagh, D. 1982

Crewe, I. 1983a 'The Disturbing Truth Behind Labour's Rout' *Guardian*, 13 June

Crewe, I. 1983b 'How Labour was Trounced all Round' *Guardian*, 14 June

Crewe, I. 1984 'The Electorate: Partisan Dealignment Ten Years On' *West European Politics* 7

Crewe, I. 1987a 'A New Class of Politics' *Guardian*, 15 June

Crewe, I. 1987b 'Tories Prosper from a Paradox' *Guardian*, 16 June

Crewe, I. 1992a 'The Thatcher Legacy' in King, A. *et al.*

Crewe, I. 1992b 'Why did Labour Lose (Yet Again) ?' *Politics Review* 2 (1)

Crewe, I. 1992c 'Changing Votes and Unchanging Voters' *Electoral Studies* 11 (4)

Crewe, I. and Harrop, M. (Eds) 1989 *Political Communications: The General Election of 1987* Cambridge, Cambridge University Press

Crosland, T. 1964 (original edition, 1956) *The Future of Socialism* London, Jonathan Cape

Denver, D. 1987 'Great Britain: From Opposition with a Capital "O" to Fragmented Opposition' in Kolinsky, E. (ed.) 1987

Denver, D. 1989 *Elections and Voting Behaviour in Britain* Hemel Hempstead, Philip Allan

Denver, D. and Hands, G. 1993 'Measuring the Intensity and Effectiveness of Constituency Campaigning in the 1992 British General Election' Paper presented to ECPR Joint Sessions, Leyden

Devine, F. 1992 'Social Identities, Class Identity and Political Perspectives' *Sociological Review* 40 (2)

Downs, A. 1957 *An Economic Theory of Democracy* New York, Harper and Row

Drucker, H. 1979 *Doctrine and Ethos in the Labour Party* London, Allen and Unwin

Drucker, H. 1981 'Changes in the Labour Party Leadership' *Parliamentary Affairs* 34 (4)

Dunleavy, P. 1988 'A Non-nuclear, non-NATO Britain: Is There an Electoral Pathway?' in Burt 1988

Dunleavy, P. and Husbands, C. 1985 *British Democracy at the Crossroads* London, Allen and Unwin

Dunn, J. 1984 *The Politics of Socialism* Cambridge, Cambridge University Press

Dunn, J. 1993 'The Heritage and Future of the European Left' *Economy and Society* 22 (4)

Duverger, M. 1964 *Political Parties* London, Methuen

Edelstein, J. D. 1967 'An Organisational Theory of Union Democracy' *American Sociological Review* 32

Edgell, S. and Duke, V. 1986 'Radicalism, Radicalisation and the Recession' *British Journal of Sociology* 37

Entman, R. M. 1989 'How the Media Affect What People Think: An Information Processing Approach' *Journal of Politics* 51 (2)

Epstein, Leon 1980 *Political Parties in Western Democracies* London, Transaction Publishers

Esping-Andersen, G. 1985 *Politics Against Markets* Princeton NJ, Princeton University Press

Esping-Andersen, G. and van Kersbergen, K. 1992 'Contemporary Research on Social Democracy' *Annual Review of Sociology* 18

Evans, G. 1992 'Is Britain a Class Divided Society?' *Sociology* 26 (2)

Feldman, S. 1982 'Economic Self-Interest and Political Behavior' *American Journal of Political Science* 26 (3)

Ferguson, M. (ed.) 1990 *Public Communication: The New Imperatives* London, Sage

Forgas, J. P. (ed.) 1981 *Social Cognition* London, Academic Press

Franklin, M. N. 1985 *The Decline of Class Voting in Britain* Oxford, Oxford University Press

Furnham, A. 1982a 'Why are the Poor Always with us? Explanations for Poverty in Britain' *British Journal of Social Psychology* 21

Furnham, A. 1982b 'Explanations for Unemployment in Britain' *European Journal of Social Psychology* 12

Gapes, M. 1988 'The Evolution of Labour's Defence and Security Policy' in Burt 1988

Gavin, N. 1992 'Television News and the Economy: the Pre-Campaign Coverage' *Parliamentary Affairs* 45 (4)

Gibson, H. and Tsakalotos, E. 1993 'Does the City now run Economic Policy?' *New Economy* Autumn (sample copy)

Glasgow University Media Research Group 1982 *Really Bad News* London, Writers and Readers

Goldey, D. B. and Johnson, R. W. 1988 'The French Presidential Election of 24 April–8 May and the General Election of 5–12 June 1988' *Electoral Studies* 7 (3)

Golding, P. 1990 'Political Communication and Citizenship' in Ferguson, M. (ed.)

Golding, P. 1992 'Communicating Capitalism: Resisting and Restructuring State Ideology – the case of "Thatcherism"' *Media, Culture and Society* 14

Golding, P. and Middleton, S. 1982 *Images of Welfare* Oxford, Martin Robertson

Golding, P., Billig, M., Deacon, D., Middleton, S. 1992 'Two Shows for the Price of One' *British Journalism Review* 3 (1)

Goldthorpe, J. H., Lockwood, D., Bechhofer, F. and Platt, J. 1968 *The Affluent Worker: Industrial Attitudes and Behaviour* Cambridge, Cambridge University Press

Goldthorpe, J. H. (ed.) 1984 *Order and Conflict in Contemporary Capitalism* Oxford, Oxford University Press

Goldthorpe, J. H. *et al.* 1987 *Social Mobility and Class Structure in Modern Britain* Oxford, Clarendon Press

Gould, B. 1989 (a) 'Introduction' in Industrial Strategy Group 1989

Gould, B. 1989 (b) *A Future for Socialism* London, Jonathan Cape

Gould, P., Herd, P. and Powell, C. 1989 'The Labour Party's Campaign Communications' in Crewe and Harrop

Greenleaf, W. H. 1983 *The British Political Tradition Vol. Two The Ideological Inheritance*, London, Routledge

Haas, R. G. 1981 'Effects of Source Characteristics on Cognitive Responses and Persuasion' in Petty *et al.*

Hall, P. A. 1987 'The Evolution of Economic Policy Under Mitterrand' in Ross, Hoffman and Malzacher

Hamill, R. and Lodge, M. 1986 'Cognitive Consequences of Political Sophistication' in Lau and Sears

Hare, D. 1993 *Asking Around* London, Faber and Faber

Harrop, M. 1990 'Political Marketing' *Parliamentary Affairs* 43 (3)

Harrop, M. and Shaw, A. 1989 *Can Labour Win?* London, Unwin

Hattersley, R. 1985 'An Alternative to the Alternative: Labour's Economic Strategy. Interview with Roy Hattersley' *Marxism Today* October

Hattersley, R. 1987a *Economic Priorities for a Labour Government* London, Macmillan

Hattersley, R. 1987b *Choose Freedom* London, Penguin

Healey, D. 1985 *Labour and World Society* London, Fabian Society

Healey, D. 1989 *The Time of My Life* London, Michael Joseph

Heath, A, Jowell, R., Curtice, J. 1985 *How Britain Votes* Oxford, Pergamon Press

Heath, A. *et al.* 1991 *Understanding Political Change* Oxford, Pergamon Press

Heffernan, R. and Marqusee, M. 1992 *Defeat from the Jaws of Victory: Inside Kinnock's Labour Party* London, Verso

Hewitt, P. and Gould, P. 1993 'Learning from Success – Labour and Clinton's New Democrats *Renewal* 1 (1)

Hewitt, P. and Mandelson, P. 1989 'The Labour Campaign' in Crewe and Harrop

Higgins, E. T., Herman, C. P., Zanna, M. P. 1981 *Social Cognition* Hillsdale, New Jersey, Lawrence Erlbaum

Hill, R. and Lodge, M. 1986 'Cognitive Consequences of Political Sophistication' in Lau and Sears

Hirst, P. 1991 'Labour and the Constitutional Crisis' in Andrews

Holland, S. 1975 *The Socialist Challenge* London, Quartet

Hollingworth, M. 1986 *The Press and Political Dissent* London, Pluto

Hovland, C., Janis, I. L. and Kelley, H. H. 1953 *Communication and Persuasion* London, Yale University Press

Hughes, C. and Wintour, P. 1990 *Labour Rebuilt* London, Fourth Estate

Industrial Strategy Group 1989 *Beyond the Review* Edinburgh, Industrial Strategy Group

Iyengar, S. 1989 'How Citizens Think about National Issues: A Matter of Responsibility' *American Journal of Political Science* 33

Jamieson. K. H. and Campbell, K. K. 1988 *The Interplay of Influence* Belmont California, Wadsworth Publishing Co.

Jenkins, P. 1987 *Mrs Thatcher's Revolution* London, Cape

Johnston, R. J., Pattie, C. J. and Allsopp, J. G. 1988 *A Nation Dividing?* London, Longman

Jowell, R., Witherspoon, S. and Brook, L. 1987 *British Social Attitudes: the 1987 Report* Aldershot, Gower

Kavanagh, D. 1982 *The Politics of the Labour Party* London, Allen and Unwin

Kavanagh, D. (ed.) 1992 *Electoral Politics* Oxford, Clarendon Press

Kelly, R. 1993 'Taxing the Speculator' *Fabian Review* 105 (4)

Keohane, D. 1993 *Labour Party Defence Policy Since 1945*, Leicester, Leicester University Press.

King, A. *et al.* 1992 *Britain at the Polls 1992*, Chatham, New Jersey, Chatham House

Kinnock, N. 1986 *Making Our Way* Oxford, Blackwell

Kircheimer, O. 1966 'The Transformation of the Western European Party Systems' in La Palombara and Weiner

Kitschelt, H. 1992 'The Socialist Discourse and Party Strategy in West European Democracies' in Lemke and Marks

Kolinsky, E. (ed.) 1987 *Opposition in Western Europe* London, Croom Helm

Krieger, J. 1991 'Class, Consumption, and Collectivism: Perspectives on the Labour Party and Electoral Competition in Britain' in Piven (ed.)

La Palombara, J. and Weiner, M. (eds) 1966 *Political Parties and Political Development* Princeton, Princeton University Press

Lafferty, W. 1990 'Political Transformation in a Social Democratic State' *Comparative Politics* 23 (1)

Lansley, S. 1985 'The Phony War' *New Socialist* July/Aug.

Lau, R. R. and Sears, D. O. 1986 'Social Cognition and Political Cognition' in Lau and Sears

Lau, R. R. and Sears, D. O. 1986 *Political Cognition* Hillsdale, New Jersey, Lawrence Erlbaum,

Lau, R. L., Smith, R. A. and Fiske, S. T. 1991 'Political Beliefs, Policy Interpretations, and Political Persuasion *Journal of Politics* 53 (3)

Leadbeater, C. 1987 *The Politics of Prosperity* London, Fabian Society

Leadbeater, C. 1988 'Power to the Person' *Marxism Today* Oct.

Leadbeater, C. 1989 'Back to the Future' *Marxism Today* May

Leapman, M. 1987 *Kinnock* London, Unwin Hyman

Lehmbruch, G. 1984 'Concertation and the Structure of Corporatist Networks' in Goldthorpe J. H. (ed.)

Lemke, C. and Marks, G. (eds) 1992 *The Crisis of Socialism in Europe* London, Duke University Press

Lindblom, C. E. 1977 *Politics and Markets* New York, Basic Books

Lipset, S. M., Trow M. A., Coleman, J. S. 1956 *Union Democracy* London, Collier MacMillan

Lipsey, D. 1992 *The Name of the Rose* Fabian Society, London

Lloyd, J. 1990 'Europeans by Default' *Marxism Today* Oct.

Lukes, S. 1974 *Power: A Radical View* London, Macmillan

McGuire, W. J. 1989 'Theoretical Foundations of Campaigns' in Rice and Atkin

McKenzie, R. and Silver, A. 1968 *Angels in Marble* London, Heinemann

McKie, D. 1992 "Fact is Free, Comment is Sacred or, Was it the Sun wot Won it?' Paper prepared for the PSA Conference on Elections and Public Opinion, Essex University

McSmith, A. 1993 *John Smith* London, Verso

Mandelson, P. 1988 'Marketing Labour' *Contemporary Record* Winter

Marquand, D. 1988 *The Unprincipled Society* London, Jonathan Cape

Marquand, D. 1991 *The Progressive Dilemma* London, Heinemann

Marshall, G., Rose, D., Newby, H., Vogler, C. 1989 *Social Class in Modern Britain* London, Unwin Hyman

Martin, R. 1968 'Union Democracy: An Explanatory Framework' *Sociology* 2 (2)

Media Research Group (Goldsmiths' College) 1987 'Media Coverage of London Councils: Interim Report.' Unpublished paper.

Milburn, M. A. 1991 *Persuasion and Politics* Pacific Grove, Calif., Brooks/Cole

Miller, A. H. and Wlezien, C. 1993 'Social Group Dynamics of Partisan Evaluations' *Electoral Studies* (12) 1

Miller, D. 1991 'A Vision of Market Socialism' *Dissent* Summer

Miller, D. 1993 'The relevance of Socialism' *Economy and Society* 20 (4)

Miller, D. 1993 'The Beeb at Bay' *British Journalism Review* 4 (1)

Miller, W. L., Clarke, H. D., Harrop, M., LeDuc, L., Whiteley, P. 1990 *How Voters Change* Oxford, Clarendon Press

Miller, W. L. 1991 *Media and Voters* Oxford, Clarendon Press

Milner, H. 1989 *Sweden: Social Democracy in Practice* Oxford, Oxford University Press

Minkin, L. 1991 *The Contentious Alliance: Trade Unions and the Labour Party*, Edinburgh, Edinburgh University Press

246

Mitchell, A. 1983 *Four Years in the Death of the Labour Party* London, Methuen

Mitchell, A. 1979 *Can Labour Win Again* London, Fabian Society

Moran, M. 1993 'The Labour Party: Options after 1992' *Talking Politics* 5 (3)

National Institute of Economic and Social Research, 1990. 'Policy Options Under a Labour Government' *National Institute Economic Review* Nov.

Newton, K. 1992 'Economic Voting in the 1992 General Election' Paper prepared for the Conference on Elections and Public Opinion, Essex University

Noelle-Neumann, E. 1974 'The Spiral of Silence' *Journal of Communication* 24

Nordlinger, E. A. 1967 *The Working Class Tories* London, MacGibbon and Kee

O'Shaughnessy, N. J. 1990 *The Phenomenon of Politcal Marketing* London, Macmillan

O'Shaughnessy, N. J. 1993 'Why a "flawless" campaign flopped' *Independent on Sunday* 12 April

Padgett, S. 1993 'The German Social Democrats. A Redefinition of Social Democracy or Bad Godesberg 11?' *West European Politics* 16 (1)

Padgett, S. and Paterson, W. E. 1991 *A History of Social Democracy in Postwar Europe* London, Longman

Pahl, R. E. and Wallace, C. D. 1988 'Neither Angels in Marble nor Rebels in Red' in Rose, D. (ed.)

Panebianco, A. 1988 *Political Parties: Organisation and Power* Cambridge, Cambridge University Press

Panitch, L. 1989 'Socialist Renewal and the Labour Party' *Socialist Register 1988*, London, Merlin Press

Paterson, W. E. and Thomas, A. H. (eds) 1986 *The Future of Social Democracy* Oxford, Clarendon Press

Peffley, M. 1984 'The Voter as Juror' *Political Behavior* 6 (3)

Peffley, M. *et al.*. 1987 'Economic Conditions and Party Competence: The process of belief revision' *Journal of Politics* 49

Perloff, R. M. and Brock, T. C. 1983 '. . . And Thinking Makes it So: Cognitve Responses to Persuasion' in Roloff and Miller

Petty, R. E. and Cacioppo, J. T. 1986 *Communication and Persuasion* New York, Springer Verlag

Petty, R. E. *et al.* 1981 *Cognitive Responses to Persuasion* Hillsdale, NJ, Lawrence Erlbaum

Pfeffer, J. 1981 *Power in Organisations* London, Pitman Publishing Ltd.

Pimlott, B. and Cook, C. 1991 *Trade Unions in British Politics* London, Longman

Piven, F. F. 1991 *Labor Parties in Postindustrial Societies* Cambridge, Polity

Pontusson, J. 1992 'An End to the Third Road: Swedish Social Democracy in Crisis' *Politics and Society* 20 (3)

Price, V. 1988 'On the Public Aspects of Opinion' *Communication Research* 15 (6)

Przeworski, A. 1985 *Capitalism and Social Democracy* Cambridge, Cambridge University Press

Radice, G. 1992 *Southern Discomfort* London, Fabian Society

Radice, G. and Pollard, S. 1993 *More Southern Discomfort* London, Fabian Society

Rentoul, J. 1989 *Me and Mine* London, Unwin Hyman

Rice, R. E. and Atkin, C. K. 1989 *Public Communication Campaigns* London, Sage

Roloff, M. E. and Miller, G. R. 1983 *Persuasion: New Directions in Theory and Research* London, Sage

Rose, D. (ed.) 1988 *Social Stratification and Economic Change*, London, Hutchinson

Rose, R. 1967 *Influencing Voters* London, Faber and Faber

Rose, R. 1992 'Long-term Structural Change or Cyclical Fluctuations? The 1992 Election in Dynamic Perspective' *Parliamentary Affairs* 45 (4)

Ross, G. 1992 'Party Decline and the Changing Party System: France and the French Communist Party' *Comparative Politics* 25 (1)

Ross, G., Hoffman, S., Malzacher, S. 1987 *The Mitterrand Experiment* Cambridge, Polity

Sainsbury, D. 1990 'Party Strategies and the Electoral Trade-off of Class-Based Parties' *European Journal of Political Research* 18 (1)

Sainsbury, D. 1993 'The Swedish Social Democrats and the Legacy of Continuous Reform: Asset or Dilemma?' *West European Politics* 16 (1)

Sanders, D. 1992 'Why the Conservative Party Won -Again' in King, A. et al. 1992 *Britain at the Polls 1992*

Savage, M. 1991 'Making Sense of Middle Class Politics' *Sociological Review* 39 (1)

Scammel, M., Nossiter, T. J. and Semetko, H. 1992 'The British General Election Campaign on Television: News Content and Potential Effects' PSA Conference, 'The 1992 Election: Voters, Parties and the Media', Essex University

Schlesinger, J. A. 1984 'On the Theory of Party Organisation' *Journal of Politics* 46 (2)

Seaton, J. 1991 'Trade Unions and the Media' in Pimlott and Cook (eds)

Seyd, P. and Whiteley, P. 1992a *Labour's Grass Roots* Oxford, Clarendon Press

Seyd, P. and Whiteley, P. 1992b 'Labour's Vote and Local Activism: The Impact of Constituency Campaigns' *Parliamentary Affairs* 45 (4)

Seyd, P. and Whiteley, P. 1993 'Inactivity Rotting Labour's Grassroots' *Guardian* September 25

Seymour-Ure, C. 1993 'Campaign Strategies: the Challenge of the Tabloids', paper prepared for ECPR Joint Sessions, Leiden

Sharples, A. 1982 *Socialist Economic Review*

Shaw, E. D. 1988 *Discipline and Discord in the Labour Party* Manchester, Manchester University Press

Smith, M. J. 1992 'Continuity and Change in Labour Party Policy' in Smith and Spear

Smith, M. J. and Spear, J. 1992 *The Changing Labour Party* London, Routledge

Snow, D. A. and Benford, R. D. 1988 'Ideology, Frame Resonance and Participant Mobilisation' in *International Social Movement Research* 1

Stokes, D. 1992 'Valence Politics' in Kavanagh (ed.)

Strom, K. 1990 'A Behavioral Theory of Competitive Political Parties' *American Journal of Political Science* 34 (2)

Tait, R. 1992 'The Parties and Television' PSA Conference on The 1992 Election: Voters, Parties and the Media, Essex University, pp. 3–4

Tajfel, H. and Forgas, J. P. 1981 'Social Categorisation' in Forgas

Taylor, S. E. and Crocker, J. 1981 'Schematic Bases of Social Information Processing' in Higgins, Herman and Zanna

Thomas, D. 1986 'Labour's Smooth Operators' *New Socialist* October

Tilton, T. 1990 *The Political Theory of Swedish Social Democracy* Oxford, Clarendon Press

Tumber, H. 1993 'Taming the Truth' *British Journalism Review* 14 (1)

Tyler, R. 1987 *Campaign! The Selling of the Prime Minister* London, Grafton Books

van Praag, P. forthcoming, 'Conflict and Cohesion in the Dutch Labour Party' in Bell and Shaw

Ware, A. 1992 'Activist–Leader Relations and the Structure of Political Parties' *British Journal of Political Science* 22 (1)

Webb, P. D. 1992 'Election Campaigning, Organisational Transformation and the Professionalisation of the British Labour Party' *European Journal of Political Research* 21

Westergaard, J. 1984 'Class of '84' *New Socialist* 15 Jan/Feb

Wilder, D. A. and Shapiro, P. N. 1984 'Role of Out-Group Cues in Determining Social Identity *Journal of Personal and Social Psychology* 47 (2)

Willman, J. 1992 'Slaughtering Labour Shibboleths' *Fabian Review* 104 (6)

Worcester, R. 1991 *British Public Opinion* Oxford, Blackwell

Windahl, S., Signitzer, B., Olson, J. T. 1992 *Using Communication Theory* London, Sage

Wright, T. 1993 'Now or Never' *Fabian Review* 105 (4)

Wright, W. E. 1971 *A Comparative Study of Party Organisation* Columbus, Ohio, Charles Merrill

Young, K. 1987 'Nuclear Reactions' in Jowell *et al.*.

Young, K. 1992 'Class, Race and Opportunity' in Jowell, R., Brook, L., Prior, G. and Taylor, B. 1992 *British Social Attitudes: 9th Report* Aldershot, Dartmouth Publishing

Zysman, J. 1983 *Governments, Markets and Growth* Oxford, Martin Robertson

INDEX